GATHERING STICKS

Lighting up small fires

IAD PRESS

GATHERING STICKS

Lighting up small fires

by

MARGARET HEFFERNAN

with Gerard Waterford
and Frances Coughlan

IAD PRESS

Published by IAD Press
PO Box 2531
Alice Springs NT 0871
Australia
phone + 61 8 8951 1301
sales@iad.edu.au
www.iadpress.com

First published in 2018
Gathering Sticks : Lighting up small fires
Margaret Heffernan with Gerard Waterford
and Frances Coughlan

 A catalogue record for this
book is available from the
National Library of Australia

National Library of Australia
Cataloguing-in-Publication data:

Title: Gathering Sticks : Lighting up small fires
ISBN(s): 9781864651478 :

Designed by Tina Tilhard
Printed by Graphic Print Group, Australia

This book is supported by

FOREWORD

Margie and I sat together on our back verandah one sunny Winter's afternoon in June 2015 pouring over a working translation of a song into Arrernte. As usual, there were too many Arrernte words to fit the rhythm of the song which led to an intense culling of some words and exploring the option of other possibilities.

A stroke in 1991 caused Margie to lose her Arrernte voice. Her tongue no longer went to the places necessary for creating the flowing sound and rhythm of the Arrernte language. From that time, Margie has expressed herself with simple hand signals and carefully considered English. I have never heard her speak her traditional language.

Because Margie was unable to bring sound to the Arrernte words of the song we were translating, it was my task on that particular day to look up the English words in the dictionary and search through the range of Arrernte options that fitted the subject, then speak aloud the word that I had found.

'What's that?' was often her response as I exposed my languid language skills to her meticulous ear and sought to annunciate the word in Arrernte. After several attempts that all sounded the same to me, she finally responded 'Yewe!' with a broad smile on her face and hands raised with a muffled sound like one hand clapping.

A few days previously, Margie's friend Sister Robyn Reynolds, had sent me a cassette recording of some short talks in Arrernte prepared for young people preparing for their confirmation in the Catholic Church at Santa Teresa back in the 80's. I wanted Margie to listen to the tapes to see if they were relevant for young people today. It was a female voice, strong and sure. She listened intently and was silent at the end. I waited. 'That's my voice,' she said.

There are times when one is taken aback by an insight to another that changes the whole scene. This was that time for me. I felt a grief, a loss, that I had never heard or seen Margie in those days when she was without restraint and full of the life that is found in this book.

From her childhood Margie was inspired in her culture by the women's circles and the strong men in her family. At night she would sneak her bedding close to the fire and listen to the family stories. She experienced her initial schooling at the Bungalow, later schooling and living in the Dormitory at Santa Teresa Mission. She was encouraged into teaching by the sisters at the Mission and later stepped confidently into a world of linguistics and the translation of cultural stories for children. She was instrumental in working with others to set up Yipirinya School, to provide a bi-lingual education for four different language groups in Central Australia. She was the first President of Ngkarte Mikwekenhe Aboriginal Catholic Community in Alice Springs.

Margie's desire, in telling this story, has been to pass on to her children and future generations of her family, the story of her life, a life in transition from traditional culture to a very different world that is still unfolding.

Her story was begun over 30 years ago with David Wilkins, and has continued in more recent years with Franny Coughlan and Gerard Waterford, working and reworking the text. It is a team effort with Margie holding the melody line and Gerard filling in the at times discordant harmonies of life in two worlds.

David Woods

CONTENTS

Ilewerre – Margaret's country.
Courtesy of Jenny Green

CHAPTER 1

The storylines of my birth

As a kid, I was a small ball of energy topped by a mop of yellow hair, the colour of the wet, dusty river sand. All my brothers and sisters had this yellow hair. It was easy to pick us Heffernan kids out in the crowd because of it. And we got teased about it. But what's a bit of teasing!

These days, I'm a white-haired great-grandmother, surrounded by my kids, grandkids and great grandkids. But I was young once; born at the women's sacred site called Werlatye Atherre, just a little north of Alice Springs. So I'm a girl of the Yeperenye caterpillar dreaming, one of the three caterpillar stories. There are Yeperenye, Utnerrengatye and Ntyarlke caterpillars. They all connect through Mparntwe country with the Seven Sisters, Puppy Dog and other important creation time stories crisscrossing our homelands.

As young kids we could run like the wind, jump like wild horses. We raced around in our own little world of games and adventures. All of us in one mob. All us sister girls and brother boys being looked after by a watching group of mothers and grandmothers. Protected by our fathers and grandfathers; our family caring for us like a warm blanket on a cold night. We felt safe; and much loved.

This is my story as I was told by senior members of my family. Before I was conceived, my father took my mother and brother back to stay with their families at their sacred waterhole of Apmere Yetwernte. This place is a few kilometres east of Aileron Station homestead, and a hundred kilometres along the Stuart Highway north of Alice Springs, in Australia's Northern Territory; along the southern edge of my father's Anmatyerr country.

This was in 1942 when the Second World War was at a very bad stage for Australia. Before the move my family's camp had been at the Little Flower Mission on the Todd River, in Alice Springs. But this had been taken away from us by the Australian Army. Many of our families had been taken by the army, east to a new mission being set up in Arltunga. There were also big fears being spread of the Japanese army invading Australia through the Top End, and coming down to kill everyone. So this gathering at Apmere Yetwernte allowed the senior Anmatyerr people to meet and talk about some of these things.

The Apmere Yetwernte wetland has been the permanent water source for our tribe since creation. The place is very important and a very sacred site for us, honoured in our cultural rituals and traditions. But the water hole had been badly damaged in the changes since the arrival of the white man. Some things could be repaired; but other things have been lost forever.

Since ancient times the Anmatyerr mob lived near this clay-pan country, close up to the sweet water of Apmere Yetwernte. All this allowed for the gathering of the local families, with each family caring for their part of the Apmere Yetwernte story in the performances of their songs and dances of renewal. Everyone was connected through ritual and culture. Everyone shared this responsibility for looking after our country. Our families met there in the spring of 1942, and looked after the soakage points, cleaned out the sand and the weeds to keep this supply of sweet, clean drinking water going. This was important so that their kids and grandkids would keep hold of their knowledge of this sacred water source.

The Spring of 1942 was the time, and Apmere Yetwernte was the place where mother first knew she was pregnant with me. It is known as my conception place. My father, mother and older brother David camped there with close family members building a humpy out of leafy branches from the witchetty bush, or what we called the atnyeme bush. These branches were tied to bigger branches of mulga bushes, called artetye, to form a windbreak and a place to store precious things.

One morning at my family's camp, my mother and aunt went to get water from their soakage place. When they got there they saw a big old kangaroo just lying right there next to the sacred water. My mother ran quickly to get my father. He was able to creep right up close and spear the kangaroo dead.

All this was very unusual. Our people don't like unusual things, especially in troubled time. They became a bit worried and afraid. Why was this kangaroo just lying there at the side of the water? It didn't make sense. But my father had killed it 'traditional way' using the 'proper' rituals. They brought the meat for sharing back to our camp. It was cooked with ceremony, and the families all ate together. That kangaroo had a lot of fat. The elders decided that this kangaroo had let them kill it. So it must be a sign. But what did it mean? That is what the senior people of the tribe needed to work out.

After much talking the senior healers said they believed that the kangaroo appeared from out of the sacred site itself; out of nowhere, out of thin air. So they knew it was a spirit. Spirits were part of our home and landscape. They were often attached to a particular site or object. These were the ever-present spirits of ancestral beings reborn into new bodies. These spirits had been released on the death of a person of an earlier generation of the tribe. From their body's dying place, these spirits journeyed back to their ancestral place.

But sometimes other spirits might be wanting to trick people. Other times spirits might come as a messenger. And sometimes the spirit was looking for a woman to have a baby.

The elders thought that this was a spirit that had selected my mother to have this baby. And I became that baby. The kangaroo had let them kill it so that its spirit became part of my mother. The spirit lives on in me. Anyway that's what I've been told, and would like to think happened.

Not long after the kangaroo was eaten, a very big frog came right up into the family humpy. My father killed it too, with his boomerang. The frog caused a lot of talking too. This type of frog usually lives in the sand, waiting for rain before it comes out. But it had been dry and everyone knew that frogs come out after rain. They feared the frog might be an evil demon. But after that, a big rain did come. So was the frog a messenger telling of the big rain coming? This big rain became a flood.

So when the rain came my family decided to go back to Alice Springs, back to Mparntwe country in our Yeperenye caterpillar dreaming place of Middle Park, near Spencer Hill. When it was her time, the Arrernte midwives took my mother to the birthing place at Werlatye Atherre, just north along the Todd River. So I was born and became a Yeperenye caterpillar dreaming baby.

Because Apmere Yetwernte was my conception place, the Anmatyerr elders said I belonged to this water dreaming. A senior man gave me the name of Ampelyerrke, the Anmatyerr word for those little dark storm clouds appearing below the thick rain clouds. It's a good name for me. Some people say I've always showed the little storm cloud within my nature. Even now as an older, more tired elder of the tribe I can become a bit stormy. Just ask my children.

My brother David was five years older than me. I called him Akngerrepate. His birth site was also along the Todd River, closer to town beside Atnelken-tyarliweke Athirnte, a sacred site at the foot of Anzac Hill. It's a white rock, partly covered with sand, and also belongs to the Ntyarlke caterpillar dreaming line which tells of the Ntyarlke caterpillars moving across the country from west to east. The story goes that they crawled across the plains of Mparntwe meeting up with the Yeperenye and Utnerrengatye caterpillars at Ntaripe, Heavitree Gap. These caterpillar chains became frozen, forming the Macdonnell Ranges and surrounding landscape. You can clearly see the line of caterpillars as you pass through town.

This Ntyarlke dreaming is also part of my grandmother Old Big Dorrie Peltharre's story. I share that dreaming story with my grandmother and my brother. With my grandkids born in Alice Springs Hospital, we all share these Ntyarlke, Utnerrengatye and Yeperenye caterpillar dreaming stories.

....

Nobody was keeping track of the date I was born. I only got registered on the government system later on. Perhaps it was when I started school at the Bungalows or at Santa Teresa. There was no kid's money or baby bonus for Aboriginal kids. We were born wards of the Commonwealth Government.

I grew up being told that 1 April 1943 was my birthday. The same records say my mother was just nineteen years old and already the mother of my five-year-old brother. Whitefellow way, my birthday is April Fool's Day. A day for telling tall stories and yarns. So maybe it is my true birthday. I've told a few survival stories in my time. Back in the old days, unless some district officer or cattle station boss made a note of your birth, they just guessed the age of us kids running around in our Aboriginal camps.

Often birthdays were recorded as the first of January. Sometimes it was the first of July. So there were lots of birthdays shared on those two days. I got slotted in between those two dates. Lots of the Santa Teresa mission kids had this date. Some in my family say they got the year wrong. Many decades later, when I went to the Registry Office to get my birth certificate the bit of paper said I was born in 1944. But my family know they got that wrong.

The end of the war years were tough. We were living poor in our raggedy clothes whether it was summer or winter. None of the white town mob wanted us living next to them. They were scared of us because we were a different colour, spoke a different language, and had lots of rituals and dances. The white mob was easily spooked. We knew that when the white people got scared they could get very nasty. Sometimes they stole us kids away. They might lock us up or hurt us. We were told to hang back in the shadows if we ever saw a white man. And we knew to stay away from their houses and dogs, even from the priests and church ones. We knew to stay clear, and be careful. Otherwise there might be big trouble, and more sorry business for everyone.

Our families had their own stories too – of wild women, boogie men, spirits and demons. These were repeated around the fires at night. Our parents wanted us staying near them and away from danger, especially at night. They tried to hold us close, and with great love.

We had nothing really; no house, no electricity, no running water, no toilets, not even any furniture. We didn't have cars, horses, camels or even donkeys for moving around. Our family owned only what we could carry to our next camp. Just two feet to walk around on, and two hands to carry things. Most of us families living so close together. And we were living on some other tribe's country, away from our own sacred places. We were being blown around by the wind like the spinifex, on the fringes of this ever-changing white man's nightmare.

Our fathers and mothers were busy working when they could. But in those days they were likely to be paid with food. When our families didn't have enough food and couldn't get work, we went hungry and sometimes starved. That's the truth. Other times Government men or someone from the church might help us out for a while.

But mostly our community had to just tough it out. The men had to travel further away, hunting in the old ways. Our women, and us kids would be chasing goannas, lizards and bush food. We'd go into the bush trying to knock down birds or track down insects for a feed. In the cold time, we often got very sick and many of us died. There was not a lot of fat on our bones but we had to make do with what we had. Sharing and caring. Sometimes when we had nothing, we had to beg, and rely on the generosity of strangers. And there wasn't always a lot of that about.

The families along the river would all be hungry together, the dogs and us kids as well. We would all be hunting around down the local dump and in back lanes, looking for food that might have been chucked away. When we couldn't find enough food and there was no work, my family would try to get extra government rations. It was always hard times. We lived mostly on rations. Many times we had no 'good' choices to make to survive.

But still we had lots of happy times along the dry river bed; especially for us kids; with not a worry in the world. The school teachers could be real cruel too. And any old white boss could order you about. They might hit us if we didn't move quickly enough. And we were often cold and hungry. Alice Springs gets bitter frosts and cold winds during winter. But we had our small campfires burning, sitting all close together, and shared the thin blankets. Us kids got rolled up together like little puppy dogs. And real puppy dogs got tucked in with us, close up with the bigger dogs. When the frost hits the ground, sleeping holding onto a dingo pup, keeps you warmer than a blanket.. On the 'three dog' nights, our mothers and grandmothers would all together sleep around us, holding us in against the cold winds blowing along the river beds.

....

It took a long time to get any schooling happening for us kids. The bosses just didn't have enough schools. Plans for building houses for us didn't exist either. Our bosses were the police and welfare officers always keeping a close eye on us. Some of these workers tried to be really good people; but us kids still got taken away. Our fathers often got treated badly, were sent away to work or locked up if someone said they weren't doing what they were told. There was not enough food or anything. And it was often much harder for our families out on the cattle station camps.

Things are still really tough today. But there has been a lot of progress too. My grandkids don't have the big lives they might have dreamed of. Some days it can be a struggle for them to just get out of their bed; let alone going out to hunt and gather a bit of work, money or food for their family. But our people aren't starving any more. Those few Aboriginal families with houses might be overwhelmed by their own homeless family members; and the impossible rules about family visiting. Did you know Territory Housing has started employing their own security guards to harass us and our visitors? Its 'three strikes and you're out'. They have their lawyers waiting to kick us all out. The money they spend on security and lawyers could have built a hundred houses. It's crazy really, but slowly more houses are being built

None of my family have managed to get a chair at the big table; not yet anyway. None of us are there when the big Government or mining royaly money gets split up. We don't get the flash houses, or the well-paid jobs and consultancies. We just don't seem to get much respect at all. We are the 'poor things', and there are lots of us. Today many of our families are still living in humpies and tin sheds, hopelessly overcrowded. Most of my kids and grand-kids don't have places to stay. Every night they have to look for somewhere to sleep. 'Couch surfing', the young white fellows call it. Territory Housing calls it overcrowding, a reason for our families to be evicted.

At least in the old days we had our own campfires and dogs. Nowadays, you get into trouble for lighting a fire; and any 'cheeky' dogs get shot or dragged off to the pound. We have no money to save ourselves, let alone a dog in the pound. They get the bullet or the needle. Or if they get real lucky they are given away to nice white families with lots of food.

I'm hoping my stories help build some understanding of what's happening here in Central Australia. Us Aboriginal people want things to get better. To do that, we need people to know about the problems and to work with us to build change. We need to work these things out together. We need to get better at sharing the wealth of our beautiful land, and learn about living together and looking after it.

It really shouldn't be too hard. We are the most researched mob in the whole world. Working together, we might be able to fix a few things before I become a great-great-grandmother. How about some bilingual Aboriginal teachers for our kids? Building some new hostel beds for our older students so that they can go to school? They are too old to be staying with their grandpar-ents. We need to keep our family leadership working and our own language and culture strong.

How about we create real jobs for our young men and women when they finish their schooling, so they can grow confident? And what about some good places for young couples to live when they are starting out raising a family? Give them a chance, without the humbug of a whole lot of drunk, older family about messing things up. Let the young people grow into leaders without being overwhelmed. They will still need support from their families, but give them a chance to work it out for themselves. Let them make their own mistakes and take responsibility for their own kids. Too many parents these days don't do anything hard to love their kids and keep them strong. It is often us grandpar-ents and white foster carers raising the kids instead.

Lots of these things are just the same as what youngsters wanted back in the

1960s and 1970s, and into the 1990s. But we still need them now, more than ever. And we need new ideas and a stronger, younger leadership, with better funded programs that 'work with' our young people. It would be cheaper than all the new police officers, detention workers, prison guards and 'case managers'. Cheaper than building bigger jails, juvenile centres and cemeteries to hold our young suicides. We need to punish our own family members to teach them ways we are proud of. They need to be held accountable to their own cultural identity.

We want our own kids to grow up properly here in Central Australia. Young parents today can still learn from our ancient traditions. But some of our customs need to be adapted to modern times. The violence against our women and kids must stop. Our men need to get healthier. Our culture needs good ways for our young people to belong in their own worlds.

We need our local families to be better educated and stronger within our own Aboriginal circles of women. Holding our kids strong; and with great love; this is our "Grandmother's Law". We need better understanding and respect between all our families and cultures so we can all learn to stand up strongly within our local community leadership councils.

In this book I am writing of my own hopes and dreams. This is my story and my wisdom, such as it is. Writing it is my way to help my family with our own lives. It is about what happened and what I have learnt. If it helps others I am really very pleased. But people can disagree. I don't mind. I might be wrong sometimes. But I've tried my best. And I hope those old women in the circles are proud of me. I hope my ancestors are happy with me.

I still get up early every morning, with hope in my heart. But I'm greedy for change too. In recent times we have seen some very bad government policies. I'm really angry about the Intervention. It is not good enough to say we have failed as a people, and now need to be battered into submission. Lots of our leaders have been talking about our problems for a long, long time. They need to be included in your planning so we can get some new understandings about how to build a better place for future generations. We need our own mob to lead the changes and be employed in the rebuild.

Like our mothers and grandmothers before us, my generation is just the 'old women, gathering fuel in vacant lots'. But the struggle still goes on for another generation. Hopefully the rebuilding of our language, our stories and our culture will grow stronger too. And hopefully, within our ancient culture, ever-changing as it is, my great-grandchildren will have a better place to grow up in.

CHAPTER 2

Stories of first contact
for the Arrernte tribes

The campfires of my childhood, and the close circles of our senior women, are a long way from the crowded spaces on the edge of town where my grandchildren live today. For me, as a young girl, there was the quietness, the open desert skies, the time to tell slow, complicated stories as a family group. There were fields of wildflowers after rain and ripening bush tucker to open us up to new ways of looking at country. We had respect for our elders. We had respect for the knowledge that they held. They fed us and held us with love, so we listened to them carefully. If we did the wrong thing we were ashamed. This held me close to my culture. Maybe later we might be shamed by our community, and punished too.

....

Central Australia has been the home of my Arrernte and Anmatyerr people since the Dreamtime. These days, the experts say we came here at least 50,000 years ago, maybe even 60,000. A long, long time to be calling a place home. My mother's side of the family are now called Northern Arrernte. They were neighbours of my father's family from the Southern Anmatyerr tribe.

In my linguistic training, I learnt that my father's language is an Arrernte dialect. You can tell from the shared language structures. The Arrernte and Anmatyerr were one group, separating later on. This is why Arrernte and Anmatyerr were both part of the same dreaming and ceremony rituals. They shared the same law, many of the same stories, the same ceremonies and the same ways of living in the world.

Linguists tell us that the Western Desert mobs – the Warlpiri, Luritja and Pintubi – were similar languages but different. They had separated earlier from the Arrernte. About three-quarters of the 300 Aboriginal language groups were from the same original language. Only some of the Northern Australian and Top End mobs were really different.

Our dreamtime stories tell of the creation of our desert homelands. Before the coming of white men, the Arrernte's influence and trading went all across our country with trading routes throughout Central Australia. These trading routes continued across the continent. The trading kept the tribes changing, and built our language and culture. It shaped the advances in lifestyle and understanding. Our ancient laws, our Tjukurpa, were how we created our largely peaceful and spiritual way of being in the world over many tens of thousands of years. Through this sharing of our knowledge along the trade routes, we grew wiser across all our tribes.

Our senior Arrernte men were the powerful desert lawmen. They were important in the big ceremonies and the decision-making about law and the proper ways of doing things. The desert mob was always a bit harder than the others. The hardness of desert life kept our culture strong. Our laws were respected for their strength. Our magic was feared for its power. Our knowledge of these stories, songs and rituals made us senior in the councils of the tribes.

Our Arrernte Dreamtime stories tell of godlike beings that made the spirits of our land. These spirits shaped our countryside and waterways with their powers. This was in the time of magic. These spirits performed great deeds. They filled their new places with all the animals, the native trees and grasses. It was these spirits that created our ancestors. Our human nature comes from these spirits, and our Dreamtime stories tell of the creation of all our Aboriginal tribes.

As well as creating and protecting their places, these spirits could be jealous and vengeful with each other, even towards their own creations. It was a time when many good and bad acts were done as the spirits walked about the earth and made our sacred places. These stories were retold in sacred dances and within our ceremonies. Our Aboriginal law and culture is maintained by the re-telling of our stories. Following these laws protects our people and our land. Renewing these stories is essential to holding everything in proper balance.

My ancestors walked everywhere on our lands. They had no horses or cars. They walked to visit their family places and their sacred sites. They completed their own circle of ceremonies following the rules of birth, death and rebirth. They tried to understand and live according to these Dreamtime rules, following the cultural laws passed down through our creation stories. The elders of our tribe had the responsibility for carrying these stories as a way of teaching younger generations how to complete the essential rituals of our life cycles. Through these rituals and ceremonies, skills and knowledge were passed on so that the next generation would be able to care for their own family and land. Following the ancient laws allowed us to survive, even through the hardest of times.

Building our understanding of culture started as babies, in the learning of our language and our relationship to family. Knowledge was sacred. It was held concealed in our storytelling. When we were teenagers we were told more hidden knowledge of our land and history. This knowledge grows throughout our lives, in the telling of our stories, the learning of our rituals, and the performance of our songs and dances.

Our teachings slowly introduced us to the sacred wisdom of our ancestors. The stories were re-told as they had been to our grandfathers and grandmothers by their own fathers and mothers. Each generation has a responsibility to sustain our laws and ways of being in the world. We each shared the responsibility to train up our own children to care for our families and the country. We are charged with passing on these stories of our place in the world to future generations.

Our sacred knowledge was kept hidden by the adults within our secret language and stories. Passing on the essential knowledge was done when there was a readiness. There was danger in everybody sharing knowledge they couldn't understand. Knowledge is power and can be misused. We needed our children to grow our knowledge in the circle of their elders, so that in the passing on we could all become wiser. We must pass on our knowledge in this proper way. This is our sacred duty.

As a grandmother and great-grandmother, I carry sacred knowledge within my own stories. It is captured in all that I learned within the circles of our senior people. I have carried this knowledge, held the stories with love, and started the passing on of these stories to my own young ones. What I learnt from my grandparents around the campfires, or when they took me out visiting country, or through their dancing in the ceremonies, I'm now seeking ways of passing on. I'm an old woman now, an elder. It is important that my children and grandchildren learn my stories now.

....

Our Arrernte homelands are a beautiful part of the world, on the big plateau that shapes the middle of the Australian continent. The MacDonnell Ranges run east–west across this landscape, following a fault-line where volcanic activity pushed up the ground. We believe spirits made the mountains and carved the rivers through the limestone levels of this land. These spirits still inhabit our sacred places.

According to our stories, the rivers and waterways flow along the tracks of our ancestor spirits: the rainbow serpent and other magical creatures that were on the land in the Dreamtime. This land is where a raindrop falling can go either way. Raindrops can be swallowed up in the underground river systems that go south and maybe east. But two steps away, another raindrop might fall and go north, or maybe west along completely different underground waterways.

The underground water will travel a long way before bubbling up in our springs and waterholes. Arrernte country is a series of permanent waterholes surrounded by the huge deserts that form much of the interior of Australia. Our ancestor spirits created the Arrernte to live in and care for this land. They created the animals and plants, and the countryside that we sit in. And these spirits tell us to keep our stories and ceremonies strong. They remind us that we are responsible for looking after our land.

It wasn't the Warlpiri or other tribes that upset the balance in our Aboriginal lands, but the white settlers and their 200 years taking over our sacred places. At first it was just a few bands of explorers. But these men on horses were followed quickly by land-hungry families with their sheep and cattle looking to steal our lands. The whites with their horses and camels first travelled through our Arrernte and Anmatyerr homelands in the 1860s.

Some of these explorers came here because South Australia wanted to build a telegraph line to connect all the way to London. The government in Adelaide wanted to control this connection, and so the line needed to travel all the way through Arrernte country to get from Adelaide to the Top End.

The first white explorers following our Arrernte trade routes was John McDouall Stuart and his small group of men. They followed earlier white explorer groups of northern South Australia. These groups succeeded, following the water courses in good seasons and by learning where the permanent waterholes existed. These men all brought their guns to protect themselves and to kill things along the way. None of our tribal leaders were happy. Many of my ancestors were killed. These white explorers were sent by governments that didn't respect our ownership or our laws. They never asked permission. Nor did they make any attempt to acknowledge us as owners and caretakers of the land they travelled on. They didn't look after our waterholes and sacred places. It was an invasion, a stealing of our land. The white history of Australia is like that.

This part of the book tells of many of the bad things that happened to our Arrernte and Anmatyerr families a long time before I was born. It was called the 'killing times' by white historians. There was a sickness in the world of that time that taught white people that they were superior to anyone else, or any other culture. What happened to my ancestors was what happens when one group of people don't respect another culture.

I am not saying that there were not a lot of courageous white people who did good things for Aboriginal people. Or that there were not a lot of good white people who were kind and thoughtful, and worked hard. But our basic rights were ignored. The white government bosses and white colonists everywhere were making decisions about what happened to our land and culture that at worst were genocidal in their intentions; at best they were assimilationists, and didn't think or behave in ways that respected our culture and laws. We were just collateral damage to their dreams of wealth, power and privilege. Sometimes we were just accidental damage to white people surviving as best as they could. What happened to our Aboriginal tribes in Australia remains a sin on the white families that benefitted from the theft of our land, and the massacre of our families. If there is no atonement for the sin there is no genuine repentance, and no genuine forgiveness..

In 1870, the British government awarded South Australia the contract to build the telegraph line. The building of the Overland Telegraph Line started in that year. The single copper wire line was stretched on posts all the way from Adelaide through to Darwin. From there it went north and east sometimes underground, sometimes underwater on the ocean floor and underground across continents, all the way to London. From Adelaide it headed to Australian eastern states.

Telegraph lines vibrate. They use a system of taps and dashes on the line spelling out words using a system that was called the Morse Code. But the vibrations lose strength over a distance. The Australian Overland Telegraph Line needed relay stations every 200 kilometres along the way. The telegraph operators who lived there would listen to all the messages and re-send them along to the next telegraph station all the way to their destination possibly 10,000 kilometres away. In Central Arrernte country a relay station was built on a waterhole in Mparntwe country, that they named Alice Springs. It sent and received messages from further north in crossover Anmatyerr–Kaytetye country at a place the white people called Barrow Creek, after the round hills there. Going south was a relay station called Charlotte Waters.

So in 1870 big mobs of construction workers, with their guns and horses, started travelling through a lot of Aboriginal country. All that copper wire and the posts and timber to build the telegraph line and relay stations were carted up on teams of horses and camels or by ship to the Top End. They took big mobs of sheep and cattle too, plus all the supplies needed for feeding everyone.

And after that the white fellows never left. Things soon got much worse for our people. The white government in Adelaide started to sell our land to strangers, people who had never even seen our country, white people wanting more places for their horses, sheep and cattle.

In 1872, a rich important man called Edward Bagot was granted huge pastoral leases at Undoolya and Owen Springs, covering all the Mparntwe land surrounding the Alice Springs telegraph station and beyond. The granting of this lease entrenched the permanence of the white invaders. Soon their sheep and cattle were drinking at our waterholes and eating out our grasses all around Alice Springs. The Arrernte custodians and traditional owners were very angry. But when there was a dispute, it was our people that were often killed if they fought back. The white police and the cattle station bosses had guns, and were murderous in their protection of the pastoralist's sacred cows and precious flocks of sheep.

Further up north, in 1874, a fight broke out over the taking of Aboriginal women by the white staff at the Barrow Creek telegraph station. When the Aboriginal husbands of the women couldn't sort out the problem they attacked the telegraph station, killing some staff.

There was no real tradition of Arrernte tribal groups getting together to fight a common enemy. The desert made it hard to feed a large force of warriors for a long time. And different family leaderships were allowed to follow their own paths. Even individual men didn't need to become involved in someone else's fight.

It was clear to our desert lawmen that our old powerful magic wasn't strong enough to defeat these white ghosts on horses with their guns and their greed. The Arrernte healers had no chance. But what could the senior people do? They carried the responsibility for this land. We had to stay. These were problems without known solutions within our culture.

But the white men had been fighting big wars for thousands of years. They were organised, experienced and travelled in numbers wherever possible. They had horses to carry food and water, and could move long distances quickly. They had guns that could shoot people from a distance. They would scout out Aboriginal groups from fires in the evening, make camp for the night and ride into peaceful family camps just before dawn. They would kill indiscriminately. We had no Aboriginal stories about this.

········

The deaths and injuries in Barrow Creek caused the police in Alice Springs to be joined by other white men in town to ride their horses up there, picking up white station workers, and prospectors on the way. Once at Barrow Creek they rode at dawn into the local camps of defenseless Aboriginal families, trying to kill as many as they could with their guns and their stirrup irons. Not just Aboriginal warriors. They killed our mothers and babies too. They massacred many of my grandfather's tribe. This was white fellow payback to the entire mob just close around Barrow Creek. It was any group they ran into. They didn't take any prisoners back to Alice Springs. Our people scattered as best they could.

All these changes in the 1870s brought the outside world so much closer to our Arrernte heartland. My cousin, Rosie Rice, once told our class how her father's father spoke of seeing the first white men on their horses. Her grandfather thought the men and their horses were spirits, the horse and rider just one animal. They were all terrified of this animal with four legs and two heads. They thought it could point a stick at people and kill them dead over long distances. They learnt it could chase after you faster than you could run away, and that it would kill anyone without pity. They were shocked and horrified. Terrified too.

········

Throughout the 1870s, 1880s and 1890s, the white invaders inflicted terrible pain and suffering upon our people. Our tribes that had survived 60,000 years didn't stand a chance. The government of South Australia never once talked to any of our senior Arrernte or Anmatyerr leadership. The police and the white bosses just made it clear that our tribal lands were now ruled under their law. Aboriginal ownership and sacred traditions were worth nothing. The police were the bosses.

By 1884 a police station was established on the southern edge of Alice Springs through Heavitree Gap. Among the police were two constables: Wiltshire and Wurmbrand. These two men, people say, led the most murderous attacks across Central Australia, mostly against Western Arrernte families along the Finke River. Any Aboriginal group accused of spearing cattle, or that might have been in the wrong place at the wrong time, were likely to be killed off.

Then in 1885 rubies were found by some white stockmen droving out east of Alice Springs. The find led to miners coming up to have a look. It turned out it wasn't really a lot of rubies. Many of the stones were garnets. But in 1887 gold was discovered nearby at a place called Arltunga. Gold was a white fellow madness. Thousands of whites invaded the Eastern Arrernte homelands. Our mob didn't get much of a look-in.

As well, our people were sometimes poisoned with flour laced with strychnine or contaminated water given to them by settlers that had taken over their sacred waterholes. Thousands of others died of starvation and lack of water. Then there were all the new diseases: smallpox, measles, influenza and syphilis, all brought to Central Australia by the white people. In the end it was the sicknesses that killed so many of the vulnerable among our Arrernte and Anmatyerr people.

It wasn't until 1891, after complaints from Pastor Carl Strehlow at the Lutheran Mission called Hermannsburg, and Frank Gillen, an Alice Springs-based government official, that things started to change. Pastor Strehlow and Frank Gillen were appalled at the police killings, and complained to the South Australian authorities. Wiltshire was charged with murder. Wurmbrand had already left town by now. But when Wiltshire was taken to South Australia for trial, the all-white jury of settlers found him not guilty. The white invaders backed Wiltshire and applauded his acquittal.

The white bosses looked after their own, and Wiltshire was soon away again. This time he was employed as a policeman across the Western Australian border in the East Kimberleys. Same job: killing Aboriginal families up near the Ord River, Halls Creek, and Margaret and Mary river systems. Wiltshire even wrote and published books justifying all this killing. He ended up dying as an old man in South Australia. The government bosses in Alice Springs named one of their streets after him.

Only in the 1900s did the South Australian government start handing out food rations in places where the telegraph stations were located. Big Aboriginal camps started to grow up nearby in the Ilyerenye, Inarlenge and Anthepe areas, just south of present-day Alice Springs. There was some safety for our families in these camps.

·········

Central Australia was always good grazing country when the rains came. There were plenty of kangaroos and animals living here. But the white fellows never wanted to share with us, especially the flatter, high plateau country of the Anmatyerr and northern Arrernte lands. These grasslands had springs and could fatten a lot of sheep and cattle. And the Aboriginal families were easier to hunt away or even kill in the grasslands. Whole family groups were left to die without food or water. When the droughts came, even the sacred knowledge of the land and its secrets couldn't stop our families starving. We were nearly wiped out.

All through this time the government in South Australia continued granting more and more cattle station leases on any piece of land that might be okay for sheep or cattle. Soon, all the Arrernte and Anmatyerr lands were said to be owned by these white station owners. Lots of the owners never even got to the Northern Territory. They paid managers. There were more police stations and government men spreading out across Central Australia, and the sheep and cattle continued eating out the best parts of our Arrernte and Anmatyerr lands. Everywhere our tribal elders looked the white mob had settled in.

·········

I have talked with some of my white friends who have taught me more about the invasion of our Arrernte nation a long time ago. The local Arrernte population is thought to have died out from around 30,000 of our people before white settlement to about 5,000 in 1900. There didn't seem to be any sense of shame about the murder of Aboriginal families on the part of the colonial government. That was just how things were done in those days. They say these massacres happened everywhere. It wasn't anyone's fault, some say, just human nature at work.

In any case, in the 1870s when our families tried to stop the white fellows coming in and stealing their land, they were just killed. The lucky ones sheltered in the marginal edges of their country. Or they moved into the Christian missions, onto government reserves, or camped on the fringes of towns. They became refugees, forced off their own land and out of their own country.

For a while, many members of my family got to stay on their country, living close up to the cattle and sheep stations with the new station bosses. Aboriginal men were needed to work as stockmen, looking after the animals that were destroying our traditional Aboriginal way of life. Our senior men and women were surviving as well as they could, powerless to stop the new bosses from taking whatever they wanted. Local Aboriginal women often were forced to become sexual partners and domestic helpers, or chose to get married up to these powerful new white bosses. Our women became part of the recognised wage structure for the white stockmen, according to some government reports. Our ancestors were treated like slaves.

Only after 1900 did the government men in Adelaide and London say that the killings had gone on long enough. They ordered a stop to the slaughter. They did this in most other places too, after these tribes had been largely destroyed by the 'killing times'. The government would even pretend to be saddened about the massacres once any fighting by the local tribal owners had been utterly squashed. But that didn't mean the government gave back any of our land, or ever tried to share power with the Arrernte and Anmatyerr.

The end of the 'killing times' only meant that the police and cattle station bosses had to be a bit more cunning and careful when they were murdering our people. That was all. In the old days, if any of our mob got cheeky or angry they could still be shot and secretly buried close to where they fell. We know this from our family stories. There are still lots of places where the bodies of our dead can't be found.

Big Dorrie Peltharre, Margaret's mother's mother, at Santa Teresa.
*Courtesy of AIATSIS **

CHAPTER 3

Campfire stories of my Anmatyerr grandparents

I was a young girl when I heard some of these stories, sitting around in the Alwekkere within the circle of women. This was near the Telegraph Station in Alice Springs. Around the campfires I learnt about my father's father's side, and my father's mother's side. I would lay awake at night trying to imagine these people, especially my grandfather with his old name, striding through the countryside, reading the signs as he went. I saw him as a big hero, with an important story to tell. But I never learnt much more of his story till later in my life. He was a long time dead by that time.

In these childhood campfires I would watch closely as my Anmatyerr grandmothers drew circles and lines on the ground, showing us kids our family stories. I learnt about culture and my traditional responsibilities for country. They would talk up the old ways of being on country.

My father's father's Anmatyerr name was Ingkeperle-perle and he was born in Ilewerre country, near modern-day Laramba. His name means 'Big Foot'.

His skin name was Pengate. Today the white fellows call his family homeland of Illewerre Lake Lewis. Ilewerre is associated with the Amantye Aknganentye, a corroboree dreaming line that includes many women's dance stories. Amantye is the Anmatyerr word for the place of 'women dancing at ceremony time'.

Ilewerre is maybe 10 kilometres off the Tanami Highway, about 180 kilometres north and west of Alice Springs near Tilmouth Well Roadhouse. At Ilewerre the water, if it isn't evaporated in the salty lakes, travels north and west. The land is grassland, and good hunting country.

A few kilometres east along Napperby Creek is Napperby Station. Our family homeland called Laramba was won back in a land rights claim in the 1980s. It is an excision, or slice of land, cut from the Napperby Station stock route. Today it is where our Anmatyerr family members call home.

My grandfather Big Foot had two wives and many children. He was born at a time where, in culture, men might have more than one wife. This was if your brother died, or if you were a good hunter. Sometimes you might have to take your brother's wife to feed her and any children she had. In culture you might marry an old woman to make sure she got food. That was the proper way for the Anmatyerr, to make sure the kids and old people were all looked after. You might also take another wife because of love. But only if you had the right permissions. Old ways it was the man's responsibility to feed his family. He had to be a good hunter.

Ingkerperle-perle's first wife was my biological grandmother, Jenny Mpetyane. The Mpetyane skin name was Pengate men's first choice marriage partners. Jenny's family was Anmatyerr from Ti Tree Well way, about 60 kilometres east and a bit north of Ilewerre. Big Foot's second wife was called Nellie. In culture we called her our 'little grandmother', because she was married to our grandfather, after he had married our grandmother. She was also of the Mpetyane skin group. Nellie was from Twenty Mile Creek, the first creek you pass going into Napperby Station coming from the east out of Aileron.

When I was a girl I heard that my grandfather and his own father, and his own father's father, all the way back to the Dreamtime, had lived at Ilewerre. If they moved away from Ilewerre it was mostly to visit other close-by Anmatyerr family groups, or to travel in the circle of men during 'ceremony time'. Men's business might take him into Arrernte country, and sometimes further away. He and his wife might also have moved away to live with his wife's family after they had a new baby. But Ilewerre remained my grandfather's home and his responsibility.

White cattle men had bought the lease of that land from the South Australian government in the 1880s. Soon there were cattle in the waterholes, and white men on horses following them. Before long, the bosses of Napperby used some of the local Anmatyerr to work with their cattle. Ingkeperle-perle became a stockman, keeping water up to cattle that were feeding nearby his family camp. Like all the stockmen he didn't get paid. But his family probably was given rations from time to time.

Ingkeperle-perle grew into a senior man in the time of first contact with the whites during the 1880s and 1890s. It only took a little while for the cattle men to set up all across Anmatyerr lands. My grandfather would have heard what was happening. He would have talked within the circles of Anmatyerr men. He would have been witness to the loss of Anmatyerr control and the spiralling loss of life among the Anmatyerr and Arrernte tribes. In 1900 the anthropologists Walter Baldwin Spencer and Frank Gillen described the Anmatyerr as 'almost wiped out'[1].

My grandfather lived through these killing times, but many of his friends and family wouldn't have. He had first-hand knowledge of the sacred waterholes sites being desecrated, his ancient way of life being destroyed. He would have seen senior custodians killed and their sacred objects taken away or destroyed. This happened everywhere. He must have been really angry.

There was great fear within the families living in small groups on their own lands. The invaders weren't respectful. Traditional Arrernte or Anmatyerr spears and boomerangs couldn't stop men on horses. The station bosses had too many guns. They had the police to help out if there was a fight. Cattle and sheep took over the Ilewerre waterholes.

In the past the senior men had been the bosses and always had the right answers. But this new enemy was too powerful and cruel. Even when these white men didn't know country or the right stories, when they had no 'magic' powers or knowledge, they were still winning. They were able to take the land and smash the ancient Anmatyerr way of life. The sacred knowledge and rituals hadn't been able to protect them. They must have become very sad.

Many senior Anmatyerr and Arrernte leaders tried to make sense of what was happening. With the land being desecrated the traditional custodians and caretakers' duties couldn't always be done on their sacred sites. And there were no Anmatyerr stories about these new white bosses. What had seemed impossible before the coming of the white men, had now become the new reality. Our people were dying. There might even be an ending of our families' entire connection to our ancestral land and stories.

Within proper Aboriginal traditions every initiated man was his own boss, and was entitled to be heard and decide his own path. This made local leadership different in many places. Some decided to spear the cattle and were hunted down. Others thought that because they had no answers to what was happening they must hold their family close and wait. These senior men would say they needed time to find a new way to stop the white men who could destroy everything.

But waiting was hard. How did the senior people find a way to pass on their sacred knowledge and ancient skills to the next generation? They needed ways to continue 'ceremony' and rituals. So they worked for the new white bosses on their own country where ceremony could still happen. This is a problem faced by every new generation of Aboriginal leaders since colonisation.

Everywhere it was the old leaders who died first from the new sicknesses. Our nungkaris, or traditional healers, couldn't make medicine to keep our people alive. So there was always sadness and loss. Young people would become the new leaders but often there were lots of problems between different Anmatyerr groups, lots of fighting. These young leaders didn't always know all the stories. Sacred knowledge would be lost.

It was mostly the young boys who got the stockwork from the station owners. These boys became men who were kept busy on their horses. They learnt the new culture of the stock camps. The head stockmen and bosses became their leaders. And they were working the same animals that were messing up the sacred waterholes. And while you got no payment for work, you got privileges from the bosses. Your family would be looked after. So it could be difficult for these young men when they were living across two cultures.

There was the complication of marriage partners too. In traditional way, young Anmatyerr women would be promised in ceremony. But many were being stolen to work with the white bosses and their stockmen. Sometimes the young women were marrying up to these bosses and living at the station homesteads. They would leave with their husbands when he moved to a new job. They could become lost to culture.

What could the senior men and women do? If they stopped the young people working for the white bosses the whole family might have to leave their own country. But if some young ones were allowed to live outside the ancient laws, then culture could lose even more power. Often the senior men had to decide these things. Some wanted the hard punishment laws to be followed. But many took work on the stations, keeping the water flowing for cattle. It helped to keep the young men closer. On the stations the old people, the women and the young families could be kept safer. The old people could continue to run the ceremonies and follow our old ways.

It was in 1908 when my grandfather Big Foot was a senior man that the Australian Commonwealth government took over running the Northern Territory. This government had more money. They built new ration stations to feed our surviving family members. Now the rations included not just flour, sugar and black tea, but sometimes even salted meat and chewing tobacco if people were lucky. They got thin blankets and even clothes maybe once a year. There was more work on the stations.

In 1911 the Commonwealth enacted its own Aboriginal Ordinances to put their 'boss' status into law. All Northern Territory Aboriginal people became 'wards of the state'. Police were appointed to be the official Aboriginal Protectors. The police, of all people! And it didn't work. In fact, putting the police and government men in charge of looking after our families was a very bad idea. Central Australia was a long way from Canberra. The station bosses felt they could do anything they liked.

Under the Aboriginal Ordinances of 1911 the Commonwealth government got to decide where all Northern Territory Aboriginal people could live, work or go to school. They decided whether we got paid and whether we could manage our own money; whether we could get married or not; whether we could own land or property; whether we could travel about; whether we could drink alcohol; and whether we could make agreements, sign contracts or even be represented in the courts if we were charged with something. Parenting arrangements for Aboriginal kids were legally in the hands of our white bosses. There was nothing much that the police or government officials couldn't tell an Arrernte person to do. Under these new laws, everything was legally okay for the white bosses.

Like other colonised people, the Arrernte and Anmatyerr tribes were left homeless in their own country, starving, and without a way to protect themselves or their children. The senior tribal men met often to try to change things. But it seemed the white fellows had no ears for our pleas. Not even the ones who wanted to save you, the priests and the sympathetic ones. They thought our mob were too stupid to make our own decisions. We were treated as pagans and savages needing to be corrected and brought kicking and screaming to the new gods of whiteness and light. Our ancient culture and traditions were seen as nothing.

·········

My grandmother Jenny spoke two languages fluently: Warlpiri first, and then Anmatyerr. She was born near Ti Tree Well and had seven children to my grandfather. Her third child was my father, Dick, who was later called Heffernan. Later on, when my grandfather was an older man, he married Nellie. Grandmother Jenny helped to look after Nellie's three young children when they were born. Big Foot, his two wives and all the young children were able to live together, mostly within the traditions of the old culture and laws, camping at a small soakage spot east of Napperby Station on the border with Aileron Station. There they were protected and a fair way away from their white bosses. Small outstation camps were ideal for this.

My grandfather seemed to travel around a lot. By this stage he was senior in the circles of men and played teacher roles in men's ceremony. These ceremonies weren't like the short events of today's busy Aboriginal world. In Big Foot's days culture and ceremony continued throughout everyone's life. People could be away for many months, even years. The women would live in their circles with families surrounding them.

Sometimes I imagine Big Foot stalking through the countryside taking culture and stories across the Anmatyerr world. And I can feel the pain of all these old people, working so hard, but struggling to hold their family and culture together.

How to keep culture and language strong are the same questions I ask myself all the time. What can I do when the old culture and magic has lost its power? How do you keep fighting when the old life seems impossible anymore? Even holding our grandkids solid seems too hard at times. Going back to an older way of being, it seems, is not going to happen.

·········

The First World War years and into the 1920s were increasingly settled times in Anmatyerr country. But still lots of the senior men died. Some had been killed, others died of diseases. Perhaps my grandfather married Nellie as a consequence of her promised husband's death. I didn't ask and I don't know.

I'm told my grandfather died in the early 1920s. I used to think that perhaps it was the Spanish influenza epidemic that killed him. They say it killed lots of Arrernte and Anmatyerr, particularly our elders. Because the rules of culture say that we don't talk of dead people until a long time after, I didn't hear any stories of Big Foot until much later. More recently, some older people say he died in a culture fight closer to Ti Tree.

The funeral, or 'sorry business', for Ingkeperle-perle involved taking his body back to his home at Ilewerre. From everywhere people came to pay their respect. In line with ancient rituals, his clothes, weapons, bedding and other possessions were destroyed, burnt or given away. Our family cleansed his camping place where the memories of my grandfather's life were strongest. His two wives and their children showed their sadness with 'sorry cuts', hair cutting and wailing. These rituals allowed my grandfather's spirit a peaceful journey into the afterlife, and back to his spirit's sacred place. This was proper way.

After my grandfather's death and the grieving, his wives and children returned separately to their own parents' families. My grandmother Jenny returned to the Aboriginal camp at Ti Tree Station. There she stopped with her older daughter Mompie and her older son Charlie, and his wife Ruby, and their children.

Living in the family camp near Ti Tree Station seemed a settled time for my grandmother and her family. It was good rain years in the early 1920s, with plenty of fresh grass for the cattle. Plenty of ground water too. The families were allowed to move off their station camps to visit their sacred sites, where they continued the ancient rituals of renewal.

During these summer months my grandmothers and their children would walk away from station life with the whole Aboriginal camp. They would visit and clean up the sacred waterholes, like Apmere Yetwernte. It would be time to harvest some bush tucker, the grass seeds, acacia seeds and other bush food in their seasons taking only enough to eat. Their lives would revert back to the ancient ways of our ancestors.

The white world and its often cruel rules would disappear for a while. And during these few peaceful summers of good rain young boys were commenced on the pathway into manhood. Young girls were taught the dances and the knowledge needed to become the women of the tribe. This suited the white bosses, who in good rain years often went walkabout themselves. They might travel to their town houses, or go even further to visit family and friends living in southern states.

In good summer times the station could mostly look after itself. It became deserted with just a few stockmen, maybe a cook or a book-keeper in charge. Someone might occasionally wander around to do maintenance jobs and check that there was water for the cattle. Young horses might be mustered and broken into the saddle. And these lonesome cowboys had their own cultural gatherings, sometimes at race meetings or at a local party, where they'd drink and celebrate the season.

In the old days different families held and performed different stories. They were invited to ceremony gatherings to perform their parts in the ancient dances and songs of revival. Every sacred story represented at the gathering would need to be sung and danced, so that the whole cycle was told. It would include all the local creation stories that needed to be passed on and renewed. The gatherings remained a sign of hope for the tribes.

I am old enough that I still remember the thrill of seeing my Aunt Mompie, Mary Leo and some of the other older Anmatyerr women do their dancing during their special parts of these nights. Re-wakening songs of Ingkerper-le-perle's country. They were representing our mob. Ilewerre was a big name for Central Desert people, both for men and women. All our stories are linked together, telling how people survived hard times, and how to keep things strong. Keeping the dance cycles happening is still very important. Not just within the Anmatyerr and Arrernte cultures, but for Aboriginal people from west to east.

And the Ilewerre name carries great respect even through Warlpiri country, Kaytetye country and Luritja country down Finke River way. Even across to the east through Alyawarra country. Ilewerre still carries its name to the old traditional senior people everywhere.

I learnt this from the old people of Napperby, Ti Tree, Aileron, Yuendumu and even old people from the east. Whenever the Ilewerre mob travel around from place to place, they'll be known by all Aboriginal people, no matter which way they go because of the Kelenthwelkere language, dances and rituals. We'll be known to these other groups represented because we can still explain ourselves properly. Because we know who we are and from what country we belong. Because in our culture the knowledge of Ilewerre explains how we fit in the wider cycles of tribal creation and renewal.

Those big ceremony events might take five nights or a week; longer if you included the preparation. After they finish, in accordance with ceremonial timetables, the gathering might move to the next sacred place. It might be three months or more before senior lawmen came back after the cycle of ceremony into our community life. Some senior men and the new young men could be away longer. In the old days, it took many years to complete the ancient initiation cycles. This was before the coming of the white men. And in the old days you needed to be careful not to wander into other people's ceremony business, especially men's business if you were a woman. That was serious trouble, even possibly death.

....

In the new order of life on the cattle stations, if it was a good rain year then the men might not be back at work until towards the muster time of April or May. The stockmen would return to prepare for the muster. There were always lots of things to do beforehand. Saddles to be repaired, ropes to be plaited, camp equipment to be got ready. The women and kids would settle back into the routine of camp life. If it was busy they might get work around the homestead or do other station jobs.

The stockmen would hunt down and round up their stockhorses that had been allowed to run free on the station. The good ones were kept closer to the homestead. Then they'd break in the young horses to the saddle and settle their older stockhorses back down. They would need to get enough horses ready for the whole season.

If it was a bad summer rain year, then the stockmen were needed earlier to keep the water flowing in all the smaller waterholes and soakage points. You needed to keep moving the cattle to where there might be grass. Cattle won't live further than half a day's walk from water. So they needed to keep every bit of water happening to spread the feed out. Otherwise the cows would eat out all the grass from the main water places and start to starve. They would bog themselves in the muddy holes that were left when the tanks and soakage points dried up.

On most stations the traditional owners and custodians were allowed to set up around their sacred sites as long as they took responsibility for keeping the water going. They would work in with the stockmen who camped out on the river soaks and wells to fill up the water troughs for the cattle. And when the rain came the cattle station cycle would begin for another year.

But in the mid-1920s there were hard droughts all across Central Australia. The cattle died or were in too poor condition to be sold. Station work dried up. Whole families died in Anmatyerr country. It was the same everywhere. My grandmother Jenny and her family all ended up camping in Alice Springs. There was a big Anmatyerr camp there.

My other grandmother, my 'little grandmother' Nellie Mpetyane, was also in town. She had remarried to Jimmy Lynch from Yambah Station. He was a good father to Nellie's kids, particularly her youngest son, my uncle Huckitta. Ingkerperle-perle's two wives would often be found living together in the Anmatyerr river camps. They always remained very close within the Alwekkere where the circle of senior women trained up us young girls.

But by the time my parents were married in the 1930s, the once fierce and dominant desert warriors of the Arrernte and Anmatyerr tribes had been forced to live as beggars away from their own land in Alice Springs to get rations and keep their families safe. Many of my ancestors were camped along the Todd and Charles rivers in Alice Springs, mixing up with other refugees from homelands further away. They would sit down quietly with the once proud Mparntwe family groups on Mparntwe country.

Our senior Arrernte and Anmatyerr men and women persisted with their own cultural obligations when they could. They kept telling their stories to each other, and to new generations of their children. They even tried to build a shared way of being in the world with the priests. Our elders tried to keep our families strong within our ancient laws and rituals. They knew that this knowledge had to be saved and kept alive to protect us all.

But in the towns our people continued to die. Babies struggled to get enough food to stay alive. Women and girls, even some of the boys, might be grabbed from the camps by welfare. They could be forced into having sex for food and drink. Some became infected with syphilis and gonorrhoea, which slowly killed them. Sometimes these diseases even infected their babies. Up until 1935, our Aboriginal tribes continued dying quicker than they were giving birth to more kids. I was one of the first of this new generation, born when our community started growing again.

........·

In recent times Rita Dixon and the old women of Laramba would sit me down with them telling me stories about my grandfather's family and country. Our younger children and grandchildren would be coming in and out from time to time, just like in the old days when I was one of those little girls. I would listen to the talk of the women's sacred site within that Lake Lewis, and the storylines that run through the area.

It is the same with my father's mother's side of the family. During the year I might catch up on visits to Ti Tree or Yambah. Other senior women would tell these stories of place. Sometimes it was the same women. Often we would catch up when they came into Alice Springs.

All these visits would also be about the gossip, funny stories and talk of family troubles. There was lots of laughter and tears. Lots of cups of tea, and kids being chased up, fed and cared for. The cycle of the days would finish when the married women needed to go back to their houses to cook food or to take kids home to sleep. The circle would re-form as new visitors came and went. It might go on for many days before I too had to take my family back home.

Our Aboriginal camps always had these women's spaces, the Alwekkere, in the centre of the main camp. Outside the Alwekkere was where the married-up families camped. Outside this again was the single men's spaces, guarding the edges. It was a way of protecting, looking after the old people and the children, holding them all strong, and with love. Still we try to keep holding onto these ancient ways.

At Laramba I would often visit my uncle Huckita, my father's only surviving brother. He still sits me down and straightens my understanding of family stories. He now lives next to Ilewerre, with his family around him. When he was younger he would sometimes stay with my family or at my mother's family home around Yambah. Now he is old and mostly stays home.

I didn't get to hear a lot of these stories as a young woman. I had to learn some of them a long time later on. I am still learning. This is proper way and respectful. Sometimes with being away as a child, or growing up in the dormitory at the mission, or with important people dying, you can miss out on knowing and understanding the details of these stories.

CHAPTER 4

Moving to town, the big drought and the Coniston Massacre

None of my grandparents ever lived in houses. They built shelters from tree branches with kangaroo skins to protect them from the desert cold and the summer heat. I was a teenager in the Santa Teresa mission dormitory, but still most of my family all lived in their humpies. It was only in the 1980s that many of us lived in buildings. We moved back to town and got given a few overcrowded raggedy houses and tin sheds in segregated Aboriginal camps. It's for my grandkids that I am telling these stories, so that they can understand how quickly life changed around us.

It was hard to get fat as an Arrernte person in the old days. Every day you were moving about all the time and working hard to feed the family. Especially us women. There was not always a lot of bush tucker to go around in any one place. Life revolved around getting enough to eat every day. It was hunting and gathering, and moving from place to place. You shouldn't eat out a place. Our families ate a little and moved on. You kept the waterholes clean and running.

There were always family coming behind you. Everyone needed to know that the family ahead was looking after them. This allowed the plants to regrow. There was no refrigeration, no packaged food, or takeaway shops. Just everybody sharing and caring. Our ancient laws said you had to do this. Our sacred places were always looked after, so they could look after us all.

The women were the ones gathering food every day. Hunting the perentie and smaller lizards, raiding the birds' nests for eggs, digging up the sugar ant nests, hacking into the bush honeycombs, finding the witchetty grubs, gathering the different grass seeds and fruits in their seasons. Sometimes it might be echidnas and smaller animals that we tracked. Our grandmothers and mothers took the young children with them to teach them the skills of tracking, catching and digging up food. As we walked along singing the country up, they taught us the ways to hunt properly. We were also told about our relationships to the land and the things in it. As individuals and families we had strong rules about being safe and respectful in our world.

Our men hunted the larger animals – the kangaroos, emus and bush turkeys. They guided the young men through the long rituals of culture and continuity. They fought battles to keep the law strong and worked together to keep the relationships healthy across all the family groups and tribes. This meant holding our young men in small groups, showing them country, and teaching them the skills and knowledge they would need as older men. They would make sure the next generation learnt the law and their responsibilities to our land, its sacred stories, and our rituals and ceremonies of renewal. Our senior people instilled in us all a map of how to survive when the rains went away or if food became hard to find.

But the white men came with their bags of flour, tea, sugar and tobacco. In some of the deep desert places this was less than forty years ago. We became dependent on the white man and their rations. And the land got sick and couldn't feed our families.

The white fellows didn't worry about looking after the land for the next generations of family coming after them. They didn't care about their kids and grandkids living here forever. There were too many new animals with their big hooves churning up our waterholes. They stripped the grasses from our country. Some of our animals and plants were shot or eaten out, and are now lost forever. We were forced to survive on the edges of a selfish culture that didn't care about us.

The new invaders didn't want to understand proper culture and our land was abused. Our ancestor spirits became angry. The rain didn't come, and the soil was blown away. Our people died. Our whole way of being was dying. We couldn't the pay proper respect to our sacred rituals. And we couldn't fight back. Any trouble and our families got punished and kicked off their own land. The station bosses had come to stay. They had their guns and horses and had taken over.

The station bosses took our young men and put them on the back of horses from an early age. They were taught to ride and muster cattle on horseback. Later, they learnt to work as teams to take the animals to markets far away. The bosses took our boys into their stock camps and taught them the new culture of being stockmen. Our men became harder and tougher. It changed things forever. For long periods, our men would be away from their families and country, separated from their wives and children. Culture changed. Relationships and parenting roles changed. Men and women lived more separated existences.

The station owners were always tough and often cruel. They always needed to be the bosses. Sometimes they didn't even want to feed everyone, even when the government was paying for our rations. In harder times they sometimes hunted our old people away to die. In the really dry times, sometimes they forced the whole camp to leave. They didn't want to feed them if there was no work to be done. Many bosses were best avoided where you could. They raped our women, young girls and young boys. They seemed to enjoy being feared. And they killed people too. Just shot them like dogs.

There had always been dry times. Droughts had always been hard for the tribe. Our culture and law told us to save the permanent waterholes and the hidden gardens for these dry times. Sometimes these dry periods lasted for years and many people who were unlucky might die. It was especially hard on the old people and children. It was often a long walk between places to get a feed and some water. If there was no water then you died. After the white fellows came we didn't have the old ways of saving ourselves. Our country had been taken away from us, often destroyed by their animals. We had nowhere to go. There were so many deaths that often there was no-one who could follow all the rituals.

The droughts in the 1890s saw many white bosses walk off their stations forever. But when the rains came again, so did the white bosses, even if they were new ones. Our families weren't so lucky. So many people died horrible deaths with no food or water. They couldn't survive. They couldn't just get on a horse and go interstate.

Even after this big drought, the station bosses didn't learn much. They still had too many animals on their stations. Again, the animals died when the rain didn't fall. Again, the white bosses didn't seem to know that the dry times always come back. They didn't care how many Arrernte died.

In 1924, the good summer rains didn't come, and 1925 was the same. A lot of stations didn't even get any storms. There wasn't enough new grasses. This was the start of a huge drought all across Central Australia, continuing for many years. It changed everything across our lands. All the cattle and sheep stations were affected. With the water drying up, everything started to die.

The drought meant our families were left without a way of getting clean water. Work on the stations slowed down to nothing. And when the station didn't have any work they stopped feeding our families. It was the soakages with our old people and children that were the worst off. In many places they were left to die even before the animals. Sometimes whole families and tribal groups died.

The station owners started fencing waterholes that still had water. They guarded them with their guns and dogs. Rations stopped. They pushed our families off the stations. They told the government they couldn't feed people. The government was shamed into bringing families into town. But not before thousands died. This dry period lasted eight years and nearly everybody from our tribes ended up in Alice Springs.

The Great Depression came as well in the late 1920s. Because there was no money down south, the demand for meat and its price dropped to nothing. Even when there was a little bit of storm rain and enough grass for sending the cattle away, it often cost the stations more to get the animals to market than the prices they would get paid. The stations didn't need even their Aboriginal stockmen then. They didn't need anything, except rain and meat prices to go up again. A few stations closed down entirely. Some bosses walked off again, and didn't come back. Other white men didn't seem to have anywhere else to go. They just sat on their verandas with a big gun and nasty dogs and ate from their gardens, watered by hand with what little water was left.

Our families were doing it so tough on the stations that they needed to come into town. There was no pay. Even in the good rain years there was little clean water and not much good food in our camps. With our lands long since taken away, and our waterholes now dry, and with dead cattle polluting them, my parents and grandparents were forced into moving off their own country to stay alive.

Proper Aboriginal way, the drought was blamed on the coming of the white men, and nobody looking after country. The traditional rain-makers had been locked out and ceremonies weren't happening. Sacred obligations had not been met. Our law had been broken. The drought was punishment for our failures.

Across Central Australia the permanent waterholes were nearly all ruined. The government built wells along the stock routes but these began to dry up too. A report in 1928 said that hundreds of our Anmatyerr families had died of thirst around Conner's Well, just one of about forty wells built along the stock route between Tennant Creek and Alice Springs.

Eventually our senior men and women accepted that there was nowhere else left to go except into town. Else there might be nobody left to carry our ancient stories and renew the sacred rituals when rain and better days came again. My mother's families moved to permanent water, into their traditional camping spaces near the junction of the Todd and Charles rivers near the Alice Springs Telegraph Station. My father's family came behind them, camping in their own Anmatyerr camping grounds a bit further north.

From these camps the government employed new welfare people to give our families rations. Sometimes our fathers might even get some work in town chopping wood or labouring. Our mothers might get work cleaning houses or shops. But in town everyone was doing it tough too, but it wasn't as bad as on the stations. Bits of work gave them small amounts of extra food to add to their rations and bush tucker. They could feed their family better. But with all the tribes living close together, diseases spread. Our people's spirits were already weak. There were a lot of deaths from sickness.

....

In 1928, in the middle of this long drought, a white dingo scalper called Fred Brookes was killed in Anmatyerr country at a place called Yukurru, near Coniston Station. Our Aboriginal story says his death was payback carried out by an old senior Warlpiri man. Mr Brookes hadn't let the old man's wives come back to him when he needed them now that he was moving on. So he fought with Mr Brookes and killed him. The old man and his two wives buried Mr Brookes's body in a rabbit hole and ran away to Warlpiri country.

When the Coniston Station boss, Randall Stafford, found out about the death, he got scared and sent a message to the police. Sergeant Murray from Alice Springs Police Station, Randall Stafford, some other local station owners and the stockmen from different local stations all got together with their guns. There was lots of anger, with massacres in lonely waterholes, where whole families were killed, their bodies burned and buried where they couldn't be identified.

In the first couple of weeks they killed as many as fifty people. They would ride down the rivers and creeks, killing every Aboriginal person they were able to hunt down. It was easy. In the drought everyone had to camp near water-holes and soakages. The result became known as the Coniston Massacre. But it wasn't one massacre. It was like 'the killing times' again, with our defenceless families hunted down and murdered.

We always knew some cheeky white people wanted us all dead; but these killings just spread out across all the Anmatyerr, Warlpiri and Kaytetye coun-try, and even into further away tribal areas. All the way past Tennant Creek, some people say. The massacres continued throughout 1928 and 1929, and even later on. Hundreds of our people were killed. Some of the whites were killing every Aboriginal person they could.

These massacres and the legal cases afterwards spread even greater fear among our families. Some witnesses were taken by the police all the way into town. They were terrified. The murders also created some compassion in sec-tions of the churches and more generally in white society. The government men, the Christian missionaries and local families started helping the Aborig-inal families to come into Alice Springs like they'd never done before. At the same time, with the railway just come to town, there was a big new mob of white people moving into Alice Springs too.

Sergeant Murray was called before a special government Board of Inquiry set up to investigate the deaths. It was mostly another white-wash. No-one was even charged with murder. Not even when it was old women and our kids. They said maybe only thirty people died. So that was okay, wasn't it? Just more 'collateral damage'. Murray was disciplined, whatever that means, and sent back to South Australia. The other people involved didn't seem to get any punishment at all.

It was only because Alice Springs had changed a lot during the 1920s that this investigation was even held at all. By 1921 the white population of Alice Springs was recorded as just thirty. There were said to be about forty-two mixed descent women and kids living in an Aboriginal refuge called the Bun-galows[2]. But by 1930 the white population of Central Australia was record-ed as having grown to 590. The mixed descent population was said to be 260. The Aboriginal population of Central Australia was estimated at 5,500.[3] Many of our people were now living in or around the Todd River and Charles Creek camps.

When the railway line from Oodnadatta to Alice Springs was finished in 1929 there was a big explosion of new white families, many of them part of the construction teams. A lot of them railway workers stayed. Many didn't like the government men much either. And this new mob of white people weren't so scared of the police. They didn't agree with the old town and cattle station bosses. They had grown up with the Australian idea of giving people a 'fair go'. And many thought us Aboriginal mob should be looked after properly. There became too many sympathetic white people to get away with the old-style 'Aboriginal protection' system. Never again did the cattle station owners have the same control of the police, government men and town management. There was more local administration, and more reviews of what was happening here by senior white people coming up from down south on the train to Alice Springs. The isolation and secrecy was reduced.

One result was that in 1930 the government changed the rules, reducing the payments to cattle station owners for providing rations to the Aboriginal families. There were standards put into place. Some in the government saw it as just a cash bonus for station owners and a rip-off. In retaliation, many station owners decided to force our old people and children off their Aboriginal camps by stopping their miserable rations. They were forced into town to survive.

....

Alice Springs was always cross-over country, a meeting place for all the tribal groups. It was Mparntwe ceremony country where many of our tribes had the big dreaming stories passing through. In the 1930s, north along the Todd and Charles rivers there were us Northern Arrernte and Anmatyerr mobs camping. Towards the south-east along the Todd, the Central Arrernte mob were camped close by the Afghan cameleers' shops and camps. The Eastern Arrernte and Alyawarr families stayed east near Ilypi Ilypi at the back of the coolabah swamps. The Southern Arrernte and southern tribal groups camped south of Heavitree Gap, while the Western Arrernte and Western Desert tribes camped west and south-west of town. Now people from tribes even further away, who weren't even Arrernte, ended up stuck long term in and around Alice Springs.

There was also a growing population of Aboriginal people of mixed descent. Many had been 'stolen away', grown up in the cold charity of the Bungalows Children's Institution. Most were related to our Arrernte families. They had a camping place on the southern edge of town in a collection of hovels and sheds known as Rainbow Town. There was a new post office and telegraph station, and the name was officially changed from Stuart to Alice Springs. This left the old stone buildings of the Telegraph Station empty. The place became the new Bungalows Institution for mixed descent Aboriginal kids, with the children moved back into the safety of town from Jay Creek. In 1932, the government also forcibly moved in more than thirty mixed descent boys from the Top End on the back of the mail truck.

There was overcrowding in the river camps. It was a very stressful time for families that had to move onto other people's country without proper permission, a huge change to the ancient traditions. They became permanent residents without enough food, water supplies or toilets. Having all the different tribes together led to the breakdown of the cultural authority systems. Senior leaders of families had less control of our young people.

In the early 1930s too, the churches started sending their priests and ministers up on the railway into Alice Springs. The new railway families, now resident in town, had been asking for their own traditional spiritual guidance. So the Catholic, Anglican, Methodist, Presbyterian and other churches all sent up their preachers to join the Lutheran missionaries in the new parishes in Alice Springs.

My mother's family, the McMillans, connected with Father Moroney and the Catholics. By 1936, Father Moroney had been joined by Frank McGarry and Brother Bennett. They started to build a Catholic Arrernte mission in the middle of our camps. It was called the Little Black Flower Mission for the Arrernte, and was at the junction of the Todd and Charles rivers, just north of town.

The McMillans, from the Northern Arrernte homelands, were among the first to relocate into town. Their kids were also the first to be baptised as Catholics. They had worked around Yambah Station about 70 kilometres north of Alice Springs. My mother's father's father's name was Packhorse Jimmy Perrule. These great-grandparents were part of the first contact stories for the Arrernte tribes. Packhorse Jimmy married Jenny Penangke and they had five children: Clara, Brandy, Dick, Mary and Harry.

Brandy was my grandfather. Kemarre was his skin name. Their McMillan name was given by an old white linesman for the Overland Telegraph Line who had lived nearby. Big Dorrie Pultara was a Luritja woman from Mt Zeil, 200 kilometres to the west. They had seven children, my mother, Mabel McMillan, being the oldest. My mother grew into a young woman in Alice Springs during the 1930s.

Back in the 1920s drought, Brandy Kemarre McMillan, his wife Big Dorrie and their children walked into Middle Camp along the Todd River just north of town. Related families – the Golders, the Rices, the Lynches and the Goreys – who had all been forced off Yambah Station, were all sitting down near

Middle Camp.

Brandy and Tim Golder were like full brothers, but cousin-brothers white fellow way. They had the same skin name, Kemarre. They were brothers-in-the-law, having gone through ceremony together. They had always roamed the Northern Arrernte countryside together, hunting for food to feed their families. Later, when I was a small child I would see them together everywhere. Sometimes it was in our camps or at the waterhole swimming together or doing their washing at the soak. They would be sitting in the shade sharing food together, or moving camp with our families. They were always together. You couldn't separate them.

Our senior men were like that. They hung around as brothers-in-the-law, sometimes two together like Brandy and Tim. Sometimes all together travelling as a larger group. They went kangaroo hunting together. They sang and danced their songs together. They organised and did ceremony together. And they met regularly as a group to make decisions for our group.

When families were fighting it was the senior men who gathered to sort it out. Of course, the senior women would talk to them, but the men mostly took responsibility for decisions that kept everything settled. A lot of our men could be away at station work or maybe law and ceremony gatherings. It might be for a long time or a couple of days, depending on what was happening. When they weren't hunting, it was all this talking meeting, dancing and singing that kept our men busy.

When I was little I would see the younger men come and go. But they would be away a lot of the time, out in bush camps or working on the stations. We might see them in the ceremony gatherings. Or they might turn up after the muster season, or for the races. It added a bit of excitement for everyone when the younger single men were around. Lots of playful energy happening then.

I was given a collection stories written up from notes kept by the early missionaries of the local Catholic church put together by the Church in the 1990s, where I read that that our family leadership sent my grandfather and his mate Tim Golder along with other senior Central Arrernte men to help find a way to straighten things out with the new church leaders In the writings the priests said our men came to the priests because they thought that the church would know about sacred knowledge and ancient ceremonies. My mother, her brothers and sister were among the first to be baptised into the Catholic church. This was said to be in 1935. The priests and missionaries started a small Catholic mission in Charles Creek to give out rations. And they started a school to teach us about their God.

By 1936 the Catholics had set up a camping area with huts and shelters for our families. Later, five Irish nuns from the Our Lady of the Sacred Heart (OLSH) order arrived in Central Australia to help out in the mission. They started an Aboriginal school at the presbytery. The government census said there were 112 Arrernte people living at the Little Flower Black Mission at Charles Creek in 1937 – twenty-six women, twenty-seven men and fifty-nine school-aged or younger children.

The Catholics made their own Arrernte Advisory Committee of eight senior Arrernte men. My grandfather was part of this. The committee tried to get the priests to understand Arrernte sacred traditions. The priests were invited to ceremonies. They gave the priests some of their sacred objects, their churingas, and tried to get them to understand our ceremonies and rituals. But the priests didn't seem to want to hear the stories or understand our ancient wisdom. The churingas ended up being taken to Sydney, and I heard they have been lost.

The Catholic priests thought our belief system was a poor thing for savage pagans that needed to be forgotten. They thought our families needed to be swallowed up in the rich traditions of their own Catholic faith. They believed they could save our children's souls by converting them. This was very sad for the men and over time some of the old men drifted away. But because our families needed the protection of the Catholics and the practical help they offered, the old men kept their families close to the safety of the church. There were fewer conversations between the priests and the Arrernte leadership though, and the Arrernte Advisory Committee seemed to fade away. The census in 1938 said the mission had grown to fifty men, forty women and at least fifty children living in thirty-nine huts at Charles Creek.

Many decades later the Catholic church became more open to connecting the two ancient knowledge systems. Today Aboriginal Catholicism is different, and the church and the Arrernte families are richer for this new Catholicism that works with our Aboriginal leadership. When I grew up I became a part of the new group of Aboriginal parish leaders, and I'm proud of what we were able to do. But this was much later on.

Dick Heffernan, Margaret's father at Santa Teresa.
*Courtesy of AIATSIS ***

CHAPTER 5

My parents' story

Aboriginal men don't cry. All our families knew that.

My father grew into a young initiated man over many years in our ceremony camps. He learnt about the country from our old men of culture. You get teased and tricked. You get to do lots of things that hurt very bad. You were taught not to panic, and how to keep strong. And how not to cry.

To pass, you had to show the senior men that you were the boss of yourself. This was how you earned their respect. This was where your brothers-in-the-law saw that you would be still there for them at the end of a long day.

My father Dick Heffernan was a very tall and strong man, bigger than all the men around him. His skin name was Penangke and he spoke Anmatjerre, Arrernte and Warlpiri. He was wiry and very fit from his days in the stockyard and bush camp. Always busy, he was good at getting up in the morning and making things happen. He became a senior man of his tribe.

People say my father was a wonderful man for looking after his family, his land and his culture. He was always helping out, sharing and caring. It wasn't an easy time to be taking care of your family. He had little power or influence in the outside world. But my father tried really hard to honour his obligations under our ancient rules.

He had also learnt how to behave as a stockman in the world of the cattle camps. There were no schools when he was a young boy. He learnt his trade by hanging around the stockyards with the older stockmen, earning their respect. When you ride the station horses you learn to be tough. If you got chucked off, you had to get back on. Even with a broken leg. You had to show that you were the boss of your horse. At a young age Dick could sit in the saddle like a rodeo rider. The Heffernan owners of Ti Tree Station gave my father and his brothers their own surname as a mark of respect for their horsemanship. The Heffernan bosses were very tough and even harder to impress.

Dick learnt to be a stockman around his older brothers. My uncle Charlie said my father was a natural horseman. He could out-think the cattle and work out what they would do. When the stockmen were out looking for the cattle, my father knew where to ride. He knew exactly where the cattle would be. This was even before the cattle knew where they heading themselves! And he was clever. He could take charge of the mob and turn them home alone. Walk them as a mob to where the bosses wanted them. He could read the country like that.

As an older man, it broke his heart when he couldn't be a stockman anymore. There was no work for him. It had been his life and his pride to get on any horse and go work the cattle. But the station bosses said they didn't need horsemen anymore. This was when the bosses closed out the Aboriginal stockmen working the stations because of the equal wages decision in the High Court in 1968. None of them could get work after that.

When I was young, I thought my father was bullet proof. He was the lone ranger on his horse, travelling the countryside, making things better. He could fix anything. My father could tell a joke too. And he kept on smiling even through the hardest times of greatest pain. He was tough and kept going even when he was exhausted. And he had enjoyed the respect of his mates, his bosses and his horses. He was known as Long Dick Heffernan by those who knew him well. We loved him for his toughness. But he had his scars too. He was smashed up badly in the end, dying all alone in the old Alice Springs Hospital.

··········

In traditional culture, our Anmatyerr fathers always stood a bit apart from us kids. The men were very powerful, and mostly absent or silent in our children's world within the noisy circles of women. Strong men, they were mostly quiet within their family circles. In the old days the fathers were often many years older than our mothers. Their age and our cultural traditions made them the main decision-makers. It was a patriarchal world.

Our fathers needed to able to command respect and talk up strongly within the men's circles. Without permission, no-one could talk for other initiated men. You could only talk for yourself and your immediate family. But the clever men of the tribe would always be talking quietly with the senior men and women of their family. Outside the family they were always persuading and arguing for the right decisions to be made. Sometimes it was only later that our mothers found out about the important discussions. As kids we might never be told.

At certain times during the year small meetings of senior men were held. These were to share news and discuss difficult problems within the tribe or outside in the world of our white bosses. Our senior men needed to make their decisions according to our ancient laws and knowledge of what was happening. Then the senior men would go back to talk to other men of the family. Every initiated man could be part of decisions. Any man could stand separate in their opposition to a decision. These different opinions had to be respected. Later, the senior men re-gathered when the family discussions were complete. Decisions could only be made when everyone had a chance to be heard. Our way of deciding things could be too slow for some of the white bosses. But it was proper way. The white bosses tended to do whatever they wanted anyway. It didn't matter what we said.

In traditional Arrernte culture, with its hard desert environment, the senior tribal leaders had to make sure our family groups were joined together. There were lots of rules. If one family group was struggling, promised marriage was a way for the old law to restore the storylines and keep all the rituals and country and the tribal group strong. Planned marriages were used as a way of balancing things across the different family and kinship groups. It meant that families were connected through the different family lines, and had obligations to look after each other.

In law, a senior man could offer his daughter as a future partner to an initiated man. The wishes of daughters didn't get much of a look-in when marriage partners were discussed. But it could also be a man asking a father for his daughter in a promised marriage. If it was a senior man, it could be hard for fathers to say no.

Marriage promises were often discussed as part of men's business as a way of holding the tribe together. It could give great offence if an offer was refused.

If the man accepted the offer, they had to make a commitment to the senior man's family that when their daughter grew to marriage age he could marry her. In the old ways, this relationship had to be acceptable to both families. It had to be agreed by the senior lawmen of the tribe. That was proper way.

These promised marriages had status in our law as long as the man kept looking after the woman's family. Traditionally, gift-giving was seen as sealing the contract. It showed the tribal elders that a young man was able to look after his future wife and any children that came along.

These promises could sometimes happen even when the young girl was still a baby. When the girl grew up her family had obligations to keep the promise. Family honour was at stake. But these promised wives often ended up with older men. They might be thirty or more years older than the girl and have to look after him. It even happened in reverse. Sometimes a young man could be promise married to a much older woman, to make sure the older woman was being looked after. But it could upset young people who had found love with their own choice of life partner.

·········

In the mixing of the tribes in the Alice Springs camps, the marriage rules got harder to keep. Families couldn't always stop young people falling in love. This became part of my parents' story.

My parents met as they had been running in the same extended family circles in town. There had been many deaths in this time of the big drought and massacres. Perhaps my mother didn't have a promised partner, or else he had died in the tragedies that were happening everywhere. Perhaps my father had settled all other claims within the council of lawmen. Anyway, they married for love.

My mother's mother, Dorrie Perrule, was a Luritja woman from out west, between Glen Helen Gorge and Haast's Bluff. Under the laws, Penangke men can marry Perrule women. It is right way along skin names. My grandparents' marriage was arranged within culture. My grandfather was a Northern Arrernte man from Yambah Station, and culture lines run west towards Mount Zeil. My mother Mabel McMillan was their first baby, born in 1925. This was when the drought came and there was no work on the stations. So both my father's and mother's families ended up coming into town.

It was only thirteen years later that my parents got married and my brother David was born. To get married the senior people for both my father and mother sat down to reach this decision. My dad's status would have been talked about. Payment by my father's family would have been worked out. Then the decision was made. They were married under Aboriginal law. The old people had given it their blessings.

From that time my mum and dad were able to walk together as a married couple. So my parents' marriage was more like the modern-type of love marriages. They had met and fallen in love, even given the social dislocation to traditional Aboriginal life in the 1930s.

David was born in Alice Springs in 1938. The drought had long since broken by this time. Rain had been plentiful in the mid and late 1930s. But like many families, my mother was still living in town at the time of David's birth. She was held within her women's circle when he was being born. It was good to be around your family and the women who know you at this time. David was born into the caterpillar dreaming stories of Mparntwe country.

·········

When David was a baby, the government became worried about a war that was spreading through Europe and Asia. They started enlisting men to build an army. By the end of 1940, when David was two, they had over 2,000 army troops in the Top End[4] and Central Australia. In 1941 all of Alice Springs became a military zone, with camps training and supplying the army bases in the north. Then Japan entered the war by bombing Pearl Harbor on 7 December 1941.

Alice Springs became full of army people. The army bosses took over running the town. Later, with American help, they decided to build an all-weather road between the end of the Adelaide to Alice Springs railway and Birdum, where the Darwin railway started. Lots of white and many mixed descent women and children were sent away down south. Many of the Aboriginal kids were sent to missions and reserves down in South Australia or even to New South Wales. Others were fostered or adopted out to white families. Some of these kids were never heard from again. They were lost, poor things, and lots of them didn't find a way back home.

The Old Telegraph Station buildings were set up as an Aboriginal workers' compound where Aboriginal people with jobs in town could camp. Later, when the army took over, they tried to set up missions and ration stations out of town to keep Aboriginal families safely out of Alice Springs. But the camps persisted everywhere. There was better paid work in town. Many in our family were employed at the abattoirs or cleaning up around town. So they stayed near the Telegraph Station.

At the start of the war nearly all the McMillan family and lots of Arrernte people were living at Middle Camp or around the Little Flower Black Mission at Charles Creek. The rain had stayed good for a few seasons. And there was work happening again on the stations. Cattle prices had gone up and the bosses needed Aboriginal stockmen. Many of the white men in town and Aboriginal stockmen out bush had joined the army. For Aboriginal soldiers it was the first time they had proper wages and been paid the same as the white soldiers.

My grandfather Brandy, my father Dick, and lots of the other stockmen decided to go back to their station work. Our family settled down again on Yambah Station. For a while the bosses were happy and living was easier. The stockmen started getting a bit of cash. Many families were able to return to their homes on their traditional country.

But when the cattle work finished some families decided to come back into town. The army was paying wages for work in town. Other town work started to be better paid too. So most families crossed over both these groups, staying mainly in town, with the men working in season on the stations.

My uncle Alex McMillan was a little boy about ten when the army set up in town. He told lots of funny army days stories to us as we grew up. He would show us how he and his friends would stand up on the highway to watch for army trucks and jeeps going by. They would be heading off to or coming back from Darwin. He and his friends would be waving their hands, jumping up and down, shouting patriotically as the army trucks lumbered past. The boys would try to look cute but hungry.

He was a very funny man, my uncle Alex. We would be roaring with laughter, tears rolling down our faces. Alex would mimic being real hungry too, one hand outstretched. Our kids were always hungry. If Alex and his mates got lucky, the army blokes might throw them out some oranges, apples, or packets of chocolate or lollies as they thundered past. There would be a scramble for the goodies. Alex would tell how all the proud young hunters would come back to camp to share what was left over with their families. They always brought back what they hadn't eaten straightaway up on the highway.

In the early days of the war there were lots of stories. Things were going bad for the white fellows. One uncle, Henry Ross, said that he heard from the army people that the Japanese were coming down the highway. There were stories of massacres of families in other places when the Japanese took over. Our mob knew about massacres. So many were terrified by all these army massacre stories. They worried that the Japanese soldiers were going to be marching into town any day.

These army bosses were also worried about all their soldiers mixing up with our families. What they really wanted, as well, was the land at Charles Creek that had become the Little Flower Black Mission for the Arrernte. They needed it for a training camp for the soldiers coming up from Victoria to help defend Darwin. Anyway, the Catholic church was given orders to pack up. As a reward for helping with this, the church was given land out of town in Eastern Arrernte country at the old mining area of Arltunga. The army would arrange the move.

On the appointed day, when the army trucks rolled into the mission and our camps along the Charles and Todd rivers, most of the families and all of their possessions got put on the back of army trucks. Even the camp dogs were taken on the trucks. The army drivers drove them out. Later, they pulled down the sheds and village structures. These too ended up out at Arltunga.

My family members who went out there said Arltunga was a real hard place to live. The army trucks dropped everybody off near Paddy's Plain, west of the old goldfields. But the creeks ran that way and water was bad. Our people died. When the army tested the creeks and wells they found the water full of cyanide left over from the gold mining days. In the old days rocks with gold in them were washed in a diluted cyanide solution to extract the gold.

So the army came back again and the Little Flower Black Mission was moved further up the creek, a little past Arltunga, above where the old gold mines had been. At this new place the people erected a church and some houses for their new mission. Dormitories were built for the girls. An Aboriginal camp was created near the church. A school was started. And the mission stayed there for about ten years.

The new mission still didn't have much water anywhere. And the whole place was too rocky and dry, the ground too hard to dig. There was not much local bush tucker. There was not much soil. It was hard to start gardens or water anything. It was hard to grow much food. So when the mission was set up, it was arranged that the local cattle station bosses would move the Eastern Arrernte families out of their camps at the station and onto the mission. The stations also helped out with meat and other food. They got their Aboriginal workers and families looked after. Government rationing for our people was restricted to the mission.

Food was a big problem, so any help was really good. The new mission was a long way out of town. With the war on, the army and government mostly forgot about looking after the mission. It was a hungry place for the families out there. And a lot of the 'out of country' families, especially the men, drifted back to their old camps along the Todd River hoping to find work.

The women and children stayed out there on the Little Flower Black Mission. Them and some of the local station families. Many even stopped at Arltunga after the war finished. It was the right country for them. Some stayed because they believed the church would look after them. But my parents never stayed out at the mission at Arltunga, just visited family later on. By the time the army trucks first came, they had already headed back up north getting work at Yambah.

Later, when the army was busy and the station work slowed down, our families headed back to town and set up again in Middle Camp. My dad found some work in town. He even got paid proper money sometimes. Our family didn't go so hungry during the war years.

But it became a lot tougher for my family and the Aboriginal workers in town when the war finished. The army packed up and went away. The old bosses came back. Work dried up with the young men coming back into town. Families were put back on rations instead of wages. Everyone had to go back to being told what to do and think by the police and welfare people. Not that our families really did what they were told as soon as the bosses disappeared back into their nice offices.

CHAPTER 6

My early years at Middle Camp

My first memories are from after the war ended. I remember running around after my big brother, David. He was always happy, running about with all his friends. One time, it was just him leading with me trying to chase along behind. I might have been three or four years old. It was when we were in town. David was always getting further away. I was being left behind. Then I woke up frightened. I was still lying there safe with my family. I'd been dreaming.

I was a baby living at Middle Camp on the Todd River during the Second World War when the army was still running the town. But after the war, the army sent the soldiers back home and pulled out. The old town bosses came back to run the council. Then in 1947 the Northern Territory elected its first Legislative Council, including with local Central Australian people. As well, the new Commonwealth government created the Department of Native Affairs. This saw the police replaced by district officers and welfare workers. It was their job to tell Aboriginal people what they couldn't do, and to control our money and lives.

Most of my earliest memories are of our family camp on the eastern bank of the Todd River. My mother's family and lots of the Northern Arrernte families lived around Middle Camp. Each family had their different camping places. And I had friends and family in all these. Life was sweet. The women's hunting team included big groups of us kids herded together to chase things down.

David was five years older than me. I called him Kaka. Later, when my sister Sandra was born, I had to lead her into the world like my big brother did for me. I was a very proud big sister, six years older than her. I taught her how to take her place in the big world of us sister girls. But I also taught her how to be very respectful of her big sister too.

Through my mother's side I was part of the Northern Arrernte mob. We were visitors in town, living in the traditional lands of the Mparntwe families. It was the same for the other out-of-town Arrernte. Anyway, we hung around together with all the other tribal groups that had been forced from their homelands in the 1920s and 1930s. And all my family dreaming stories crossed over with the dreaming tracks crossing through Mparntwe country. So we were related by these ancient stories. We had our place in the circles of the Mparntwe people.

Since the late 1920s there had been lots of us kids born in Mparntwe country. This didn't mean we were Mparntwe. But we had a special connection through being born and growing up here. Me and my older brother had these relationships with Central Arrernte people through the dreaming stories and rituals. When we left town, we knew we had our places to come back to.

As family groups we were still visiting other places. Travelling was always a long walk. In the summer months you walked in the cooler hours; fathers first, kids in the middle, old people and mothers walking at the end. Everyone carrying what was needed. You would sit down quietly during the middle of the day. Get a little bit of sleep. You had to get water sometimes from the secret waterholes hidden away. Our fathers and mothers knew these places. We would also get water from the government wells and station dams. Sometimes we had to dig in the rivers at the soakage points. In winter time travelling could be easier. But it was also colder, and you had to carry more things.

The old men and women would be singing up the country as we passed through. They would be repeating the old stories to let the spirit people and traditional owners know that we were travelling through. Within culture you needed to let them know. You needed to wait for their permission before coming through their country. And the old people's songs would be telling the owners and the spirits of the land who we were and what we were doing. We had responsibility to look after the places along the way as we went, gathering only what we needed, and leaving the rest.

·········

When I was a small child in town, at special times in the year other Arrernte families would visit and gather together for ceremony near Alice Springs. At these times our camps along the river would swell. We would hold our women's and men's dances, and the corroborees. These were celebrations as well as cultural rituals. Most weren't secret. Almost everyone was there to dance their own songs. We would all get dressed up and painted in those days. Our grandmothers would lead us mobs of kids, the older kids helping them teach us. We had a really good time watching the dancing and singing by our families. Those were the days when there was hardly any grog around.

My mother, Mabel, was one of the many strong McMillan women that formed this side of my family. She was a very good and gentle mother to us. She was always there for all her family. As the oldest daughter, she had spent all her life helping out with her younger brothers and sisters. She was always the carer. It was very important for her. She really wanted us kids to be good at everything. I grew up in this world of powerful Arrernte and Anmatyerr women. Our mothers and grandmothers, our little mothers and nannas, always with their eyes on us. Shaping us and looking out for us.

Hunting with them was the most fun. Afterwards we sat down with them when they were cooking our food. We watched them when they were keeping the camp going. They were always teaching us, showing us the right way to do things, and telling us our connections to the people around us and the country we passed through. They were there for us when we fell over and hurt ourselves. There to wipe our tears away and make us happy again.

At our home in Middle Camp the older women would sit around together. The married couple camps and the single men's camps would circle them. But all the women would come together during the day, caring for us kids and telling their stories. We would play our own games, comforted by their presence.

Sometimes we visited my grandmothers, Jenny and Nellie, stopping together in their Alwekkere. A lot of the older Anmatyerr women were often living within their own circle of women. These senior women sat down close to their daughters and grandkids. The older women, strong in culture, taught the older girls to do the jobs that senior women didn't always want do for themselves. Everyone was happy. Our mothers and aunties gathered there during the day. There was always lots of laughing and gossip. They were always making jokes and looking after the babies and young kids together.

People came and went from these Alwekkere and from our camps in town. The circles of women were busy places where families came to find out what was happening. Some families might only stay in town for a little while. Then other business might take them back into their own country. They might be replaced by another family coming into the Alwekkere.

During the day, when the men were stopping in our camp, they would often be going one way, and their women heading the other. There was usually a male and female separation. It stopped some of the jealous talk and fighting. Slowed it down a bit anyway. Later on, the husband, wife and kids might move together as a family, packing up and going back home to their own camp. Some years later, families mostly got lifts on the back of station trucks coming in and out of town. But in earlier times, or when a family had to travel fast, they usually needed to travel alone.

So with the comings and goings, there was always a bit of a party feel to the river camps. With the opportunity to catch up with old friends and family, there would be stories being told and food being shared. There were deaths and births to be talked about; rituals of sadness and renewal. There were new marriages and bad behaviour to be discussed. Things to be celebrated and people to be growled. Sometimes there was a settling of scores. But I was only a kid. And I didn't always know much about what was happening.

In culture, little boys stayed with their mothers and grandmothers until they were ready to become young men. They could be living with their family all the way until they got taken into the young men's camps ready for the start of men's business. So around the Alwekkere there was lots of us young girls and boys running around everywhere, falling over, crying, laughing and playing together. The camp wasn't a quiet place. Us kids just raced around till we fell over or got hungry. Then some grandmother or mother would feed you or pick you up, tucking you into blankets near the fire.

All the women would be looking out for each other's kids. So there was always someone to take you back to your family and tuck you safely into some blankets. There was always food being gathered, always women cooking on small fires, stories being told, always a flow of visitors travelling through. As you slept and woke up you would hear the voices or the snores of your family.

Later on, I was one of the younger women sitting down for a time with the senior women in the Alwekkere, in the cycles of learning my own culture. We were all getting to know these old women's knowledge and learning, our Dreamtime stories. We were being taught the proper way of being young Aboriginal women in an Aboriginal world. And like old grandmothers everywhere, those senior women could sometimes get a bit bad tempered and bossy. So could us girls. There were lots of women visiting. Sometimes they came just to let you escape if things were getting too much. The mothers and aunties would cover for us, keeping an eye on things, to smooth things over and stop trouble.

As a young girl, I'd hang around with the senior women for a few hours each day. We might go hunting in smaller groups and they would talk about the places we were passing. As I got older it might be for a few days, learning about the different bush tucker stories.

Sometimes, if it was a nice day and we had plenty of food, everyone would be sitting down together outside, or down in the creek telling stories and catching up on family news. They would talk around me, sometimes to me, about who was family and what it meant. They let me know how I was related to the different families travelling around the camp. They taught us not to be rude or think bad things about people if we didn't know their story. You can never know everything about people's stories so you should always be respectful, even to people we thought might be enemies. Same as the Catholics. Treat people like you want to be treated. It is a good idea. But always easier said than done. If all our families re-learnt these skills, we would be a long way to solving our fights and payback problems.

The women taught me the proper way of placing people into land and into their stories. This was how us kids learnt our place in the world. We watched and listened as the cycle of visiting family and relations came past us. At the same time, other people would be hearing my story and learning about my dreamings. It was how the old people kept all the family together and looking out for each other.

My father's sister, Nancy Heffernan, was often living at the Alwekkere when I was at Middle Camp. She had no husband then. But she had her first son, Sonny Gorey, with her. Another of my father's sisters, Mompy, was living nearby, staying at the Anmatyerr camp with my grandmothers, Jenny and Nellie. Mompy had got married into the Yambah families, living with an old white man, Bill Gorey. She had sung him, the women laughed. Her husband and the men would be sitting in their own places laughing, telling stories and working things out. That was what created the harmony and the connectedness. There was plenty of time and places to straighten things out. The old men and women would be joking a lot, but worrying and working sideways, trying to keep things straight. These days you don't see those things happening. The old people don't have the same places to sit together within their family groups to keep things straight.

After the war, the Anglican church built a place for holding Aboriginal kids and taking them to school. This was out through Heavitree Gap and was called St Mary's Village. The welfare mob would often be taking Aboriginal kids from their parents to stay at St Marys. Sometimes these taken-away kids would be sent further away to Top End kids' institutions, or to the Methodist mission on Croker Island, or the Catholic mission at Garden Point on Melville Island.

Later these kids were sometimes sent to the Retta Dixon Children's Home and became part of the Bagot Reserve in Darwin. There were lots of these children's institutions set up after the war. Like the earlier homes for kids, they were terrible places, full of bossy, often abusive white fellows. These taken-away kids got treated really badly. They missed out on being loved and held strongly by their own family. They weren't shown how to behave properly. Because they didn't get their mother's love as babies or young kids, they had to try to learn all this later on.

There were other big changes happening in the Aboriginal world of Central Australia at that time. In 1946, a new ration station for the Warlpiri was set up by the government at a place named Yuendumu. Then in 1948, a government settlement 250 kilometres west of town at a place called Papunya was built for the Luritja Warlpiri and Pintubi tribal groups. And around the same year, a government Aboriginal reserve was set up south of Tennant Creek; it was called Warrabri, now renamed Ali Curung. This was for Kaytetye, Alyawarra and Warlpiri tribes.

All this setting up of reserves and kids' institutions was part of the government push after the war to turn us into workers. In 1946, the whites made rules so that they could stop people's rations being given to them in town. Instead, families were sent to get rations in one of the new settlements. They wanted to move all us families that had moved into town back out to our homelands. Native Affairs used their powers under the Aboriginal Ordinances to force many of our families to stay out in these new government reserves and settlements. Some tribal groups stopped being rationed in town altogether.

Anyway, we stayed in our camps as family groups until the Native Affairs mob suddenly said we couldn't get rations in town anymore. This didn't happen for a while. And they thought we were making the places along the river untidy. In any case, finding work in Alice Springs had become much harder, so a lot of us wanted to pack up and go anyway. The Native Affairs mob started organising work. My father was forced to take whatever work they found him. This time we had to go. We were soon enough on the road out bush again.

·········

At first there was a lot of jobs mustering. Most of the stations had become very run down in the war years. Cattle hadn't been mustered. Bull calves had grown into feral bulls that were running wild. The cattle bosses wanted our fathers back as stockmen to fix things up again. But in these years after the war, the old cattle station bosses told the new Native Affairs mob they couldn't pay the Aboriginal stockmen properly. They said they were struggling because they didn't get any money unless the cattle got mustered up and sent to markets down south. And the prices were bad. There hadn't been many young bullocks born in the war years, and many were too wild to take to the markets. So the stations didn't have much money coming in.

But even if the station bosses had money they didn't like the idea of paying Aboriginal stockmen. They preferred the 'good old days' before the war when Aboriginal staff were paid in government rations of salted beef, sugar, tea, flour and tobacco. They wanted to go back to the days when the government paid for the 'rationing of Aboriginals', and the station bosses got to tell us what to do. So it was a bit of a stand-off. But the station mobs won this fight, and Native Affairs were told to take over the employing of Aboriginal people and the rationing for our families out of town on the cattle stations, to force us back out bush again.

During the war the army paid its Aboriginal workers proper wages. But after the war these jobs disappeared. There was only a bit of building work happening with our men employed making concrete bricks for new white fellow houses. Later, when all the soldiers came back, there was less work and money in town. The trade unions came in to force proper wages for their members. Not that the unions cared much about what was happening in the Aboriginal camps out bush. But there were a lot of white stockmen who weren't getting paid properly. Soon both white and Aboriginal stockmen started heading across the border into Queensland where the wages were better.

The unions forced the stations to build better houses for the stockmen they employed. And bosses now had to pay proper cash wages. But the station owners again went to Native Affairs. Then the politicians stepped in to make Native Affairs set up 'trust funds' for Aboriginal workers. This stopped our fathers from getting their pay properly. The government said they would collect our wages and look after it for us. That was the last anyone in our families saw of that money.

Things turned around when the rain fell again. The men got the call from the stations that they were needed for the muster season. Once again all the stockmen answered the call, staying in cattle camps during the cold winter months. They even stayed out longer sometimes to do mustering in the back country, clearing out and selling feral bulls and unwanted wild horses, breaking in others.

Even the stockmen staying at the Little Flower Black Mission at Arltunga were getting mustering work. The missions and reserves were asked to manage the contract muster teams. The mission also got big fencing contracts. So everywhere there was a time when it was just us women and kids in the camps with a few old cowboys sitting down together keeping an eye out. It was difficult times, with the cheeky government men still trying to push us all out of town.

But our circles of women were tough. They could see off most threats. Us little ones didn't notice all that much. Life went on as usual if the men were away. Many families tried to stay in the town camps. They were more protected from the humbug of white bosses. But Native Affairs made sure my father and other men had to take the bush work when it came up. Plus our fathers loved their horses and being back on country. So when they got the call to go mustering, they all answered the call.

They mustered all the feral Hereford bulls and sent these animals away on the train. Then the station bought new Brahman bulls out of India. The government scientists said it was time to change the herd. Cattle prices got better in 1947. Our fathers did the work to send all the cattle to markets down south.

Margaret and Huckitta Lynch at Ilewerre (Lake Lewis).
Courtesy of Jenny Green

CHAPTER 7

Living out at Jervois, Aileron and Arltunga

It must have been around 1949, when I was about six, that my father got sent to work out in the Jervois Ranges. This is way out east, towards the Queensland border. The Native Affairs mob had organised this job for him, working in a copper mine.

Dad's new boss was Mr Kurt Johannsen. He had bought a lot of army surplus trucks, called Blitzers, just after the war. He also bought up an old copper mine that was abandoned. Now he needed people to work there. So it was arranged for Dad and my uncle Huckita to come along. Huckita was perhaps sixteen years old. He was promised some wages if he was good enough. Even David at twelve got a job helping out. The next thing we know, all our family were packed up and taken down to where a big truck was being loaded.

Kurt Johannsen was a very clever fellow. He had not paid much to take up the lease of this copper mine. Other people had tried but it was hard to get workers to stay. Plus it was really expensive getting the copper ore carted into town. So Johannsen designed and rebuilt his trailers. He invented a new type of truck axle where each set of trailer wheel axles turned separately to the others so they could all follow the same track. This allowed trailers to be pulled along together down the narrow dirt roads of Central Australia. The invention was used to build the first road trains. Like on trains, one driver only was needed to pull these huge loads of attached trailers. He sold his invention all over the world.

Mr Johannsen bought the army surplus trucks and the scrap metal for his trailers for practically nothing. He knew how to build in metal properly and was really good at keeping those engines going. So he had solved most of the transport cost problems. Then he got the support of Native Affairs and they organised an Aboriginal workforce for him. It was the days when if you didn't work you didn't eat. There were no rations if you didn't take a job when it was offered. You did what you were told. No sit down money or pensions in those days. People knew Mr Johannsen as a pretty good boss who always paid a bit extra in cash. He helped with families allowed to come along, feeding them too. And a lot of men took the work.

We knew we would be staying a long way off our own country. Mr Johannsen's truck had lots of supplies loaded up on it and empty 44-gallon petrol drums used for carting the copper ore. There was plenty of room for us all on the trailers. But you didn't want to be down the back. Anyway, the truck started up and we bumped along the narrow track heading east, camping overnight near Harts Range. It was a very narrow, winding road with lots of sandy places and parts where you nearly bounced off with big rocks poking up through the track. It was slow going and very dusty.

The next day we bumped the rest of the 300 kilometres or so through dry grassland along the edge of the Simpson Desert. Just before dark there was a little turn-off track to the mine. A couple of miles further on our driver stopped in the mines work camp area. The whole place looked a bit miserable, raggedy hill country. I remember just being grateful we were stopping.

A local family came out to greet us. My mother knew them from around Loves Creek Station and the Arltunga Mission. Like us, after the war they later drifted into town. Like my father, the family hadn't been able to get stock work. We were distantly connected up so they said to set up camp with them. Our driver helped chuck off our gear before heading off to their camp. We met some of their kids, Ruby and her sister Queenie about my age.

·········

The Jervois Range is in crossover Alyawarra country that travels alongside Eastern and Northern Arrernte stories, all the way north towards the Barkly Tablelands. I remember in the mornings and at night great mobs of budgerigars would swoop down into the trees and shady areas where there was water. There were different coloured parrots and finches that I hadn't seen before. Then, just as quickly, the sky would empty of birds. During the day there might be only a lonely hawk or kite floating above us.

When we were at the mine it was really hot and dry. Then in winter, it was freezing cold with the wild desert winds driving you under your blankets. We lived in humpies with big windbreaks. A few white workers camped nearby, but they weren't living much flasher than us really. It was easy to see why it was hard to keep mine workers.

Our meals were just tins of meat, with supplies of tea, sugar, flour, jam and water. Anything that would keep unspoiled for a long time. There was no refrigeration out there in those days. Bush tucker was a bit scarce too. You sure would get sick of the same old food, and not enough of it. It was hard country and we got sick of the constant wind and the dust. Nobody liked being off their country, and all us kids missed the fun of being in town.

Ruby was the same age as me and Queenie, her sister, a little bit older. We all became good playmates. We would run around together, keeping close to the camp. There wasn't a whole lot of things to do so we would make up games. Our mothers would make us toys to play with. Bush dolls and cubby houses. Often the women would go hunting, taking us with them to look for bush tucker, usually down where the birds headed in the mornings. My brother had his slingshot out, hoping to knock a bird down out of a tree, where they might be sitting in the shade along the way.

But the Simpson Desert area around there was really just small lizard country, and a hard place to feed off. Still, every bit of bush tucker helped, and it must have helped keep us kids busy too. It was always good getting something fresh to eat. And sometimes you would wander into echidna or bigger lizard tracks. That got us more excited. There was never enough fresh food for us kids. The campsite didn't run to a school or teacher either. Just our mothers' bush teaching. We spent a lot of our time hanging around in the shade of camp all the time.

Many years later, me, Ruby and Queenie were part of the Catholic church parish in Alice Springs and in 2001 worked together getting a Catholic family healing group called Ngarte Mikwekenhe started. Ruby and Queenie had married two Doolan brothers, Paddy and Walter. And we all had a big mob of kids. They had stayed out in that Queensland border country longer than us, and even stayed in Mount Isa later on. But we had overlapped at the Santa Teresa mission and Amoonguna where we all met our husbands. After starting Ngarte Mikwekenhe, we later set up our own little school called Irrkerlantye Learning Centre. It had adult education places and an art centre. Ruby and Queenie became good painters.

In 1949, it was my father and my uncle Huckita working at Jervois. No paid work for my mother. And I wasn't any use, running around and getting in the way. I'm not sure if my brother David even got paid much beyond being chucked a few coins. Maybe it was just my father on proper wages. His job was drilling holes and putting dynamite in them to blow up the rock. It was dangerous work. The young white blokes had the driving roles.

One day us kids followed my father and some others who were going to work at the side of a big hill. I saw my father drill the hole and put the fuse in the rock. He told us to get out quick. Then we heard a big explosion. This time I was hanging out in the open and wasn't quick enough to hide. The rocks flew down around me. One got caught down the back of my shirt. My dad hadn't even known I was there and he was very angry. I got a really big fright and I guess he did too. A bigger rock might have killed me. But it wasn't my time to die. We were all a lot more careful after that. We weren't really allowed up near the explosions again.

After these explosions we would see big clouds of grey dust hanging around until the wind finally blew it away. We hoped the dust wouldn't blow back into our camp. When the dust finally settled a bit and you could see again, the men would go back into the blast site to smash the rocks that had been blown off the hillside. Everybody carted the copper ore down to flat ground. They used big sledge hammers. Once the rocks were smashed about you could pick out the copper globs within the rock. These were loaded on wheelbarrows and put into old 44-gallon drums. When these were filled there was a heavy lid jammed on. The men had a ramp for getting them onto the trailer. When the trailers were all full they would be driven into town to the railway sheds, then loaded onto the train to go down south.

We got to come into town with the truck sometimes. After we got into town, the boss paid everyone up. It was pounds, shillings and pence money in those days. I don't know how much. But not enough for my father to want to stay out east there once the rain came back and stock work was on offer.

·········

My younger sister, Sandra, was conceived during that time. In early 1950 my mother knew she was pregnant again. I think it was maybe one year that we spent out in that mining country. With the baby coming it was time for my mother to head back to town. She wanted the support of family midwives for the birth. Plus there was no schooling for us older ones. We ended up stopping back with family at old Middle Camp for a while waiting. I was really happy. We were all happy. Sandra's conception story was from budgerigar dreaming country. She was born in town on 17 August 1950.

After Sandra's birth we went to visit my mother's country at Yambah. It was late spring time, not long before ceremony time. Some of my father's family were staying there too. Dad got some stock work for a little while.

One time Dad took us all to see family around Aileron. We were stopping with his younger brother Willie and his family, and relations. This was just 40 kilometres further north from Yambah. I had the biggest mob of family around Aileron and I was real excited to be seeing them. We camped at the edge of a big station dam called Ten Mile. It had been made for the cattle to drink at. The main Aboriginal camp was nearby. But there were no bores, pipes or taps going out to our camp. The station bosses said putting water on was too expensive. Aileron Station had never put in many bores.

At Ten Mile they had dug out a soakage in the creek at the side of the big dam to get water to drink. Problem was there wasn't enough clean water from the soakage for all the families staying at Ten Mile. People were getting sick. Plenty of water in the dam for the cattle. None coming for our families. The owner of Aileron Station tried again to move families from place to place, dam to dam, when water or feed for the cattle became a problem. But this time people got angry and didn't want to move. The bosses came out and told all us visiting families to move away. There was a big fight with everyone moving away.

Perhaps this was also the time when the union was trying to get better wages and conditions for all the stockmen. I was just a kid, so I only know this story from later on when things were talked about as adults around the fire.

·········

We left Ten Mile and from there visited the Little Flower Black Mission at Arltunga. Some of my mother's sisters were still out there, with other relatives. My grandparents Brandy and Dorrie came with us. They had sometimes lived out there or went to visit their kids and grandkids going to school there when the season was good for travelling.

We travelled along the old station roads. I can still see those mission buildings when we arrived. There to greet us was my young aunty Hilda, maybe just sixteen. The girls were all living in the dormitory with the nuns. Hilda showed me a rockhole that people went to swim in on the hot days. I think all the drinking water came from a soakage further away piped into a tank.

We didn't stop there long. The rains came and the men knew there was work starting up back at Yambah Station. We were at Arltunga for a few weeks and then came back to a new camping place set up a few kilometres east of town at Ilpiye-Ilpiye past the Coolabah Swamp. We were there a little while when Brandy sent a message with the station truck saying that he had become head stockman at Yambah. He'd lined up a job for my dad. We packed up again, throwing our stuff on the truck and climbing on the back.

Margaret and her mother Mabel McMillan at Santa Teresa.
*Courtesy of AIATSIS**

CHAPTER 8

Living with family at Yambah Station

The drive to Yambah Station was 60 kilometres north along the highway. It sure was a lot faster in the truck. A special place, Yambah Station was beautiful grasslands on the Burt Creek plains. There was plentiful bush tucker, shady trees and sweet water close to the ground. We ate lots of kangaroos, emus, wild turkeys, goannas, echidnas and lizards, plus bush tucker – yams, bush raisin, wild berries, bush bananas and wild honey.

Because Dad was working on the station we were all registered for rations. There was flour, tea, sugar, jam, tinned milk and tobacco every week. The bosses shot a 'killer' when we needed beef. The head stockman was in overall charge of the Aboriginal camp. My dad's job was working with Don Lynch, putting up new steel fences around the station boundary.

Don was about ten years younger than my father and, like my mother, his country was on Yambah. All the Lynch family were living around the station. Don had recently married my cousin-sister, Nancy Heffernan, my father's older brother, Charlie Penangke and Ruby Perrule's daughter. Nancy must have been about eighteen at the time. She was employed helping to prepare the food and set up camp each night for the fencing gang.

There was plenty of fencing work for a while in the late 1940s and early 1950s. It was the time when barbed wire and steel posts started being subsidised by the government across all the big cattle stations, so steel posts were cheap and barbed wire plentiful. These fences replaced the old wooden ones built by hand in earlier times.

The cattle world was changing from open range grazing to smaller fenced paddocks, and as well as fencing the boundary many properties were being divided into separate smaller spaces allowing selective breeding to better manage the quality of the herd. The Yambah Station bosses bought the newly introduced Brahman bulls from India to increase the toughness and size of their old herds of Hereford cows.

So my father was digging the holes, putting in the fence posts and straining the wire tight. An old Bedford truck was used to move the equipment, the posts and the wire to where it was needed. It took a fraction of the time to build compared to the old wooden fences. And the smaller paddock sizes made it easier for the stockmen to work the cattle so fewer men were needed too. It was easier to catch the old Hereford bulls and take them off to the slaughter yard. Then they put in the new bulls. Most of that countryside first got fenced during the 1950s and 1960s.

When extra food was needed out in the fencing camp, Dad and other workers would come back into the station to pick up fresh meat and rations. We were always bubbling with excitement seeing them returning back home. My dad would always bring something for me and David. All us kids would share some bush honey, bush foods or honey ants in a big tin cup. They usually also had some kangaroo or emu meat for the older people. We would all get to share what they had hunted down. Then when the fencing job was finished for a while, we would have all the men back at our camp until the truck arrived back from town with more wire and fencing gear. Then the fencing gang would head off again.

....

As well as being the head Aboriginal stockman, my grandfather also became a leader for all the Aboriginal people who were living at Yambah. Mainly there was the McMillan, Lynch and Gorey families. As traditional owners for Yambah country, they all shared senior roles in community decisions around the sacred sites and living areas, working in with other local traditional owners and custodians.

In culture, Aboriginal family bosses were much more important to us than the white owners. The Gorey brothers might be the white bosses for Yambah Station, but they also had to understand this. Not that it helped us Aboriginal families during the hard times. White law didn't care then. They didn't need workers then. Our mob lost out every time the government changed the rules about the way Aboriginal families were treated. Family members always had to be careful of the white bosses or families could get pushed out. But Yambah and the Goreys were pretty good owners for looking after our families when I was there.

Brandy and Big Dorrie were now required to stay on country. Their sons, my young uncles Patrick and Paul McMillan, were starting up trained as stockmen. I was about seven or eight, and my uncle Paul only a few years older. I remember him showing me his toy truck and a toy horse he had made out of bits of bent fencing wire, tin and wood. He gave them to me to play with. He was clever at making things, even as a young boy. And now he was trying to be a stockman.

·········

During that time at Yambah Brandy's younger brother, Dick Kemarre McMillan, finally came back home to see his father's country after many years living down in South Australia. In culture he was my 'little grandfather' but I'd never met him before. There was a big gathering of our families at Christmas time to welcome him back.

Dick Kemarre had left the Northern Territory during the earlier hard times of the Great Depression. He had been getting work on the cattle and sheep stations all the way down from the South Australian border to right past Port Augusta. Now he had returned with a wife Eileen and their daughters, Shirley and Caroline. There were other little girls from the Dixon family too. We were all together in the Aboriginal camp, playing, talking and sometimes fighting every day, all day long.

The big travelling stories like my little grandfather Dick's were becoming a new part of culture. People had been thrown off their own country and some moved away for work as stockmen in South Australia and Queensland. People could leave home easier. The trains allowed people to travel further looking for jobs. And the droving bosses started using Aboriginal stockmen on longer muster trips, sometimes taking them into Queensland and a long way off their own country.

Because the stockmen had mates from their droving days, they started moving around to where there were better jobs and they got better treated. In other states Aboriginal stockmen could join unions and get better paid. These stockmen became less scared or shy after they had travelled away. Our men became bolder. They became rodeo riders and travellers. They got to have friends in other places. It was only really the Northern Territory where Aboriginal workers often didn't get paid.

But for these travelling Arrernte and Anmatyerr stockmen, the pull back home remained very strong. The travelling stories when they came back to visit were important new stories for our families struggling with the racism of many white people living in Central Australia.

Everyone was very happy to see Dick, and wanted to know about all that country he had seen. They wanted to know about the people that he had met, and what things were like in other places. In the past when young people had gone away they never got a chance to come back together again with their family. For Brandy and the other sisters and brothers it was also a time to meet and get to know their brother's new family. Time also for Dick to hear the news and pay respect to those who had passed away.

....

At Yambah there were lots of Arrernte–Anmatyerr marriages; not just Don Lynch marrying Nancy Heffernan. There were lots of my father's Anmatyerr family living at or visiting Yambah at the time of our stay.

My aunt Mompy and her husband old Bill Gorey were living with us, and Mompy's son Tommy Marshall and her daughter Violet Marshall were staying there too. Plus Dad's youngest sister Nancy Penangke and her son Sonny Gorey were there. My father's mother Jenny Mpetyane stayed with Mompy in the Alwekkere.

Other Anmatyerr people, like Stanley George from Napperby, were also living out there on Yambah Station. Stanley was looking after one of the wells on a station soakage where he lived alone, keeping water up to the cattle. People said he had left Napperby in his younger days to work at Yambah.

For us kids it was exciting to watch all our fathers, uncles, brothers and cousins. We used to hang around when they were working with the horses in the station yards. Sometimes they would be quietening them down and saddling them up, maybe riding them around, bucking away to show off for us kids. This was before motor bikes replaced stockmen on horses. You would see the stockmen in the horse paddock every morning, bringing in and saddling up horses that might be needed for the day. Then they'd mount up just like in the movies and disappear up the road. I remember how smart they looked. Sometimes us kids had fights between ourselves, saying things like, 'Your uncle's not such a great cowboy. My father is smarter!'

I remember the Yambah camp like it was yesterday. It was a wonderful time. Everyone was happy to be back on our own country. And six new tin houses had been built at the camp. Contract builders had been employed by the Gorey brothers to build them. They all had a big front door at one end and two windows on the sides. They seemed very flash after the bush camps. But mostly we still camped outside to suit ourselves, especially the old ones who always reckoned their branch shelters were cooler, breezier and more comfortable in the summer, and easier to warm up with a fire in the winter. Bush camps were also friendlier, easy for the biggest mob of family to camp right up alongside you.

The camp was some distance from the station homestead, past the big stockyards. When you came in from the Alice Springs road you had the tin houses on the east side and the humpies further off the road to the east. On the north-east there was the bore and a trough for the cattle. You would hear the cattle at night and in the early morning coming in for water. It was a peaceful sort of sound. You could hear the wild horses galloping away in the hills, or a car or truck coming from miles away. You'd go have a look to see who it might be.

At Yambah I learnt a lot more of the Arrernte names for places, colours, and ways of mapping the countryside we lived in. Arrernte is so different from English. It made you think differently about where you were, and the land that was looking after you.

At night I sat with my family, listening to their stories by the firelight. Some stories were happy. The good ones were often about before the white men came, how our families lived together, hunting for food, staying at waterholes, soakages and rockholes as they taught the kids about their land, the animals living on it and the beautiful plants growing around us. Everything was connected. Everything was peaceful and complete.

I got to know my young sister-cousins as we played together. My mother sewed me a rag doll with arms, legs, a head and two button eyes. We got given the tail hairs from a bullock and sewed it onto the doll for hair. Us girls pretended our dolls were our babies. Sometimes we wrapped a drink bottle in an old rag or blanket and pretended to feed our babies. Mum showed me how to put two safety pins on my shirt to make nipples for feeding my baby. Together we built cubby houses. Humpies of our own out of tree branches covered with old blankets and sheets. We would play there for hours.

When we left our humpy to get water, someone would call out, 'Your baby is crying.' We'd come rushing back to feed it. Very grown up, we were. Our mothers would make us little billycans from empty food tins. We'd have our own little fire going and get water for cups of tea. Our mums gave us the used tea leaves for our billies. We'd sit in the shade and pretend we were having a cuppa.

Us girls would pick leaves, pretending it was ingkwerlpe, the native tobacco chewed by the women. We would grind the ingkwerlpe on a flat rock with a round stone, small enough for our hands to hold, mix it up with ashes from the fire and pretend we were chewing it. We were a very sophisticated set of young mothers.

Our brothers and the other boys were taught by their fathers and uncles how to turn Golden Syrup tins into horses. You'd turn the tin upside down, get some nails to make holes for wire to go through and then tie on a piece of rope that would hold on their feet. They then looped another piece of rope onto the tins for reins and would ride around the camp rounding up their cattle. They'd squash the bottom of the tin so that their tracks looked like horse shoes. When they trotted around they made sounds like real horses. They would spend hours and hours running around, rounding up anything that wouldn't tell them off, run away or bite them.

The boys got into making toy trucks too. These looked like the big cattle trucks that came to pick up the cattle from the station yards. They made little tanks for water too, and windmills; and built little stockyards to push their cattle into, separate yards for bullocks and cows with calves. Then the trucks would come to take the bullocks off to town.

Us girls were not allowed to play in these boys' games. We kept to ourselves, and the boys kept to themselves. There were very different pathways as we practised being young adults.

But we'd all gather around the campfires on our blankets at night, waiting for someone to start telling a story. I loved those stories, every bit of them. Later on, as a teacher, I'd sometimes re-tell them in the classroom. I wrote some of them down in books to teach the next generation these traditional stories handed down to me as a young girl.

·········

The boss Jack Gorey lived at the homestead at Yambah. He and his wife had a son and daughter. Some of our women worked in the main house for a little bit of money and rations. Sometimes us kids might be taken up there, and sometimes our mothers would bring the two Gorey children down to our campfires to sit down and play with us kids. We taught them our Arrernte language. That's a good way of living together. We all became a bit more like family.

My mother's and aunts' job in the main house was cleaning the floors and everything. Marjorie Kemarre (Gorey) and my dad's young sister Nancy Penangke were cleaning, living all together in the Alwekere. They worked every morning, milking the goats for the station owner's missus. Yambah had a big goat yard. Other women did the cooking, washing and ironing. Most afternoons they brought some salted bullock meat from the station meat-house and some homemade bread from the kitchen.

Mostly it was the older women who would take us hunting. All us kids followed along behind, each with our small digging stick and billycan, waiting for them to tell us what to do. The search might be for witchetty grubs in the roots of acacia bushes, or we might dig up honey ants tunnelling down into the ants' nests. In season, we'd pick wild banana and wild berries, or dig down for yams.

Sometimes the women went to the wild bees' hives in the trunks of trees. They would stand under the tree to see where the bush bees were going in and out. When they knew exactly where the honey was they'd chop a hole with a tomahawk to make an opening to get the honey out. We'd share with all the families, putting some honey in our billycans to take back home. We'd look for a little forked branch and use it to get the honey out of the can, licking it clean.

Sometimes we used bigger billycans for honey ants under the witchetty tree bushes or the mulga trees. The women would teach us where to look. They'd follow ants with a yellow back and black stripe. We'd follow these ants to where lots of them were coming from under a tree. This is where we knew to dig; down, down and further down into the nest. These nests would have tunnels leading to shelves under the ground. The honey ants would be too fat to move anymore, hanging there waiting to be picked.

We'd sit on the top of the sand-pile watching our mothers dig, waiting intensely for the honey ants to be found. They would have a special twig with a hook to flick the honey ants out onto the soft sand without busting them. Then they'd pass them up to us kids with some sand too because if you don't cover them with sand their tummies might bust open.

On our walks we'd be taught how to track goannas, lizards, echidnas and other small animals. We learnt the different signs as we followed up behind. Goannas were the hardest, that's why they grew so big. They could run very fast and if you cornered them they had very sharp claws to keep you away.

They'd climb into deep holes, digging themselves even further away from their pursuers. The women would chase along behind to dig them out with their big sticks. You had to be careful or the goanna would swing around to scratch you to pieces. The women would have their big sticks ready to whack it on the head to kill it before it made its escape. Lovely to eat and lots of juicy white flesh. Everyone loved goanna.

Echidnas were harder to find and you'd have to flick them over on their backs to kill them. But very sweet meat a bit like pork; a real delicacy. Us kids didn't get much of a look in when echidna was on the menu. The old ladies got that. It was mostly the small lizards we got to practise tracking on, whacking them to death if they were too slow to escape. We'd put them in our little billycans too.

You needed to know what you were doing to find any witchetty grubs. Which trees to find them in, and how to get them out of the roots was not easy. Not a lot of tucker, and another delicacy saved for our elders.

The men came back with kangaroos. Guns were easier to come by at Yambah. This made things easier. But lots of the men still did it with spears. Cooking kangaroo was done in special ritual ways too. If you did it wrong way you were in big trouble with the ceremony bosses. It was sacred business. The men would cut open the kangaroo stomach and the guts were taken out. Everything was cleaned and stuffed back in with the legs broken. The fur was burnt off and the whole kangaroo cooked in the fire for a while. We liked it still full of blood. The men cut it up in particular ways. Different people got special parts. On smaller side fires the women cooked dampers and yams would be roasted on the coals.

The cooked food was brought back for the old men and women. The women who stayed home looking after the old people also cooked dampers and made tea, saving some for when the hunters arrived back from hunting.

·········

The time passed quickly. Our fathers were often out in the bush, camping on a bore or mustering cattle, cutting the males and branding them before moving on to another bore. One week here, one week there. They were away more than they were home on a big muster. A horseman rode in and a truck and wagon went out when the muster camp needed more food and rations.

Stockmen's holidays came around Christmas time when the races were on at Aileron. If there had been a bit of rain that made everyone feel good and relaxed. Everyone had some time off after it rained. When the day arrived to go to the races, we all got dressed up and trucked over to the track. Everyone from stations near and far came to Aileron. Some came to see the horses racing. But it was mostly about meeting up with your family and relations and having a good time. Us kids just enjoyed our sweets and treats.

The Aileron race track was some distance from the station, behind the road house and by the hills. There were plenty of camping places and stable areas. Lots of people, both black and white, would climb up the trees to cheer on their horses, especially when it was the Aboriginal stockmen's races. Other people would sit by the fence.

At night there would be parties and get-togethers. A lot of news to tell and stories to be told. Us kids would be packed off back to our camping areas with the grandmothers looking after us. Then, after a couple of days, the races were over for another year. Everyone would be packing up and going home after some hard and tiring days.

It was at the Aileron races that my father and mother decided my aunty Ruby and my uncle Charlie Heffernan would look after me for a while. I don't know much of the story but Uncle Charlie and Aunty Ruby were moving back to my grandmother Jenny's country near Ti Tree. They had some donkeys and food with them. I walked along with them or rode on one of the donkeys, a trip of about 70 kilometres. On that journey they taught me lots of new things about my grandmother's country. They showed me where the important sites connected to our family stories were.

Uncle Charlie and Aunty Ruby had a place to stay with my grandmother near Ti Tree Station. We went on hunting trips on their donkeys. We might camp out away from the station for one or two days a week. I learned how to find good spots for camping away from the wind, and how to find bush foods. They talked about what's good and what's poisonous. Later they took me back to Yambah to be back with my parents.

·········

When Dad's fencing job finished up we got a lift back on the truck to Middle Camp. We left my grandparents at the station. It was goodbye to Yambah for a while. We were back to living on the banks of the Todd River. The dry times had hit and work again became hard to find,

In 1950, the new Commonwealth Minister for Territories, Paul Hasluck, announced this Assimilation Policy. A big word for an old racist idea based on the superiority of white culture. Since we hadn't all died away, now they decided we had to become 'more white'. If they couldn't breed the blackness out, they would bleach our thinking. The Department of Native Affairs made new rules about who you could marry, what work you were going to get forced into, and where you could live.

The plan for the Arrernte and Anmatyerr tribes was to drive us all mad in their white fellow schools and reserves. We were to be separated into smaller paddocks, with lots of us kids taken away from our families and put into schools run by the new 'child welfare' workers. The next generation was going to be saved from their own parents and grandparents. Aboriginal culture and language was going to be helped to die away.

It wasn't just because of the dry season that we'd had to leave Yambah, but because the station rationing schemes had ended again. Having put in the new fences and the new bulls, the stations now didn't need a whole lot of Aboriginal workers living in camps. So the prohibition against Aboriginal people camping in Alice Springs was lifted. Old and young Aboriginals who weren't needed on cattle stations were told to go back into the big paddock of their town camps, or onto the new government reserves or into Christian missions.

Our families were told by the Native Affairs welfare officers that we had to move to the nearest reserve or mission if we wanted to be fed. Our mothers would be trained to work in the white fellow kitchens; the men would be trained for the big machines making the new roads, or sent away to look after fences further out bush. None of us mob needed to worry about finding jobs or wages. The government took care of all that trouble. They would keep taking our money and keep telling us what we had to do.

It was a lot like the scientific cattle breeding program with the Brahman bulls. The scientists had decided it was time to change the herd so the old Hereford bulls got the chop. The new Brahman bulls got to mate with the Hereford cows. These new cross-bred heifers were then bred back to the Brahman bulls. The mob was going to become bigger and more Brahman every year. The mixed descent baby bulls had their balls cut off at the first muster and were later sent away on the trains to the slaughter house. The cattle mob was going to change its colour and design. Turning them into 'proper cattle' so they would fit in the world of selling more beef.

Now it was our turn to be treated 'scientifically'. We were to be educated and managed to better fit into white fellow culture and the new economy. So it was back to town we went.

CHAPTER 9

Starting school at the Bungalows

In 1951, when I was about eight, we moved back to Middle Camp, setting up in the old place. The government mob had changed the rationing rules again. Lots of families were forced back off the stations. It was during some drier years in Central Australia. Cattle were too weak and skinny to be taken to markets and stock work had slowed down. None of the station bosses had money coming in. There was also a polio epidemic happening, with local people sick and some dying. There was a great fear of the spread of this terrible disease.

In Alice Springs, Native Affairs set up a new version of the Bungalows with the old Telegraph Station becoming an Aboriginal school again, and the rationing station. The cattle stations couldn't provide proper schools so old people and families were brought back to our old camps along the river. New welfare officers provided the new rations on Wednesdays after school. No school, no food. Just like today. The old Bungalows children's institution with its farm area and underground cellars were used to grow and store food, to be dribbled out to families living in our rubbish camps without housing, water, toilets or electricity.

When we arrived back to Alice Springs my family had to register for these rations. David and me had to start going to school. It was time we were educated just like those 'poor bugger' white fellow kids. Schooling was serious business. But the department didn't have enough school places. Us Aboriginal kids started when we were older. And they kicked us out pretty early too. No point in educating us above our station.

None of us had seen much of a school before the Bungalows. The stations hadn't been big on teaching. Us kids were going out with the women and old people on hunting trips for bush tucker, and travelling as families on ceremony events and visiting sacred sites. The station bosses thought our boys and girls weren't going to need a university degree to ride a horse or work in the station kitchen. Even their own kids didn't get much of an education. But now we were going to learn to sit still and behave properly.

The old people worried that this school business didn't fit well with our culture. It didn't allow time for ceremony and teaching the old ways. But nobody asked them. And no-one would have listened anyway. So with my big brother, I started out on our early morning wanders up river to the Telegraph Station and the old classrooms. A lot of us tried to hide, like a bunch of calves separated from their mothers for the first time. We were just a big mob of kids trying not to cry, not knowing what to do next.

But you couldn't hide for long. Welfare had their list. Every morning when we arrived the teachers lined us up and marked the roll. Then there were the showers. The one thing you couldn't do in the river camps was keep clean. So we felt like losers. Cleanliness was the new benchmark. There were two showers for the boys and two for the girls, all in one big stone building; one side of the building for the boys' showers, one side for us girls.

They've now rebuilt the Telegraph Station to its old glory. This included taking off all the signs of it being an Aboriginal compound. Our shower block was turned back into the old coach house. But I remember having all those showers there. If they could teach us nothing, they were still going to scrub us until we were white. After our showers, in turn, from big kids to small, the teachers handed us our school uniforms. We were told to stop mucking about and to put them on. Best clothes I had ever put on! But we didn't get to keep them long.

When we were all dressed, we were marched to line up in front of the school buildings in the assembly area. First day was worst because each class had its own place. So that first morning, like at the stockyard, they separated us according to age and sizes. After that, every school day was the same. In the morning it was showers, uniforms, standing in line to listen to the teachers telling us what to do and what not to do. There was always someone desperately wanting to tell us something. Not much they didn't know. We nodded if anyone looked at us. No smiling or talking on the assembly line. This was serious business. They made us stand there very still before finally marching us into our classrooms, all trying to smile so people would like us. Marching around doing what we were told. Trying to look small so we didn't get picked out.

Some 'naughty' kids would skip off to go for a swim in the waterhole rather than come to school. They missed their lessons and the teachers weren't happy about this. These kids got rounded up and got the strap across both hands. I was always trying to be a good girl but I remember getting the strap. It really hurt. I'd never felt anything like that before. Cruel, it was. The teachers told us again and again, 'Don't go swimming before school breaks in the afternoon.' But some of us kids had no ears for this talking.

It was mostly the boys who got the strap, especially when they were new kids or visitors to town. Sometimes it was the older ones who thought they were too old for school anyway. For lots of us, school was so boring that even getting the strap wouldn't stop us doing something else with our friends.

At recess, when the whistle blew, we came marching out of class to go to the kitchen area. There the white 'ladies and gentlemen' served us milk. They gave us a piece of fruit – an apple, banana or orange. They were all working for welfare, I think. But maybe it was a church mob. I'm not sure why the school didn't have some of our own families working there. But anyway, we drank our milk and ate our fruit.

After that we could run around in the playground till the whistle blew again, telling us to go back to the classroom. They used the whistle a lot at that school. In the classroom I tried to sit quietly so I didn't get in trouble. But I didn't get to learn much English at that school, and I can't remember learning much of anything else really, except how to sit quietly and not get called out.

....

We got to come out of the classroom again at twelve o'clock. They made us sit down for our lunch. Mostly it was sandwiches. After that we got to play again. We'd run around really crazy after so much sitting and holding ourselves still. Then the whistle would go for sports, which happened after lunch every day. We got to play with some basketballs and sometimes the big, heavy tunnel ball. Sometimes it might be hockey. It was always a competition. Mostly girls against each other, some combination of one tribal mob against others.

The boys played football or cricket.

Everyone had to join in the relay races. We'd be lined up and split into different teams. One half of each team would get in a straight line behind a marker; the other half of the group had to march down to another marker line maybe 50 metres away. The teachers would growl you if you didn't stay behind your marks or in a proper straight line behind each other. Then the whistle would blow and the front person holding a stick would run flat out to our team behind the other mark. They had to hand the stick over to the next person and they'd fly off with the stick down to the other line. Once you handed over the stick you had to go to the end of the line again. The winner was the team that got back to the first person first. Sometimes the teachers might give you a little prize. But we just liked winning and smiling at all the losers.

All this was practice for the big sports day carnival when we raced against kids from other schools. It was racing, high jumping, long jumping and throwing things. There were relays. Sometimes it might be racing with a spoon carried in your mouth with an egg on it that you couldn't drop. Or three-legged races where they tied one of your legs to someone else's. You had to step it out together. Or sack races where you hopped about like mad in a big hessian bag, trying to get to the other end. Then there was the tug-of-war competition where one team had to hold onto their end of a big rope and drag the other team over to their side.

It was great fun. I really liked trying to win. Sometimes you might get a ribbon. Sometimes even a better prize. I liked the prizes the best. Us kids from the bush were the usually the best. We could run fast, fly through the air and chuck things a long way. So we mightn't be winning in the classroom, but we could flog the others at anything outside. We liked to let them know it too. And they had a few ideas that they liked to share with us.

·········

At the Bungalows school we were taught to write with a short piece of lead pencil, a ruler and a rubber. Sometimes we had a special treat and were given coloured pencils, pretty short ones too. Always just one piece of paper at a time. No books. We tried to read the school readers, the story books they gave us. Usually the teacher read it out loud to us and we tried to follow our own book with our fingers and eyes. One book was about Nyree and his friend who was a girl. That book was made for us Aboriginal kids.

It was all in English in the school; no language was allowed to be spoken. Sign language was still okay, especially if they didn't see you. And if they didn't hear you it helped too. But if you got caught speaking Arrernte you got the strap. So you always had to keep an eye on where the teachers were and who might be listening. It took a long time for our English to get much better.

After school we took off our uniforms, handed them over to the teachers, and they gave us our own clothes back to put on. Then we could walk back to our camps. In the hot months this was not before jumping in the Bungalows waterhole for a swim. All us kids would be hanging around there in summer after school. That's how we met all the different language groups. It was where I met my future sister-in-law, Emily Malpiya Campbell, and her sister Joan, from Ernabella. Joan taught me Pitjantjatjara and I taught her Arrernte.

Us kids learnt some things at school but mostly from each other. Like at big ceremony times, when one mob learnt our language and we learnt theirs. Nobody was the bosses. We had to be able to talk to each other. At school there might be Warlpiri kids come in from Willowra Station, or Anmatyerr mob down from Ti Tree way. We were all stuck in town by then.

My father's Anmatyerr family was camped close to the Bungalows around this time, not far up from the west bank, near where the Telegraph Station car parking is today. The Warlpiri mob were a bit further up and north. The Pitjantjatjara a bit further away west and north again. There was every tribal group in town. So it was a proper Aboriginal language school, that waterhole. But there were no whistles, no bells and no bosses. Nobody was getting the strap or telling people off. No fights. Well, maybe a few fights. And maybe a bit of yelling names at each other too. But on a hot day the water was wet and cool. We all had lots of good fun.

Since the 1990s the Bungalows waterhole has been really dry and filled up with sand. But me, my friend Rosie Rice and others, we used to swim in the waterhole every summer's day after school. It was a big, deep waterhole that used to open up near the rocks on the east bank of the Todd where the big trees are. The water finished near the top tree up there. It had a dark, tunnel-like strip of water shaded away under a rock shelf and the big river red gums. We'd climb up the smooth rock to jump into the water. Sometimes we'd go into the cave, climb up and out through a hole in the top. We'd walk on the top of the rocks to the wild fig tree. And always we'd pick figs to eat. Then we'd climb down to the round rock to dive into the water. All the kids knew about that cave. We'd go into it in turns when we felt like going there.

When we were in the water we played 'water chasie'. We'd see when the bubbles come up, then go under the water and get them. We never swum with the boys, always made sure there were all girls in the group. The boys did their own thing. When we come out, they'd go into the water. Sometimes we'd glide along in the cool water of the tunnel. Then we'd get out to dry ourselves in the sun and talk a bit. When we were hot again we'd jump from the rock and dive into the water all over again. It was a very deep pool in those days.

When the rain came and the water flooded or trickled down from Wiggles and Junction waterholes, it would settle in the Bungalows waterhole and then flow down to Middle Camp and the waterhole there. Underground springs fed the pools as well, so there was always good water. But not anymore. Nobody has looked after it. The cattle stations were allowed to build their dams on the river and pump it dry. They created their own orchards and gardens, but stuffed up the river flow.

....

After school and a bit of swimming we would head home, walking along the river bank or on the soft river sand, splashing through any bits of water along the way. Summer was cicada time too and we'd scoop up any cicadas we spotted and put them in empty tins we'd brought along just for this. Someone would get a firestick from their camp to start a fire in the shady river bed. We would lay them cicadas out to cook on coals and then eat them. Only the young ones, fresh out of the trees. Not the old crusty ones. We burnt off the wings and the shells to eat the juicy centres. I loved those cicadas. Everyone did.

It was like witchetty grubs. They were like chips and made a crunchy sound when we bit into them. The young ones came out of the ground after rain and we looked for them everywhere, trying to catch them before they changed colour and got strong enough to fly. When they come out of the ground they are white and weak. That was the best time. Once they changed their colour – yellow with dark stripes – it was too late. Thinking about eating them now, maybe it was a bit yucky. We are spoilt for choice these days. But back then we didn't have packets of chips or ice-cream. And we were always starving hungry. You had to get your own tucker where you found it.

Sometimes after school we would climb the west bank of the river to get into the Bungalows farm. You weren't allowed anywhere near it, and you got a flogging if you were caught. But they grew date palms there and we went to collect the fallen dates to eat when they got ripe. Sometimes even before they got ripe. We'd gather some raw ones, yellow ones, green ones and black ones. When they were ripe the dates were lovely and sweet. We would put them in our tins to eat with our cicadas. We might sit down every day after school when the cicadas were about. Then the cicada noise would stop and we'd know they'd be gone for another year. They would dig themselves back into the ground. Only the empty shells left.

....

Our childhood friends at Middle Camp were Terry Rice and his brother Augustine, or Blue Tongue as we called him. Me and Terry were the same age. Blue Tongue was older, about the same age as my brother David. There was also Basil Stevens who was in between David and me, and Thomas Stevens who was a bit younger. Then there was Michael and Rosie Rice, and my baby sister Sandra.

My mother and Hilda Rice, Terry's mother, told a story about when Terry and me went missing. They went looking for us and found us sitting downriver in a pool, catching tadpoles and throwing them out of the water into the sun. Those birds with the long neck and long beak, white and grey, egrets, I think, were keeping us company. We were feeding them. When the birds saw us in the water they landed beside us. They must have known we were good at catching tadpoles for them.

After school, when we came back to our own little waterhole, our mothers were often waiting for us, collecting their washing after it had dried in the trees or sitting around a small campfire. On good days they had a damper cooked, plus sugar and jam, sometimes a tin of meat as well, and a billy of tea. They cooked these dampers in the hot ashes of the fire. We'd eat our dinner down there sometimes in the hot weather, with the cool breeze softly blowing along the river to take some of the flies and mosquitoes away.

After rain, there was a bigger swimming hole closer to the school. When the older boys got to this place first, they'd yell to us girls, 'Keep away. We got here first. You go away.' I remember David, Basil and Augustine shouting at me, Rosie Rice and the Golders. 'Don't take another step to this water or we will hit you mob.'

So if the boys got to the waterhole first, us girls had to go away to sit under a gum tree for a long time, waiting until the boys had finished their swim. Sometimes we never got our swim. Sometimes if we got there first the boys might be the ones finding something else to do.

It was a good and easy life. The boys would go hunting after birds, especially the galahs and pigeons, with their slingshots and stones, killing them to eat. Us girls would see the boys making their fires in the river bed and cooking their birds. All of us, boys and girls, were told to hang out separately, but together.

Don't travel alone, we were warned, especially at night.

We were told to stick close to the fire circle at night. And during the day we would run around pretty much keeping everybody in sight so they wouldn't get stolen away. This was the way we were taught. If we did the wrong thing the women would growl us. There was usually no hitting or getting the strap. We just got the look to remind us about looking after each other and doing the right thing.

·········

On Wednesdays, everybody from the camps all around the Bungalows area got their week's rations of flour, tea, a tin of condensed milk, butter, cheese, jam, sugar, matches and sometimes big tins of treacle. Plus a big tin of corned beef, square and long, perhaps as long of one of our rulers at school. With it would come a really big stick of nikki nikki, chewing tobacco. It was tobacco leaves dried out and wrapped together, sometimes as fat as our closed fists. People would smoke the leaves of the pitchuri plant over the coals till it dried out, then grind the leaves into powder and keep it in a tin. The ashes, it was called. They broke off some nikki nikki from the stick, wet it, then dipped it into the tin of ashes.

I still chew tobacco today, but it's Log Cabin in a tin, when I can afford it. The chewing is really good when you're hungry or thirsty. You don't notice it so much. We often ran low on food on the days before rations were due, especially if there were visitors. But nikki nikki is a little bit cheeky too. Makes you feel strong, and a little bit crazy too. The days are dreamier and a bit more pain free.

On ration days, us kids would climb the rocky outcrops alongside the river at the Bungalows. My family would sit under the big peppercorn tree, with the other families talking and waiting for school to finish. Then the welfare mob would hand out the rations. All us kids would help take it back to our camps.

One time the welfare mob gave out tents. Everybody lined up and got one. We got billycans and tin cups as well. No houses in those days. Just our humpies made out of wood and branches. Only some people used those tents for sleeping in. Most still used their humpies. The tents were used to store food. If it rained we would put the tent over the humpy to keep everything dry. Not that it rained much. But the rest of the time, the tents made the humpies too dark inside. Everyone preferred sleeping outside anyway on the sandy ground around the campfires where people told the old stories and could gossip about what was happening. In winter we might light a small fire for a bit of warmth.

You couldn't do that with a tent.

When the tent got too old to store things in, it was cut up and used to line a run-off area down past Middle Camp waterhole. You dug a hole in the sand, putting a bit of tin at the bottom. The bits of canvas were used to seal the hole. Then water from the waterhole would be heated up and bucketed in. These were our washing tubs that our own mothers made.

....

During my early school days at the Bungalows my family were friendly with the Campbell family. Later Malpiya, the daughter, became my brother David's girlfriend. She was a bit older than me, maybe eleven. The same time David's best mate, Johnny Leo, was going out with Malpiya's sister, Joan Campbell. I got the job of being David's and Johnny's secret news carrier. They would give me messages before school. I would hide them in my pocket, carefully passing along the messages when I saw the girls at school. Malpiya and Joan would then give me messages to take back.

The girls and the boys weren't allowed to cross over much. So 'secret message keeper' was such an important job. I had to be a bit tricky and really careful. David and Johnny were really nice to me at this time and sucked up to me just in case I might get 'accidentally' careless. Not that I took advantage or anything. I was a good, obedient girl most of the time. Well, some of the time anyway. I knew my brother could get me back 'proper way'.

CHAPTER 10

Living back in town at Middle Camp

Back in town we joined up with the Catholics again. Every Saturday we would go down to the church. I still remember those trips. Our families would start packing up the blankets and bedding, food, billycans and cooking things. The women and us kids would all carry them downriver to the place next to the hill below, near where the old Little Flower Black Mission used to be, where Anzac High School is today. Lots of us Arrernte people came together those nights so that we could get to the early Sunday morning mass.

Our mothers would set up camp for the night, we'd have a big feed and then our grandparents might start telling us the old Dreamtime stories as we lay in our blankets by the fire. Some of the stories were sad and made us cry. Some were stories to teach us the proper way to behave and look out for each other. Some were fun stories with happy endings. They made us laugh and roll about. It was while I was camping for mass, that my parents and grandparents taught us about the sacred site there, Atnelkentyarliweke Athirntmy. It was part of my grandmother's and my brother David's dreaming story. I remember those days as really happy ones for us kids. No drunks or fighting back then.

On the Sunday mornings we would roll out of our blankets to go to hear about God and the Bible in that little Catholic church that is still there in Hartley Street. They use it for an office today, after they built the new church at the end of the street. My parents told me that when I was a baby I was baptised there by Father Cox. That was how it was those days. My family taught us about my grandmother's dreaming on Saturday nights. And on Sunday mornings we learnt about the white fellow Catholic God and listened to the 'Word of God'. That's what I call 'Two Ways Learning'. After church finished, we would all hang around for a big feed before picking up our things and starting the walk with everything back up the river to Middle Camp.

....

My parents often took me and my brother to see my Anmatyerr family at their camp to catch up with visiting relatives when they were in town. We would catch up with Johnny Leo and his cousin-brother Sonny Gorey whose family lived there. David would sometimes play together with the Physic boys and all the other young Anmatyerr men who were living nearby. David and his friends were soon to be going into men's camp. Then it would be just me and Sandra living with the women. David would move away into the young men's spaces.

One day we went there to see my grandmothers at the Anmatjerre Alwekkere to play with Sonny Gorey and Johnny Leo. But they told us that Sonny had fallen from a tree and broken his arm. My aunt Nancy had taken him to the hospital in town to get looked after, and he was kept in there while his broken arm healed. While he was in the hospital the welfare mob came for Sonny and took him away because his father was white.

They did this without even telling Nancy what they were doing or where he was going. She looked for Sonny everywhere at the old hospital. I saw my aunt and all the families weeping and crying, thinking he must have died. Only later did everyone hear he was taken away to live down south with white people.

....

In 1952 our family met Sister Magdaline and Sister Jacqueline-Dominique for the first time. They were French Catholic 'Little Sisters of Joseph' nuns. Each day they rode their bikes from the town to come and sit down near my grandmother's Anmatyerr camp just west from the Bungalows. The Leo, Ross and Physic families all stopped there. These sisters would be close up but sit-

84

ting away from our camps when we first met them. But when the nuns didn't know how to get water from the soakage, or how to make a fire and cook on it, my grandmothers had to save them.

One day, after watching them struggling, my grandmother sent over my cousin, Violet Kemarre, to teach them how to make a proper fire. She even lent them her frying pan to cook with. They stuck like glue after that. We grew to love them. Over time us kids would stop by and talk to the sisters after school. This involved taking a long cut on our way home. The nuns loved cooking a bit of sweet food to share at school finishing time. That is how they built their mission with the Anmatyerr, and they are still out in Anmatyerr and Warlpiri country, sitting down at Yuendumu. They are well into their nineties now and spending more time in town. They are wonderful strong people, sticking loyal to our families even today.

The nuns got to know my sister Sandra very well. Sandra had very fair hair, even a lighter yellow than me and David. Sandra told the nuns her name was 'Sandra with a J'. They found this very confusing when we all nodded. My sister's real name was Jacinta, but we always call her Sandra. People still get confused. But the sisters really liked how friendly Sandra was. We were all helpful. We'd grown up in big families trying to look after people. That was our way. We helped them and they helped us.

The nuns' camp was a nice place for everyone. Soon the sisters moved a bit closer and started living near my grandmother's camp. Later, when our big Anmatyerr family was pushed out to Amoonguna, they moved there too. They were close friends with us by then. And they were passionate in their mission too. Social activists for our people's rights. The white bosses tried to kick them out, but they were proper stubborn and refused to go.

Sister Magdaline wrote of her memories of the day when my grandmother sent Violet over to give them a hand.

One day we had stopped for lunch under a gum tree, a little way from a group of wurleys when a woman came with a frying pan to help us cooking. It was Violet Kamarra, Old Jenny Mbitjina, who had been watching us battling to make fire, had sent her grand-daughter to our rescue. After that we kept coming to that same place and by and by we came to meet more people from that group.

I still run into Sister Magdaline and the other sisters a lot, even today. Over six decades they stood beside us. They were still living at Amoonguna when I was there as a young woman. In more recent times they helped us out when we started Ngarte Mikwekenhe, our Aboriginal spiritual healing service, and later our Irrkerlantye Learning Centre School in the Gap area. They are really thoughtful women and kind to us, and all Aboriginal families they came in touch with.

....

While we were living in Middle Camp my mother sometimes got cleaning work with a white family running the old Eastside bakery in Undoolya Road. She would get given a loaf or two of bread and get paid some money as well. Sometimes my father went to the Smith family nearby and did some work for them. Usually it was chopping wood or raking and watering around their yard. He would be paid a little money too. Sandra and me would sit down in the shade of a coolabah tree along the fence line. The Smiths had two sons and we played with them. Sometimes my father was given some cake and biscuits for us. We devoured these lovely treats. In summer, Dad bought some ice-cream for us at the corner shop there on Undoolya Road, where Casa Nostra is today.

A couple of times a year there would be horse races in town. This was a gathering of stockmen and their families. We went down to catch up with family coming into town. We moved our camp over to Charles Creek near the Northside racecourse. Our Anmatyerr stockmen with their families from bush would all camp close up there. There would be makeshift stables and station racehorses stabled everywhere. When it was close to the time for their race, the horses would be walked over to the stables to be saddled up for the jockeys.

The races were a mixture of a sport and a party. At night the guitars and singing would start. The races would go on for two or three days. After the races finished for the day the party started. Sometimes there were bands at the racetrack then the men might kick on late into the nights. The bush guitarists would be singing the old cowboy songs. And the young people would be up dancing. Even the older ones liked a dance. But the young ones always had the all-seeing watchful eyes of their mothers and grandmothers on them. Us kids would be sent to bed first. We would go to sleep with the singing and dancing in our heads, next to all our cousins. Then on the last day there were the Aboriginal stockmen's races. Sometimes my father would ride. This was when family bragging rights were won or lost till the next race meeting. The Heffernans were always modest and gracious winners, offering helpful advice to all the losers.

The station mob would tell you the family news from Yambah, Aileron, Napperby and across our tribal lands. Dad might hear of possible work coming up, and where old mates were stopping. And then when the last race was run, and the last dance finished, everyone from bush packed up to go home to their own country. Some were riding horses back to station properties. But more and more it was station trucks or the bosses of the Aboriginal Reserves and their trucks that took people home. We walked the shorter trip back to our own riverside camps.

The Aileron races are still a bit like this, even today. Once a year all the Anmatyerr and Northern Arrernte mob out there gather around the racetrack to see who will have the bragging rights for the year. And families still camp nearby with family and friends in from the bush community groups and their family from town. In the old days it was hard to get out there to Aileron every year. But when we could get a lift my father and his mates looked after us.

These days we drive a car or get a lift in a bus. Sometimes there are lots of our family gathered. Sometimes not so many. But still it is races and catching up with the stories. Still there is a party celebration feeling to all being back together on country. My mother's parents, Brandy and Big Dorrie, were always there with the other Yambah families at these races, when they could get there, and the Yambah horses were always well bred for speed.

·········

Sometimes my mother would take us kids out visiting other related Arrernte families in town. It was really special when my grandfather Brandy went to catch up with his old mate Dick Palmer at his place Aperalwerrkne, called Palmer's Camp out north along the river. They were great friends from droving days and stock camps. Mr Palmer had got a long-term lease for the land from the government for his droving team back in the 1930s. He lived there along with his wives and their brothers and sisters. They were a big family, generous with lots of sons and daughters, grandsons and grand-daughters.

Dick was one of the first Aboriginal boss drovers. Palmer's Camp was always a real busy place, with lots of his old droving mates calling in and staying a while. My grandfather and Dick would sit down and talk and talk of the old days. We learnt a lot about our grandfather from these visits. They were all champion horsemen and best stockmen back in their day.

Neighbours for Dick Palmer were Tim Shaw and his family, next door at Mount Nancy Camp. Tim was the father of Geoff Shaw, who started Tangentyere Council in the late 1970s. Our family was close to Tim's wife and her brother, Lesley Ryan. Back then Lesley was newly married to my mother's young sister, May McMillan. She and their young daughter, Carmel Ryan, became close friends.

So the Palmers, the Shaws and the Ryans were all living close together at Mount Nancy and Palmer's Camp. Each time we went to see Aunt May, she and my mum would sit together talking, laughing and sharing stories of earlier times. It wasn't just the men talking things up. They were just like us old ladies today, sitting around talking up the days when we were young. Sometimes you have to skip over a few details to be polite. Even when you're writing a proper history story. Many of these same families are still living out there today at Mount Nancy and Palmer's Camp.

One time, my grandmother took me south through town to see her sister-in-law, Clara Kemarre Kennedy. Mrs Kennedy had a house in the new Aboriginal housing estate in the southern side of town called the Gap. Clara grew up her family there. I met the three Kennedy daughters. They were my aunties: Maureen, Valerie and Eunice Kngwarraye. I remember this visit because it one of the first proper houses I went into.

....

Around this time, perhaps early 1952, my big brother and his friends Augustine Rice and Basil Stevens had to go to bush camp. The senior men had gathered to talk about which of the older boys they would catch to do their time at the bush camp. It was decided that it was time to put those three boys through men's business with other older boys from the tribe. They told my mother and the other women that it was the right time for them. All the initiated men – the grandfathers, fathers, uncles and cousins, everyone in the men's group – would go to these rituals and gatherings. Within a few days David, Augustine and Basil were taken away to the big bush camp gathering out of town. In those days the young men took a year to start the learning of their dreaming tracks, their totems, and their responsibilities to family and country.

At the end of the first stage of the young men's initiation, all the women with their young kids and swags, water, billycans and food, had to gather at Werlatye Therre for the Inerte-Kerte camp, or 'coming out' ceremony. Our grandmothers and mothers, aunties and cousins, all the women would cook, and the men would take this food away to feed the whole bush camp. The ceremony called up all the other tribes in the local area whose young men had been drawn together for the initiation camp. There was the Central and Eastern Arrernte, and sometimes Anmatyerr tribes there.

Maybe a week or two before the ceremony was held, all the women would gather our family to start the walk to the gathering place where the ceremony was being held. Us girls were happy and proud to be taking part in these dances. Our family and all the women would dance at this coming out ceremony. The older women would take us young girls with them to teach us the dancing. These women proudly helped put the red ochre and white feathers on our mothers and aunties who would join the dance at the ceremony. They told us kids to sit and watch and learn.

'One day it's you girls turn in years to come,' they said.

They made us sit and watch calmly and quietly while they all painted themselves up.

After the ceremony David came back from bush camp. He growing up and getting tall like our father. At this time my father was part of arrangements being made for David to marry Janie Briscoe. Janie was from my grandfather's sister's family. It was the old way of the senior men to arrange these marriages. Linking families back into storylines and country. David agreed, and him and Janie came together to be married. But a year later on when they had no kids and wanted to separate, they were allowed to go their own way again.

·········

Not long after this we heard that the Little Flower Black Mission for the Arrernte out at Arltunga was closing down and moving to a new place that was being built called Santa Teresa, in Eastern Arrernte country. A lot of the Eastern Arrernte people living in town were excited. Some of them planned to move away from Middle Camp and all the other Arrernte camps in town to move to this new mission.

It was 1953 and the police and Native Affairs mob in town were pushing us in a new direction. There had been another change in the Assimilation Policy rules. Now they wanted to get all us Aboriginal mob out of Alice Springs again. It was this year that Native Affairs became Aboriginal Welfare again. And the Commonwealth enacted new rules called the Welfare Ordinances of 1953–64. These classified our families as 'ward 2'. We became subject under the old Aboriginal Ordinance rules where we could be told where to live. We were banned again from living in Alice Springs.

The welfare officers started taking more Aboriginal kids away from their families up to the new missions. Even bigger kids were taken. Some went into new educational dormitories at St Mary's run by the Anglican church just south of town. A lot of other little kids were taken away to disappear into new Top End missions. Throughout the 1950s the welfare officers removed hundreds of Aboriginal children from their mothers around Alice Springs and Central Australia.

Before this, the 'taken away kids' were mainly children of mixed Aboriginal and European descent. Now it was any Aboriginal child that could be taken away. Under the new ordinances, many of these kids were adopted out. Some ended up living interstate with white families. Local Aboriginal families became more scared of camping in their old places along the river. They also became scared of using services like the hospital or schools because they worried that their kids wouldn't come back home from these places.

These were some of the reasons that our families made the move to this new Catholic mission at Santa Teresa. If they wanted to eat and not be chased by the police and welfare, they had to move to the mission. After a lot of talking my parents agreed it was time to make this new start. It was further off their own country, but away from the welfare mob.

By this time my brother David had got back together with his old girlfriend, Malpiya Campbell. The senior people agreed on them getting married. So David and Malpiya moved away from our parents' camp to live with his Campbell in-laws at a place called Camel Camp, near where Amoonguna is today. Within a year, my brother and sister-in-law had their first child. She was called Margaret Heffernan too, and born in the 'native' hospital' in town.

After the birth they went back to Camel Camp to pack up. Soon David, Malpiya and their young daughter Margaret and David's wife's family had to move south to escape the new ordinances. They went to Malpiya's family's country near the new Ernabella mission across the border in South Australia. David's mate Johnny Leo had also married his old school girlfriend, Joan Campbell, and they also shifted down south into Ernabella.

In 1953, my parents were as good as pushed into packing up and going to Santa Teresa. All the Middle Camp families had to go somewhere else away from the Todd River. My parents needed permission to go into other people's country but their Eastern Arrernte friends said it was fine by them. So a lot of McMillans and Heffernans, including us, were all going out to live in this new mission. One sunny winter's day my family ended up packed and waiting at the Catholic presbytery for the mission truck to pick us up and take us to our new home at Santa Teresa.

CHAPTER 11

Growing up in the mission

I still remember very clearly that day when we first went out to Santa Teresa. My family were packed up early and had dragged everything to the presbytery in Hartley Street. All we had was a few blankets, some raggedy clothes, pots and pans, knives and spoons, what was left of the rations, and the dogs. We had to wait with another family on the move. Then one of the missionaries arrived in the old Bedford truck. He was driving it back out to the mission with building supplies and food. He said we could all throw our stuff on the back. We climbed up behind our gear and the dogs, squashing in close between his loads.

When we were all settled, he tooted the horn and we left Alice Springs behind us. The gravel road travelled east and south, passing through country that was strange for us. There were yellow wildflowers, lots of spinifex and colourful bushes that you could see on the tabletop hills and the red sand dunes. There were strange smelling trees I'd never seen before. My mother said they were gidgee trees.

We all had a lot of sadness leaving town. Leaving David behind was the hardest of all. But my father stood tough and we followed suit. An old lady on the truck sat softly singing the country up as we moved along. She was naming the dreaming tracks and letting the spirits of the land know we were coming through, asking for permission.

We finally drove through a lot of bloodwood trees, the ltyente apurtes that gave the area its old Eastern Arrernte name. Behind it was the new church buildings, most still being built. There were piles of roofing tin, stone blocks and bits of wood. The church was nearly finished. There were kitchens and eating areas. Everywhere lots of people were working, helping out getting the place finished.

The driver took us past the buildings along a narrow track and through some small hills into the new Aboriginal village camp. The grandmothers and single women had already set up their own Alwekkere in a central area. We pulled in past this, in the middle of humpies made from bits of wood and roofing tin held together by wire. But the camp had a shape, and there was some love in the set-up. Water drums had been set up, and campfires. We had arrived at our new home.

The dogs jumped off, starting another turf war that we all ignored. Both families were helped to pick out our own camping spaces nearby. We picked a place within the circle of our other family members in the married families' area. Our gear was pulled from the truck. Like everyone before them, my parents were helped by family to build our small windbreak using a sheet of old tin. Soon Dad and some of the men had shaped some sticks and branches together and we had a simple humpy to throw our gear in. I helped my mother make a small outside fireplace and stack in the cooking stuff close by. Cups of tea were handed around. It felt good to be there.

My father drifted off with the men. Proper way, he visited the single men's camps stretched further out. Mixed in everywhere were lots of skinny dogs. Not that far away was a herd of goats, a few donkeys and some horses, a garden area growing stuff further down the track. The mission was obviously still being built but the people seemed happy enough and were helpful.

A lot of my extended Arrernte family had already moved into the new mission straight from the Arltunga mission. My grandparents were part of the group forced out of Yambah Station. We followed them here from our Alice Springs river camps. It was always hard to live in other people's country. But my grandparents had a big mob of brothers and sisters, children and grandchildren already there at Santa Teresa. We were safer all together. Everyone knew that. And my mother's McMillan family had already decided to link their lives to the Catholics. So we had a warm welcome.

A lot of families from the river camps who didn't come to Santa Teresa went back onto local cattle stations where the bosses were kind enough to let them stay. This way they could be nearer to their own country. Some had moved onto the new reserves and government-run settlements being set up further out in the desert country. And a lot stayed in town, being moved around and harassed by the police and welfare mobs. They were shifting around in the fringe camps, sometimes moving further out when the town bosses started circling too close. Some of the white families were helpful, giving people room in their sheds, finding them bits of work.

It had been a long battle for the Catholic church to get this land for Santa Teresa mission. The dream of building up a more sustainable and comfortable homeland for the Arrernte tribes had started before the Second World War. But the government wouldn't give the money or land to the Catholic church. They always had some other plan that saw us moving back onto cattle stations, or into a new system of government-run ration stations that always forgot to fund the training stuff. Sometimes it was just sticking families in far-away reserves. Funding Aboriginal people was never very important to the government in Canberra.

But the Catholics kept the pressure up. They developed a proposal that the new Catholic mission be on vacant Crown Land bordering Undoolya Station in the west, Nummery Station to the east, Ringwood Station to the north-east and Deep Well to the south. East was the Simpson Desert. These areas had not been taken as cattle leases because they didn't know permanent water sources on that land good enough to run their cattle. The Catholics had a lot of friends and they got them to talk it up. The parishes were told to pray harder. They said, 'Our God will provide. We will dig deeper wells to feed everyone.'

But the local cattle station bosses didn't want the churches around. And the NT Cattlemen's Association was a powerful lobby group. In the good seasons when there was plentiful rain and water pooled in the creeks, these unfenced grasslands were grazed by cattle which could be moved about to keep the better country in good shape.

Finally in 1952, negotiations between the NT government administrators and Bishop O'Loughlin were finalised. The Catholic church was allocated a block of vacant Crown Land about 90 kilometres south-east of Alice Springs. The agreement was that the Little Flower Black Mission was to be moved from Arltunga onto this new homeland.

The Santa Teresa mission was about 100 kilometres due south of Arltunga. It was well grassed and, compared to Arltunga, had good places to grow food. Plus it was big enough to run some cattle and horses. The ground water could be collected and it wasn't poisoned. And the priests knew there were good opportunities to find underground water sources since the local rivers drained into the area.

The agreement gave the land 'in perpetuity' to the mission for 'the benefit of Aboriginal families'. They had to fence the borders and had permission to drill for new bores, put in new dams and develop rainwater tank systems. The government agreed that there were advantages for the local cattle stations to have a close-by pool of experienced Aboriginal stockmen for their muster and stock work seasons. These contracts could be administered through the mission. And the mission would educate and train our kids. They got a better place to grow its flock, a good place to shepherd, educate and assimilate its Arrernte Catholic community away from the chaos of town.

In late 1952, the Arltunga mission stockmen, working under the supervision of Father Dixon and Bruce Wallace, who used to be old head stockmen at Loves Creek Station, carefully pulled down all the old buildings at the Arltunga Mission. Mr Wallace was a very hard-working and experienced builder. He had been relocated from Loves Creek Station during the war when all the Eastern Arrernte stations had sent their workers over to Arltunga.

The roofing tin, timber, iron and anything else worth scavenging was loaded onto wooden drays and the one truck they had. It was dragged along new tracks, across Loves Creek Station and other stations that followed the old stock routes and muster paths. Once at the new site they cleared an area under one of the hills.

·········

The Catholic leadership went ahead with their plan of building a mission, with a bush hospital and schoolrooms for the children. They quarried rocks nearby and also had the materials from Arltunga. Shelters were built. The priests, brothers and sisters got a temporary place to live in while the proper mission staff houses were built. The Aboriginal families set up their own windbreaks, wiltjas and humpies about a kilometre over the hill.

Over time, money for some newer building materials was donated. Some clever Catholic parishioners in town purchased these locally. Out at the mission new community gardens were ploughed and fertilised. Seed was sown and vegetables and fruit trees cultivated. Close by the church was a big kitchen and a bakery with big ovens. In front was a large communal dining room area.

Bruce Wallace led the team of Aboriginal workers. The church building was to sit under some old sandstone and limestone hills. The workers developed a quarry and cut out sandstone blocks. Some Sidney Williams corrugated iron sheds that used to belong to the army were brought to the mission from town. These sheds were linked and the walls filled in with stone dragged from the nearby quarry and cemented together. They made a beautiful new place of worship.

Next to this church were to be the wooden and stone permanent missionary houses. A large steel-framed building with roofing-tin walls was put together for a girls' dormitory. Other steel-framed sheds were fitted as a small hospital. Later two sheds were turned into the new schoolrooms.

....

Once the church was on its way to being completed, the first Aboriginal house was built out of local stone by Bruce Wallace's family at the bottom end of our village. Other families wanting a stone house were helped to gather and cut rocks. The mission had tools for this but it was still very hard work. You can still see one of these stone houses standing today. Nobody lives in it anymore. They were too small and uncomfortable. Too hot in summer and too cold in winter. Most of the families preferred their wiltjas or humpies down in the village. Much more comfortable.

Like at Arltunga mission, the new families were told by the church to put their bigger girls into the girls' dormitory, a big single space built close by the church next to the Sacred Heart nuns' houses. The Arltunga mission dormitory girls moved in as soon the place was finished. New girls from families arriving from Alice Springs were soon recruited into any empty beds.

When we arrived at Santa Teresa I started at the school with the day kids. I can still remember when my parents took me to this new school and how I met all the nuns. I never knew there were nuns who wore these long dresses and weird white hats. They were like the dresses and hats in *The Flying Nun* television show that came on TV later on. At the school they were all wearing these long white dresses with the white veils over their heads. Much different from the nuns' plain dresses worn in town. It was like a miracle really how they kept them so white. Even the dogs showed some respect. Mind you, those nuns had a big stick in case the dogs got cheeky. And they had that school teacher look that said 'don't mess with me'.

When I first saw the nuns up close I was very scared and shy. My little sister

Sandra was even more shaken up. But my mother talked with the sister in charge. I was still a stranger to the mission culture then. But I was persuaded by some of my cousins easily enough. I wanted to stay in the classroom. Sandra was still too young for school. So she got to stay at home, and go with my mother when she got a job down at the mission canteen. My father started work helping out the other stockmen getting on with cattle station dreaming stuff.

My cousins and the other school girls were dressed up in proper clothes. They told me about their dormitory. They wanted me to go into this dormitory with them. But there weren't enough beds yet. Or perhaps the nuns wanted to see how I settled in. Perhaps my family was still not sure that they were going to stay at the mission. In the end I went into the dormitory about a month after arriving. I had gone down with my mother to look at it with some other families. I thought it a bit spooky. I'd never seen so many beds and never slept in one. Let alone the idea of sleeping all by myself. This was entirely foreign to me.

Later the nun called Sister Therese Marie came around to our camp. I was told that she was the one that called around to see parents when their daughter could go into the dormitory. So when she called around to see my dad and mum I was half hoping, half scared that I was going to start straightaway. I'm not sure what my parents thought of the idea.

That day, there was no hiding away. Humpies are not built for hidey holes. So Mum stood up from the campfire, me and Sandra hanging onto her tired old dress. None of us had much English, but we could tell the nun was talking about me going into the dormitory. The decision had been made. The sister untangled me from my mother's legs, took me by my hand and gently led me to the dormitory.

When we got there the other girls were waiting impatiently. Sister Therese Marie handed me straight over. A chair was quickly found and I was sat down near the cupboard. The girls were laughing and talking Arrernte, so at least I knew what was happening. They got scissors and started my haircut. Again, there was no place to hide. The haircut wasn't quite 'sorry cut' length but all my curls hit the floor and were swept away forever. I was undressed and scrubbed in the shower. They gave me a towel to dry myself and all my new clothes. I was told what to wear and where to put my other clothes in the cupboard. The clothes that I had been wearing were wrapped up for my mother. I was shown a bed with sheets, a blanket and a pillow. Then we mucked around for a bit, me asking questions and learning everyone's family connections properly.

My mother and Sandra came down later to see how I was getting on. Sandra kept touching my new haircut and clothes. I picked up my parcel of old clothes and handed it over to Mum. There was nothing that we had at home that I really needed in the dormitory. We were all a bit teary and worried together. I showed them my bed and my other clothes. Then I could see my mother was sad and Sandra tired, so I had to let them go. But I got very overwhelmed and teary myself waving my mother off. She shrugged her shoulders and grew smaller, walking with Sandra till they disappeared around the corner.

Quickly Sister Therese Marie brought some of the other girls over to help make me okay again. They got to joking me, teasing me a bit, till I was smiling again. But I had never slept in a bed before and it was lonely, even with all the other girls there.

That night I got very sad, missing my parents, my sister and brother, even the dogs. I had always slept close up with my family. Now I was away from them for the first time and I couldn't stop thinking about them. I don't know how much of a choice my parents really had about me going into the dormitory. But my mother in particular was strong about me getting a good education. The McMillans were like that.

When I woke up the first day in the dormitory I was tired and scared. But excited too. It was a whole new world. So different from life with my family. The youngest girls were about eight, and I was about ten. I soon got to know the nuns' system where the younger girls and the boys lived with their families and walked to school. For girls this was until the sisters thought they were old enough to live in the dormitories.

Over time, the dormitories became more popular with us. You got to live and play with all your sister girls every day. So after a while I got used to the dormitory, and even started to really like it. On weekends and some special feast days us girls went home to be with our parents. But we could stay at the dormitories too. And for school holidays we went back to live with our own families.

The girls' dormitory was a large shed, about 24 metres long and 8 metres wide. The space was divided by steel columns and rafters into eight equal sections of about 3 metres each. Attached to the side of one end was a small set of rooms for the sister in charge. The other nuns had a house nearby. A single door on the opposite end was the doorway towards the church and communal dining areas about 30 metres away. At the other end was a large, central hinged door that was the main entry. A lean-to on one side was the shower area. A similar lean-to on the other side was the toilet area with the night-cans.

The youngest girls slept down the end nearest the showers and toilet. There were six beds in each of the eight sections, three on each side, with a corridor up the middle. The end section had no beds, just cupboards where our clothes and other things were kept. As you walked up the room the girls got older. Each year, as the oldest girls left to go working or got married, we all moved up the shed to make space for the next lot of girls. There must have been more than forty girls in the dormitory. We still saw a lot of our families during the day. But at nights we shared our magic world of the girls' dormitory.

·········

I started to really enjoy going to the school at Santa Teresa. It wasn't as cruel as at the Bungalows. The first year the classroom was a tin hut with a dirt floor. We had no desks or chairs and very few books. But we were happy. I remember being very excited when a year later we got given our very own books and pencils. A few years later a proper school was built and we were really proud of it. The little hospital rooms were also finished about the same time.

The mission nuns always said they wanted to learn from us Aboriginal people too. So we helped them out. There were four nuns at the mission at the start and we told them the proper Arrernte names to call all the classes, from big to small. The big girls' class we called awenke-irreme, meaning growing towards being a young woman. The smaller girls' class they called akweke, or small.

I made friends with Bessie Conway and Denise Young. We were all in the akweke size. I grew to be in the big awenke size with Myra Hayes, Carmel Conway and Philomena Wallace.

We were supposed to have been taught the alphabet and how to write a bit of English at the Bungalows school. But I didn't remember much of it when I hit school at Santa Teresa. I was about ten years old and didn't have no education. It was the nuns taught me everything about how to read and write properly.

The first book I ever read from was the New Testament. Sometimes us kids got to read the Bible in the church. Sometimes the Bible was used by the nuns as a textbook in the classroom. But I never really read the Bible much when I was young. It was too big, and too hard to read. The nuns would explain it to us though, and we tried to understand.

·········

At the mission school we played the same games as at the Bungalows, like tunnel ball and basketball. The boys played football too. Like teachers everywhere, the nuns liked anything that kept us busy. There was no money around in those days and these games didn't need a lot of expensive equipment. So we learned over again these different team sports. We had the same running races and relay races, egg and spoon races, three-legged races and bag races. The same schedule of classes during the morning and sport after lunch. But it was much better fun without welfare mob rules.

The first year we all went into town for the schools' sports competition. Even in the early years, Santa Teresa always did well in these. My first combined Aboriginal school sports carnival was held in Alice Springs on Anzac Oval. Our school came third. There was all the usual games plus a tug-of-war as well. I won the under-eleven high jump. And wasn't I excited! I got all smiley and couldn't stop feeling good. I thought I was going to win forever. I was a really big jumper. I played a lot of team sports too. And we all liked winning.

But you don't get to be a winner all the time. Even if you prayed to Jesus and Mary. We were a small school and we lost plenty of times too. Pride was a deadly sin in the dormitory. You couldn't get big headed about anything. You would be put in your place. Kids would tease you. Nobody liked a big head. Even though the nuns liked winning as much as us, they didn't think you should skite about it. It was bad luck and bad manners. You could smile a lot though in front of the other team. Even make some hand signs at them. That was okay, as long as you could run away real fast.

·········

I still remember my first end-of-term school concert. All us girls from the dormitory were training up and dancing to the music. We were great dancers. The nuns had rehearsed us for weeks before. On the night we dressed up in long party dresses in all the colours. It was so exciting. The dresses were sent to the mission from the church in town. But we had no shoes. Our feet weren't really made for fitting into party shoes.

The four nuns at Santa Teresa at that time were mostly very nice to be with. They rostered us to do work around the dormitory. I was usually on roster for washing up the cups, plates and everything. Sometimes I was cleaning the dining room. Sometimes we got tired of doing these things and hid the dirty plates and cups in the cupboard. We were always in a hurry to go out and play. The sisters usually found out and forced us to come back.

Sometimes I was in the laundry helping with washing, ironing and folding clothes. Monday was washing day and Tuesday was ironing day. We had a big copper and a tub with water and a scrubbing board. We collected the wood to heat the water for the copper. My mother and some other women would come up to help and show us what to do. Water was put in the copper and then you made the fire to get the water hot. Then you put the clothes into the big tub with soap to wash them. We had to rinse them carefully and squeeze them through a big wringer. Then we'd hang them all on the lines, and bring them in for ironing or folding up later.

It was boring work and we hated it. Some of us were even washing the brothers' and fathers' trousers and everything else that they wore. And we washed the nuns' big habits with their veils and everything. We had some fun seeing the big, oversized clothing some of them had. But for me it was not much fun. I felt funny washing the nuns' and priests' clothes.

I liked and respected the nuns and priests. Especially when they were looking at you. It wasn't like the teachers at the Bungalows who were so angry all the time, yelling and hitting. Sister Therese Marie was my favourite. When it was her turn to look after us she always got out one of our story books to keep us happy. She was good to me and the other girls. She liked us. She always called me 'gorgeous'. She said it to me lots of times. I thought it meant something like 'nice' or 'good'. She was always telling the girls' parents how good their kids were. So she was a special love of ours. A lot of the other adults could get cranky with us. I didn't like that. It wasn't fair. And I always wanted things to be fair. My family taught me that. There had been too much unfairness in their lives.

·········

The nuns woke us up every morning to shower and get dressed. Then they supervised our jobs. Sometimes I was one of the girls who milked the goats. I would get my own billycan made from a big Sunshine milk powder tin. We had to milk the goats and get a pretty full tin. The goat yard was not too far away. We all had our favourite goats, especially liking the ones with the most milk. But the big girls always got them. Later on I had a real favourite and no-one else was to milk that goat if I had a say in it. Sometimes we fought over the milking goats and sometimes we fought over our tins. We'd put the milk into bigger tins then bring these to the tables. The rest of the milk went over to the fathers, sisters and brothers, or to the communal kitchen. We had porridge with goats' milk and damper with Golden Syrup every morning for breakfast.

Sometimes, we might add a little water to the cans before we went into the goat yard. But the nuns caught on to this soon enough. Kids talk. The nuns got us all together and said, 'Don't ever use water to make your milk can full. That milk is for your porridge, not for cheating with the water.' We were learning the Catholic guilt thing. They punished us too. Extra jobs on top of our other morning jobs like picking up rubbish or collecting firewood. There were jobs in the dining room too, helping with the cooking and cleaning.

After breakfast we would get into our school uniforms. Each girl's uniform had a number on so everyone could keep track of them. All the girls were taught to embroider, starting with 'S.T.' on the pockets of their uniforms. We could muck around till the school bell rang at nine o'clock. Then it was classes till lunchtime. We mostly had sandwiches for lunch. Then a little more school till the bell rang. After we finished for the day, we changed out of our uniforms to play around or get on with sport or some work that had to be done.

·········

When my parents put me in the dormitory my father became one of the men who went away to work on the cattle stations. But my mother was always around the mission, looking after her parents and the old people. Our family still lived in a humpy so they had some shade to sit under. They used to come to the store at the mission to get their rations. It made me feel bad. I was worried about them, but there wasn't much I could do.

At short holiday times, the nuns sometimes liked to keep us at school. They taught us to knit and sew. I got my housekeeping education from those nuns. Most of it was learning how to wash clothes and keep things clean. Keeping things clean seemed really important to the nuns. It didn't worry us kids or our families nearly as much.

But you had to keep the nuns happy. And the habit of being clean stuck with you after a while. It affected the way you looked at things and saw the world. Later on, you sort of looked down more on the world of the camps. You started thinking that the church way and the dormitories was the best way. That the way the priests and nuns thought about the world was better than our Aboriginal culture.

The weekend jobs were scrubbing and mopping the sheds, doing the laundry, tending the gardens and cleaning the spider webs off the rafters with a rag on a long stick. Cleaning the rafters was a very unpopular job. You had to climb the frames to get to the high spots. And the broom could get stuck if something angry came out of the rafters to chase you. The spiders were big and quick and might run at you, making you drop the broom.

We always tried to be somewhere else when they were looking for someone to do them jobs. But the nuns had ways of finding people who didn't want to be found. It was the 'fairness' thing. If you were 'lazy' they gave you the 'look' and the 'talk'. It always made me squirm with embarrassment.

But by the end of my first year I'd settled into the Santa Teresa life. It was mostly great fun. At Christmas time we made coloured streamers from crepe paper. The end-of-year concert was to be held in our dormitory. We moved all the beds to one end and made the room like a big hall for our play and dancing. At one end were the chairs for our parents and families to sit on. And we hung big curtains up to make a stage. I remember poking my head out to have a peek at everyone coming in. We did ballroom dancing and waltzing, swaying and tapping our feet as we sang. We might have been a shy mob, but I felt like a movie star on that first concert night.

After that we put on our Christmas play in the church. Us big girls and boys played Mary and Joseph, the angels, the shepherds and the wise men. No camels, and no donkeys. We had a little white doll for baby Jesus. Black dolls hadn't been invented yet. The priests led a procession into the church grounds, waving their incense around and blessing the place. A proper Catholic smoking ceremony. The old people liked that. Then we packed up and went home with our families. It had been a good year and I didn't want to live anywhere else but Santa Teresa.

Teacher and children at Santa Teresa.
Courtesy of National Library of Australia

CHAPTER 12

Best girls in the dormitory

When the new school was built we started to make our school garden to help feed everybody. The nuns gave us watermelon and rockmelon seeds to plant. That was fun. We got to eat some of the melons when they ripened up.

Boys and girls divided into groups. Didn't matter who you were, everyone had to wait their turn. You couldn't steal the fruit. Everyone was watching out. Girls watching the boys. Nuns watching everyone. And taking fruit without asking or out of turn was treated as a great big sin against God. Like the Garden of Eden story. You might get thrown out of Santa Teresa or go to hell. But often Catholic guilt wasn't enough. Eternal vigilance helped too.

If you didn't wait your turn, you were stealing from your sister girls, your family and your friends. Nobody wanted to do that. We were good girls and we all wanted to be 'best girls'. So as soon as one of the watermelons was ready there would be a line of kids waiting to eat it. The rest of us looking on. It was a test you had to pass. Patience. Waiting. Sharing.

Patience was always a bit hard for me. I always wanted things really badly. I wanted everything to go a particular way. And when they didn't I got wound up easily. I could become a 'little storm cloud', as my Aboriginal name suggested. Nowadays I watch my own grandkids trying to be patient. And they aren't much good at it either. It gives me a little smile watching them holding themselves back. I must have been a bit like that. And I think the sisters probably smiled a bit at my efforts to be good. But I just don't have any love for waiting, waiting, waiting. Even today.

Sunday started slowly with church at 9 am. I think the masses were designed to teach us patience too. You had to fast before church. So we got really hungry and couldn't wait for the mass to be over. Sometimes the sermons would go on and on. And you had to sit 'quiet way'. Not wriggle about like a puppy dog. The older girls, the 'best girls', would be keeping an eye on us, practising their nun look. After church, you got to eat sandwiches and sometimes cakes. The younger girls went back with their family so the sisters could have some time off. The older girls could stay with the dormitory sister if they wanted to. The best girls stayed to help clean up and all that. Get more points towards going to heaven. 'Sucking up to the nuns', as the rude would say.

My brother Malcolm was born at Santa Teresa a couple of years after I moved to the dormitory. I was thirteen by then and had got more practice at being patient. Not that I was home all that often to look after him a bit as he grew up. If you asked them, I think my younger sister and brother would say that I was better at being bossy than hanging back quietly or patiently looking after people.

Later on, the mission built a boys' dormitory. It was smaller and built from local stone. It looked more like an old jail or police lock-up and the brothers were in charge of it. My brother Malcolm went there when he was big enough and he said it felt like being in a jail. It was tough. He had to learn a lot of patience too. The boys had a much harder time than us girls. We all knew that the church had us in the dormitories so that the teaching nuns and brothers could give us a good education. We were told that we were lucky to be in the dormitories. But the boys didn't get much love. Floggings was more the order of the day. Malcolm couldn't wait to get out of there. But this was later on.

·········

I went to visit my family most weekends. They were still in their humpy down at the Aboriginal camp. They had a few more belongings by then, but not much. Nor did anyone else on the camp really get ahead. Our family elders worried that having a lot of things changed our culture too much. It made people not share so much, or not look after their big family anymore.

And other people got jealous and angry if someone got extra things. Us girls in the dormitory got teased a bit by our families. We were losing culture and language, they said. And maybe they were right. It was easier in the dormitory with our clean beds, showers and toilets. We had our clean clothes and things to play with.

But the nuns kept on supporting us to go back to our camps and not forget our family life. Probably they wanted a bit of a rest from all us kids too. They said we had a duty to help our families. So it was hard for us girls both ways. But that's how we managed to keep our language going strong, and learn about the country and bush medicines and lots of other things that the old people passed on to us. I was lucky like that. That's how I remember it anyhow.

Some of the nuns in particular thought our language and culture were important. They were always talking to our parents and the old people as well. So I would go home with my 'best girl' pious look and sit down and play patiently with Sandra and Malcolm, teaching them about the Christian life in the dormitory and how to be better kids. I was leading them into the bright new future world us girls dreamed about. But Sandra and Malcolm could be a bit slow on the uptake and not very grateful. They'd start edging away from me, a bit like the old people when the missionaries wanted a chat. I'd get bored soon enough as well. Then it would be back to the dormitory for a good feed of goat stew and vegetables, leaving the family with their more modest eating options.

On Sunday afternoons us big girls would wander back up to the dormitory, put our clean dormitory clothes back on and go back to the white walls and crucifixes. It was hard shifting between the two worlds all the time. Sometimes I just wanted a simpler life with everything one way. Sometimes I would stay at the dormitory over the whole weekend.

....

Santa Teresa is very hot in the summer, day and night. There is hardly any rain. But when it rains they are heavy rains. Sometimes after these rains we had a day going bush. The nuns would take all us girls, big and small, for a long picnic. We'd be happy and excited, enjoying our day out. We'd come back late, tired and ready to sleep.

On some other Sundays, Sister Therese Marie might organise picnics for us older girls. We would walk the couple of kilometres down past Yam Creek with our picnic lunch and water. We'd go to St Christopher's Waterhole for a swim and jump in, clothes and all. Even Sister Therese Marie would jump in, still in her habit. Then we'd dry out and go looking for bush yams and other bush foods, especially the wild figs on the hills nearby.

There were no cars at the mission in those days so us older girls would walk down to the creek and into the hills with Sister Therese Marie. The magic of the nuns kept us safe from the spirits of our ancestors. They were nice afternoons. We taught the sister about bush foods, where to look and what was ready for eating. The sister would then know how to help us find the bush tucker in the hills and gullies. We would climb down the high sides of the creek that had been worn away by the water. We collected yams with a small crowbar and cooked them on a small fire. Sometimes Sister would tell us stories as we sat around. They were happy days.

I really have happy memories of living in the dormitory. I remember sitting down with the other girls beside Sister Therese Marie while she read us stories. She really was my most favourite nun. I loved the way she read the story of The Emperor's New Clothes. I thought it was so funny the first time I heard it. Especially when the emperor was parading through the streets thinking he was in all his flash clothes. And then when the little boy yelled out 'he's got no clothes on' and I realised he was naked, I laughed and laughed so hard tears started to roll down my cheeks. I loved those stories from another world.

....

The bigger boys left school to go to work much younger than us girls. They hated being in the stone buildings dormitory that were hot in summer and cold in winter. The teaching brothers bossed and abused the young men. They were hard, cruel and strict. It didn't work out. That wasn't the way we treated young people. The brothers never seemed sad to see the young men go. They didn't get any argument from our senior men who were wanting to hold them in their proper 'men's business' camps. They took the boys out of school and away from those teaching brothers and out bush as soon as they could. So there were not a lot of Catholic vocations coming out of the boys' dormitory. Some of the brothers could be brutal and bullying. It was always the women and girls who liked the church stuff.

It wasn't Aboriginal culture to tell initiated men what to do and think, so our senior men often thought the church, the priests and especially the nuns were disrespectful. The men hated the police and welfare people for the same reason. It was different for us Aboriginal women. Everybody tried to boss us around.

....

Our mothers and fathers all worked around the mission. This was the rule. Some of the women from the camp were asked to keep busy doing the laundry for the nuns. The laundry was at the other end of the dining room so we got to catch up with family there when the nuns told us girls to go and help the women so that we could learn how to wash and iron clothes. Our mothers' often rolled their eyes about when they were showing us the proper way of folding things up. We all had a bit of a laugh when you could get away with it.

The nuns taught us nearly everything. Not just washing and ironing and folding things up, but also cooking, sewing, knitting, cleaning, everything. They had a timetable on paper for us to remember everything we had to do. All these important skills for living in a humpy on the side of a river.

Our fathers did the building and big jobs when they weren't out mustering cattle, fencing or doing seasonal harvesting work interstate. Some of the men worked around the nuns' house or the fathers' house. When the church ran out of meat, they got some men to go and kill two or three goats for the missionaries and the school kids. In the early days there was also an old Arrernte man who looked after all the trees at the presbytery. He had come to the mission from Middle Camp, same place where we used to live on the Todd River.

There was a really big communal garden in the Old Village. Lots of the men got a job there with Brother Bush, helping him plant and look after the vegetables. The mission land was like a big farm with chooks and goats and all the vegetables. Our families could get fresh vegetables and eggs to eat, bullock meat and some goat meat too from this farm. It got so that the Santa Teresa farm was even able to supply vegetables to the shops in Alice Springs. This brought a little money in to the mission community for building or equipment.

·········

The main trouble for the mission was having enough drinking water. Especially at the start. Then they got lucky when they found good sweet water after drilling a deep well up at a place named Phillipson Bore. They were able to pipe this water down to the mission to keep water always flowing. There was also saltier water from other close-by bores on Yam Creek. These were used for the gardens and the mob of cattle. Once they got more water sorted out, the next problem was keeping up enough work for everyone, and finding money and materials for all the new buildings being planned.

The place grew up quickly enough. The bakery was built up bigger and every day families picked up their bread and on some days other special treats. My mother worked at the bakery. It was a good job and I was able to see her more often. The bakery was one of the bigger workspaces near the girls' dormitory. A lot of men and women worked there. Most had been with the church bosses from the days of the Little Flower Black Mission at Arltunga.

A lot of work was needed to get the Santa Teresa cattle station operating, and the mission had many experienced stockmen like my father doing it. Luckily, a lot of good stock horses had been given to the mission. For the first four years it was good seasons and a growing mob of cattle. You would see the happiness of the men when they got back on their horses. They felt strong and in charge again. These men also did a lot of the stock work for neighbouring stations, mustering or taking on droving work under contracts run by the mission. Other times, the men might be hired out to do fencing and building work.

Santa Teresa grew a lot in those early years. People saw it as their home and started building their own houses. There was more food to feed everyone. We grew up eating more meat than ever before. The gardens got bigger. There were chickens and eggs for everyone. The school got built and we had proper books and things. So we were feeling like we were the winners. Santa Teresa was the best place to live. The old culture was left a bit behind by the rush of great new stuff happening, but it was an exciting time.

·········

By the end of the 1950s I was finishing my time in the world of the girls' dormitory. Our group became the big girls, leading our young sister-cousins into the culture of the dormitories. We were the 'best girls', trying hard to impress our lovely nuns. We had our plans for becoming something different, to have bigger lives than our own mothers'. We sat at the top of the school within a circle of big ideas, being led by the Catholic sisters more than by the ideas of our own mothers and grandmothers. I was sad to be leaving the school, but happy too. My life was to change very quickly as I became a young woman of the mission community.

CHAPTER 13

Leaving school

Before we left the dormitory the nuns had one last chance to get us ready for being young women in our community. They sent us girls to biology classes where they tried to teach us things about getting married and having babies. A group of us girls would all go together. I remember us being picked and sent up to the new hospital room. When we got there, one of the nuns, who was also nurse, sat us down and taught us what she knew about having babies. I felt really shy and confused about all this talking and drawing, and spent a lot of time staring hard at the floor.

The Santa Teresa nuns weren't exactly experts at having babies so you have to admire their courage. Thinking back, I reckon they might have been better off having the old Aboriginal midwives come down from our camps and help out with this 'making babies' talk. At least the midwives would have 'been there, done that'. And our mothers should have been there too. There might have been some real stories and even a laugh or two. But I don't think the nuns were up for using the old senior women for these chats. The church didn't follow the 'circle of women' way of talking up ideas. So we didn't learn much about relationships and babies. All I can say is it was better than the rubbish my own grandkids learn in town schools these days.

Anyway, by the time we'd been in the dormitories for all those years both the nuns and our families thought we were pretty silly about the ways of being a young woman in this new world. As a schoolgirl I knew only a little about what to do with boyfriends and getting married. I had been to some family wedding ceremonies. Not long before I left school, the Santa Teresa church blessed the wedding for Mompy's son, Tommy Marshall, when he married Cecilia Turner. Lots of my dad's family came out to the mission for that marriage. It was a good party and that marriage started well. After the wedding everyone went back to their old, normal life; except perhaps the married couple. And I went back to my dormitory and didn't think much about what marriage involved.

·········

In the late 1950s you mostly finished school after you turned fifteen. This was white fellow way at the time. But the whole idea of schooling was still fairly new in our communities. And at the end of our schooling we had nowhere to go with our education. Leaving school and the dormitory was the real end of our childhood. We were pushed out into an adult world whether we wanted it or not. But it was what we wanted. We thought we were smart and would be treated like grown-ups. But the things we learnt in school turned out to not be what we needed. Instead of having respected things to do, we had nothing. We just mucked around and got in serious trouble. Becoming a proper adult takes a long, long time. You need to keep busy learning. And even then you don't always remember to do the right thing or manage to behave properly all the time.

I had to leave the Santa Teresa dormitory at a time when there was no work happening. The mission school had hopes for us but six years of schooling wasn't going to get me a high paid job. Our whole class left school into this nothingness. We had no chance of finding any real work to do. So like kids everywhere with big hopes and dreams and a lot of time on our hands, we made our own fun. Like the nuns always told us, 'The devil makes work for idle hands.'

·········

After school things got pretty boring fairly quickly. There was no women's work happening, and the men were often away. I missed the routines of the schoolyard now I didn't have to get out of bed. When I did, I'd hang around the school and church a bit, helping out with events or cleaning up. But that didn't work out much. I didn't get a sense of vocation. Mostly I was just in everyone's way. It felt like they resented having to make up something to keep us girls busy. So I drifted away.

I did help out with one Christmas pageant. A Father Christmas was coming from Alice Springs in the mission truck with presents for all the little kids and babies. A few of us older girls got the job of sitting up on the big ridge just before you turn into the community. We dressed up in our long party frocks and were driven to the lookout point in a truck. Up there you could see the dust from a vehicle for a long way before it came into sight. We made a fire and gathered some green branches to throw on it to make a lot of smoke so that everyone knew when Father Christmas was coming close.

We were mucking around a bit and somehow my dress got caught in the fire and started burning really hot. The other girls rolled me in the dirt but there wasn't any water up there. I was dragged into the truck, screaming in pain from the burns all up my legs. When we got to the clinic the nurse took one look and wrapped me in wet sheets. I was given a needle of some strong pain medicine and loaded into the back seat of a car and taken to town. Everyone was watching and I passed out soon after. I woke up in a hospital bed. The pain was still killing me so they gave me another needle.

The next day they gave me another needle and put me on the Flying Doctor's plane. Again I woke up in a hospital bed in terrific pain. I was at the old Darwin Hospital. They were pulling off my bandages and wrapping new ones on, and I couldn't stop screaming. This went on for weeks and then months. It was a long time, with my hands tied up to a bed post to stop me scratching the new skin from the skin grafts they had done.

The pain medicine was all that helped keep me quiet. None of my family could be with me up in Darwin. I was a real mess, lonely and crying all the time. Eventually they flew me back to Alice Springs and my mother and father came in to see me. It helped a lot. But then they had to go home and leave me in the hospital. At least I could see and hear some of the Arrernte mob, and family called in when they could. I would go out on the veranda, so I wasn't real worried. I had to wear these thick stockings for a long time. But finally I didn't need the pain medicine anymore. And then the stockings were chucked away and I was allowed to go back home.

....

I was wilder for some reason when I came back to Santa Teresa. Everybody came to see me. My legs were a mess but my skin got back to normal eventually. Then some of us girls started travelling around a bit, even going into Alice Springs. We saw a few things were changing. This was the start of rock-and-roll music and going to watch romantic American movies telling teenage love stories. Sometimes we got lifts into town to be a part of an event or visit family. We were all learning a bit more about a bigger world.

I quickly learnt about the world of sex and relationships and got myself into a lot of trouble a few times. Even if at first we knew nothing much about sex, there were still strong feelings about young men and even older men. They liked to make eyes at us too, especially in town or when there was a bit of grog around. We got into plenty of jealous fighting, staying up late at night, chewing nikki nikki and smoking cigarettes. Plus a bit of alcohol started floating into Santa Teresa following the visits into town by some of the men. We thought we were pretty clever but we were very stupid really.

The nuns and mission bosses didn't think 'the party' was a great idea. Nor did our parents and senior people. But they couldn't really stop us. We just ran amok. Most of us felt let down by the church. And it was easy to hang around on the edges of the mission, playing a bit of music on transistor radios and dancing. Our families fed us when we came home, and most nights we camped with them. But we weren't listening to anyone much and a lot my friends got pregnant. The worst trouble was having jealous, cruel boyfriends.

Us dormitory girls had grown up being taught that we were different. We could become Christian saints and martyrs. We were shown by the nuns' example how good Catholic women should work in the world, saving people. We were told we might be called by God to become missionaries.

And a big part of us was up for these ideas. We thought we were educated. We could even read the Bible a bit. We knew the importance of being clean. And we had these fantasies of our new God giving us these big lives dedicated to his work. We were the new generation that was going to change everything and take our people back to some new 'Promised Land'. There were times when us dormitory girls talked about how we were going to become nuns, missionaries and teachers. But we were silly really. In the end, it never happened. No-one tapped me on the shoulder to say that I had been chosen to be taken into a new life of sacrifice and do good works in the church. None of us 'best girls' ever became nuns. And we were sad and a bit angry about that.

....

The end of 1958 was the start of a seven-year drought across Central Australia. Sometimes huge dust storms would sweep across the hills covering everything in red dust. This was a really hard time for the mission, with cattle dying and no work on the nearby stations. The mission started to organise for some the men to be taken down south during harvest times. The mission trucks would drive the men to farms in Victoria, NSW and South Australia.

The summer harvest work was real exciting for the men. But none of us girls got to go. It was a way of keeping the mission and some of the men in a bit of money. But those without work quickly became sad and angry, even with their own families. They would start grumbling about the church. The priests, and us women, were blamed for everything; the drought, or them feeling useless. The men said it was the fault of the priests and their lack of respect for true Aboriginal patriarchy. They hadn't been allowed to follow their ancient rituals and traditions. Sometimes the men would talk up taking their families back into the town. But this just meant them joining the grog party. The women didn't really want that. The grog could make the men wild and bad. Us women would have to stay at home looking after things for them.

The Top End was not affected by the drought and the Catholic church was still trying to expand its missionary work, so some of the men, like my uncle Patrick McMillan, went to work on the missions up in the Top End. Patrick ended up married to a Tiwi Islander and living at Snake Bay on Goulburn Island. Some got work and stayed at the Garden Point Mission on Melville Island. Others got work building farms south of Darwin on the Daly River, at a place they called Port Keats. The Top End became their home away from home.

The world outside of our missions was changing pretty quickly. By the 1960s the Aboriginal settlements of Central Australia had expanded. As well the Lutheran mission in Hermannsburg, there was a relocated Pitjantjatjara population at Areyonga and a new Luritja mission built at Haast's Bluff. On top of this was expanded Western Arrernte government reserve at Jay Creek. By the early 1960s the government reserve at Papunya had over 500 Luritja, Pintubi and Warlpiri people. Yuendumu was rationing more than 700 mostly Warlpiri people. And these places kept growing.

Back in Alice Springs our old family camps along the Todd River had expanded. But in 1960, the Aboriginal families living in camps were moved again to a new government training reserve at Amoonguna, 15 kilometres south-east of town. It grew rapidly. Our old Bungalows school was re-created as the Old Telegraph Station recreational park.

In the Alice Springs town itself, there was also a big community of mostly mixed descent Aboriginal people who had grown up in the Bungalows children's institutions. These families were working on the railways and the main roads. Nearly 400 Aboriginal people were living in houses around the Heavitree Gap and Railway Cottage areas at this time.

....

The drought of the late 1950s and early 1960s had a big impact on Santa Teresa mission. As it continued, the men got more and more restless. Many of the senior men were calling for cultural renewal. Perhaps they were right. The boys' dormitory had been a hard place, and cruel. And the young men always wanted to escape it as soon as they could. My young brother Malcolm was very unhappy there, as I've said. Our Arrernte leadership tried the get more men's gatherings happening again to draw young men back into our ancient culture. Our young men who often felt excluded within the white world.

The senior men wanted to hold the ceremonies a long way away from the influences of the grog, the towns and the white priests. But the young men became more trapped in the circle of parties and wanted ceremonies closer to town. Some senior men moved back towards Alice Springs into the new settlement of Amoonguna to influence these young people. Some ended up in new fringe camps outside of town, trying to build up our culture again. It often didn't work out well. The young men, and even some of the older men, ended up in big parties, bigger fights and really big grog hangovers. Grog in town started to be a problem. Added to that was the mixing up of young people from all of the different tribal areas.

....

After a while, perhaps because I was hanging around and getting into trouble, my father told me it was the time I would get married. He explained that he had arranged it traditional way through his family and told me that I had been promised in marriage when I was a baby. They gave me the sign of me being carried in a coolamon when this promise was made. I was shocked and terrified. The problem was that I had grown up in the Santa Teresa dormitory, running around with the mission mob. Becoming a promised wife was not part of my hopes and dreams. But that didn't help much.

I was told that my promised husband was the right way in our Aboriginal custom and law. He was an Anmatyerr man from up past Napperby way, but working now at Yambah Station. My grandfather Big Foot and his grandmother were brother and sister. So he was my father's cousin's son. He was from the Mpetyane skin group, the first choice marriage partner for a Pengarte woman like me.

Despite me being really unhappy about being promised, my family insisted that now was the right time for me to get married. And they wanted it to happen soon. My father's big sister Aunty Mompy and her husband Bill Gorey came all the way out to Santa Teresa with my promised husband. I had never met him before. Still, I could see he was a pretty old bloke. He might have been even thirty or more. And he was a bit on the bushy side in terms of looking after himself. Not like us smart ones that had grown up at the mission.

Aunt Mompy told me that I had to learn to live with him. My father and lots of my family were worried I was losing my traditional culture. This wasn't just because of my time in the dormitory and at the mission but because there wasn't really any way forward for us young people once we left school. So we ran amok, offending against both traditional and Catholic cultures. They thought the sooner I got married and tied into the way of being a wife, the better off I would be.

The priests and nuns might have thought differently but said the same thing. What I wanted wasn't going to matter. The men had always made these decisions. Even the nuns were said to be brides of Christ. So I was told, even by those strong women, that I had to do it. I was scared. Very scared, and very unhappy. But there was no way as a young woman of seventeen that I could go up against all my family and my cultural traditions. This was just too hard for me at a time when a lot of us young ones were being pulled into line by our senior Arrernte leaders.

I hadn't really thought about getting married. Certainly not with a much older man. He didn't know my world at all. I might lose all those things I had learnt in the dormitory. But my father and even my mother's family were true believers in me getting married because I was getting into too much trouble. They pressured me to marry him, proper way. From my father's view, I'd had my fun and now had to become a 'proper' young woman. This very respectable Anmatyerr man would look after me. No-one was going to save me from this plan. Not my father's family. Not my mother's family. Not Aunt Mompy. Not the church mob. They all persuaded me to be a 'good girl', for my family's sake. In the end I was on my own.

Eventually I stopped fighting and went through 'half asleep' with this 'proper way' marriage in the Santa Teresa church. Everybody came along. They had organised the service with the priests so I was married with the bells ringing and the proper Catholic blessings. According to both Aboriginal law and church law, I now had to live as a wife to this stranger. My husband and my father's family took me back to Yambah Station where we were given our own camping place.

My husband was polite. He knew to give me some time. He knew I was unhappy, so he left me alone. He was a good man like that, and maybe a bit shy. I was never forced to sleep with him. He seemed okay for waiting for me to work things out. When this didn't happen quickly, he went back to his work as a stockman and headed away to muster cattle across the outstations of Yambah.

When he came back home I ran away each night and slept in the bush. Sleeping away from the camp was very scary. I was exhausted and had to be always on watch for trouble. I spent a lot of cold nights under the trees. And the pressure was only getting bigger. Not so much from this man, but my aunts and the older women were really worried.

Sometimes the old women threatened to hit me if I didn't sleep with this husband of mine. I would hear the old women calling me in the night, calling me to come back. They would search for me in the moonlight. But they couldn't have been trying too hard. They never found me and I never showed myself till the morning came. Only then would I go back to my camp.

Nearly everyone was really angry with me. They said I was acting like a silly girl. But I really didn't want to be married. And I was born stubborn. I just wanted to go back to Santa Teresa to live with my family and friends. I would be a 'good girl' this time. That was my only plan.

Then I got lucky. One of my family organised a lift for me on the Yambah Station truck going into Alice Springs for supplies. I was allowed my escape. Perhaps it was that even this old husband of mine let me go. When I got into town I stayed safely out of the way and waited on the road until the mission truck came in for supplies. They gave me a lift back home to Santa Teresa.

·········

My family had thought I needed to get married to be brought back into the 'proper way' to behave as a young Anmatjerre and Arrernte woman. Today I know that way of thinking. Some of my grandkids get dragged through culture and marriage for the exact same reasons. I have even been part of telling them stupid things like that, so maybe my family were right. But I was not just a really good high jumper, I could run real fast too. My promised husband never quite caught up with me.

When I got back to Santa Teresa my mother and father were scared for me. They were shamed and angry too. So I went back to hide in the single women's quarters. My mother's families were okay for letting me stay with them. Dad went to the senior men to try to sort things out. But me leaving this marriage had caused him big trouble.

Mum took me to talk to Father O'Brien. I told him that I was forced to marry this man and said I didn't want to live with him. I told him that I never slept with him like a husband and wife. I told him that I wanted to get the right man to marry and that I wanted it to be my choice.

Father O'Brien asked me lots of questions. He then went away to talk with Bishop O'Loughlin who eventually arranged to cancel my church marriage. But the traditional Aboriginal people didn't worry much about what the church said. There was still payback problems and trouble for my family. I had disrespected another family. This other family needed to be satisfied. That was our law.

The mission had become a harder place for my family to live, but the nuns found me a few things to do around the place. Being able to read and write a little was good. Knowing the cleaning stuff was good for keeping the white bosses happy. But it was a strange sort of two worlds that I had to live in and I had to be careful all the time.

For me, getting married and living in the Aboriginal camp wasn't part of my own chosen storyline. I was a more modern young woman and had a different future running through my head. When I walked out of the promised marriage, my father was left in the firing line with my husband's family. The circle of powerful men couldn't save him. He had to punish me, or accept some punishment himself. I didn't get punished. And I don't know what he suffered.

I saw that man that I was forced to marry when I was in Napperby one time. He was visiting there, with his own new family. And later again I saw him staying in Alice Springs. We had both got married and we both had families by then. He said hello shyly, smiled and was friendly to talk to. He was okay about me. We didn't become friends or anything. It was just 'settled business' for him by then. So it was all okay.

I was really pleased for him. Happy that things had gone okay for him. That freed me up from a lot of guilt about how I had treated him. I felt pleased that it had worked out okay for him as well. I heard that this promised husband passed away in the 1990s. I didn't go to the funeral or anything. The marriage had been a long time ago by then. Everything is a long time ago now. It is good for me to finally talk about these things again.

Church at Santa Teresa.
*Courtesy of AIATSIS**

CHAPTER 14

My mother's death

In 1964, my mother died suddenly of a heart attack at Santa Teresa. She was very young to die; just thirty-nine years old. But she had been getting a little bit sick. I know now it must have been diabetes. We didn't know this sugar sickness in traditional life. It came with sitting down together 'white fella' way. So our old healers didn't know about it. We were all still living at the mission when she died so she had her family around her. But it was so shocking for us all.

Mum had still been employed at the bakery when she died. And we had all liked eating her pastries. The food out at Santa Teresa wasn't all bush tucker and from our own community gardens. A lot of it came from the mission bakery and the local shop. We drank a lot more cordial than goats' milk. And everybody had lots of sugar in their tea. We liked our food fatty and sweet. Plus if there was lots of food around you had to eat it all. Our families had learnt this as part of our desert culture. The Catholics didn't like waste either. Everyone knew it was wrong to waste food. There were the sermons in Lent about the 'starving kids in India'. And we had big eyes and fast hands when it came to hunting and gathering from the dinner table. So we always ate as much as we could, beyond what we needed, till there was nothing left.

Because my mother didn't need to move around much going hunting to feed her family, like lots of our people she put on a lot of weight. And she sat around eating too much. The 'sugar bag' sickness still kills lots of Aboriginal people when they start eating shop food. Mum was always worrying too much as well. She was carrying a lot of sadness in her body.

I can see now that it wasn't just me and other young people that were greedy for changes. My mother and lots of senior family members all wanted things to be different and better. But Mum's life wasn't the 'big' life she had hoped for either. She missed us kids badly when we all went into the dormitories. But she couldn't fight the mission or the government mob. She had nothing to fight them with. And when we came out from our dormitories, we didn't really know how to be with her as older teenagers.

Mum missed the Alwekkere. She missed not having her kids and grandkids gathered around her. She missed family talking together in our old camps on our own country. But no-one had any power to change things. So she still held the dream that a mission education might make our lives easier in this new world we shared with our white fellow bosses.

My mother was a baby during the great Central Australian drought of the 1920s that saw huge dust storms. Lots of her Anmatyerr and Northern Arrernte families died of thirst and starvation. Family groups were forced into town because they had nothing left to eat or drink. My mother was just six years old when the Coniston massacres happened. In the hard years of the 1930s, she had seen lots of old people and babies dying in the Todd River camps. She got married and then pregnant at thirteen years old. That was old culture. And there was no contraception in the camps.

She was young when her father and the old men of the tribe had their first meetings to build their friendships with the Catholic priests. She was the first generation of our tribe that had the mass and the Catholic Bible in their lives. Later she watched her own children being 'grown up' in the new mission school dormitories. And when she died we were left with a great sadness. It was a really hard time for my father. What a good wife and mother she had always been.

We had to pack up the house and move away from our old home, so that her spirit would be free to go home. I was twenty years old, Sandra was fifteen and Malcolm had been taken into the boys' dormitory at the mission. He was just eight years old. My big brother David was twenty-five and working a long way away at the Ernabella mission, where he lived with his wife and young family.

A lot of the Camel Bore families, including David's mate Johnny Leo and his family, had moved south down to the Ernabella Methodist mission when this camp was closed down. They were from that way, and the government had decided to build a new reserve called Amoonguna.

When David was told of our mother's death the mission organised for him to come back for the funeral straightaway. So we were all there for our mother's 'sorry camp', sitting with Old Brandy and Big Dorrie and the McMillan family. All together, we cut our hair, cut ourselves and burned her closest possessions as a family. We gave away all those things we couldn't burn. We did what we had to do culturally to speed my mother's spirit back to its ancient resting place. Visitors came from everywhere to pay their respects to our lovely mother, as the crying and singing rose up and receded.

The funeral was at the mission church that my mother loved. Everyone came. It was a great gathering of our families. She was buried in the mission cemetery with proper Catholic ritual. The old women led a storm of weeping and moaning as the soil was emptied onto her coffin. We stood by as everyone shook our hands and went away. Then there was tea and pastries at the mission kitchen afterwards. The bakery did my mother proud with waves of her old favourites hitting the tables. There were stories of her cooking and her sense of lightness. She could make great food happen for everyone, and then would watch as it quickly disappeared. And she would have been smiling if she could have heard all the talking.

....

After the funeral, my father took all of us away with him to his own family. They were mainly living at Amoonguna. This was the second sorry camp. We all stopped with my grandmother Jenny, Dad's big sister Mompy, and her partner Bill Gorey. Aunty Nancy was there too looking after her grandmother, and Aunty Hilda who was married up to my uncle Alex McMillan. Uncle Charlie and Ruby came in from Yambah. Uncle Huckitta was living there too. It was a busy sorry camp with friends from all over coming in to shake our hands and say sorry.

Later, when the 'sorry camp' at Amoonguna was finished up, David took his family back to Ernabella. But Dad and the rest of my father's side family stayed on at Amoonguna. David promised to come back whenever he could. He always worried for his sisters and brother. He was a good brother like that. David came back later when Malcolm had been through men's business to take him to live out at Ernabella mission. Whenever David came to Amoonguna to see us he always brought presents for his aunt Mompy and our grandmothers, Jenny and Nelly. He really liked helping people and would bring presents for all of us when he could.

Malcolm didn't want to go back to the boys' dormitory at Santa Teresa. It was too cruel. But the welfare mob got involved, saying he needed to go back to school. Then Aunt Mompy stepped in, telling them he could stay with her and go to Amoonguna school.

My aunt Mompy was a big, tough woman. She held us all firmly, and with great love. As the oldest sister, Mompy was a strong woman for her family. It wasn't so much a matter of working out who was right or wrong for her. She always jumped in to help. She taught us that this was what family always did. Protect and look after your own family first. It was 'proper way'.

·········

Dad was very sad after Mum died. He got some stock work that took him back to Aileron and later to Napperby. Mompy and the family stayed at Amoonguna. But we ended up staying with Big Dorrie and Brandy at the mission. Sometimes Malcolm would hang out hiding with his uncle Alec and aunt Hilda; he hated that dormitory so much. Sometimes he hung quietly with me and Sandra.

Malcolm was sent back to Amoonguna school. But he couldn't settle there either. He had been a bit broken with his mother's death and the abuse of the brothers' treatment of him in the dormitory. He would hang around with other young absconders. Sometimes they would wander into town and get into trouble. The police and welfare would bring him home and tell the family to force him to go to school. He might turn up but then he would escape. In the end he grew old enough to get some work at the mission. Welfare let him keep this job. They gave up the school idea. In any case, the boys' dormitory closed down soon after this.

Mompy could be very bossy and stubborn. Brave in a way that could scare people. One time when Malcolm was staying with her, he got sick from a chest infection. The nurse at the Amoonguna clinic was called to our camp and gave him an injection. Malcolm turned grey, fainting away, hitting the ground hard. Some of the old ladies started crying, thinking he had died. Mompy got very upset and wild. She took off her shirt and grabbed her fighting stick, chasing after that nurse. Mompy was going to flog her. But the nurse put on a burst of speed and escaped back to the clinic. The doors were shut tight behind her. Mompy prowled and growled outside. I was watching bug-eyed as my aunty yelled and raged. Then Violet Gorey, my cousin, settled things down telling Mompy that Malcolm had woken up. She quickly headed back to our camp. The terrified nurse was 'saved'.

The Heffernans didn't get a lot of unwanted attention after that. The helping professions and our 'enemies' all saw Mompy as being too fierce and too much trouble when she got upset. They didn't want her out looking for them with her big stick. And Malcolm became even more bulletproof with Mompy covering his back.

·········

My mother would have liked to have held us firmly like Mompy did. But her way was different. Even though she too was the oldest daughter and the main carer for a lot of her family, she followed a quieter way of helping. Living at the mission, she didn't get the chance to be as wild as Mompy. Lots of people got kicked out or had to leave Santa Teresa. You had to follow the rules. The mission bosses were always in charge. They created the jobs. They could employ you or sack you. They could tell you to leave if they wanted to. There were lots of mission rules that stopped Mum from 'saving' her own kids. Besides, like me, she really liked the nuns and the safety of the church.

So my mother had been one to sit back a lot of the time, trying to sort things out from behind. She liked to keep the peace. That was the way she had to be on the mission. But she worried that her role as a traditional Arrernte mother was slipping away. It had been important for her that us kids stayed in the dormitory so we got educated in the white fellow ways. She swallowed a lot when anything went wrong at the mission. But she knew she needed to play the 'good girl'. Whether in the white fellow world or ours, she looked after people softly, but with great heart. Only in the circle of women could she be strong. There she would laugh and cry and tell all her old stories.

But us girls listened more to the nuns and priests than to our own mothers, Mum must have worried. It hadn't been easy for me going into the dormitories. All these 'rules' from the nuns, all those older girls. I wanted so bad to be one of the 'best girls'. I built a strong belief in the white Catholic world that the nuns wanted us to join. I think my mum died still trying to make everything okay for everyone in her family. My promised marriage stuff had probably been a big shock for her too.

Unfortunately my mother never got to see me as a mother with my own children, and sadly my children never met her. She saw David's kids, but they were living a long way away. I know how much I loved being able to hold my own grandkids later on. Mum would have loved them all up. But they didn't have her to hold them. And my own kids weren't able to run to her and hug her or hear her stories. So I am sad for both my mother and my own kids.

For me and Sandra, coming back to Santa Teresa after the sorry camp at Amoonguna stopped and being without our mother and father was really hard. I hung around with my friends who had nothing much to do either because of the drought. We might get a few jobs helping organise an end-of-term festival or some other event at the school. But the busy times never lasted long. Eventually I packed up and moved to start a new life at Amoonguna.

Alice Springs back then in the 1960s was very much smaller than it is today. We still had our family connections with the Palmers and the Shaws at Mount Nancy. They had a drovers lease on land there and held on. They had lots of visitors from bush staying. There were smaller camps north of town. But throughout the late 1950s the Alice Springs Town Management Board and the Northern Territory Administration had been putting pressure on the local Native Welfare bosses to shut down all the 'illegal' camps along the Todd River. The police and council rangers would ride or drive through the camps till people were forced to leave.

Officially, the whole town had been a prohibited area for Aboriginal people since the railway line came up. But there was always lots of exemptions for Aboriginal workers and their families who usually lived in railway cottages. And in the early 1950s all the mixed descent mob got houses south of the town out at a new building place called the Gap Estate.

Other Aboriginal people worked in town or in the government offices. The ones working on the road in building gangs were okay living in Eastside or in one of the boarding houses. And lots of other families were living in sheds out the back of white houses. They were working and doing odd jobs. It was friendly enough in a segregated way. Not everyone was cruel. The Aboriginal families in town sent their kids to the same schools with everyone else. There were no private schools much. And the sports teams were mostly mixed up and played against each other.

But legally, without a letter of exemption from the bosses, us Aboriginal people from out of town couldn't be in town. We could go to the hospital but we needed a permit. Before they shut down the Bungalows everyone with a permit was meant to camp there. It was called the 'workers' camp'. This was the 'dog collar' days. The police could ask Aboriginal people to show their permits. If they didn't have one or didn't have it on them, they could be taken out of town or arrested and held in jail. So many Aboriginal families started camping further away, just outside the town boundaries. They'd be able to get some work, and sneak into town when they needed to.

All this changed when I was leaving school in the late 1950s. The cattle stations were struggling. The trickle of families coming off the station camps became more of a flood. Conditions on the riverside camps became much worse with a lot of overcrowding. Plus there was more and more cheap grog appearing on the camps. Some of the pay was in grog, not money. The growing numbers of out-of-town people on the camps saw the government build Amoonguna just far enough to make it a long walk.

It was still the Assimilation Policy so employment training and teaching people to live in 'proper' houses was part of the plan. But they didn't really want to assimilate people in town. So Amoonguna was opened up in 1960 and the Jay Creek reserve was rapidly expanded. All my families stopping near the Bungalows were taken to Amoonguna. Western Arrernte and Western Desert mobs were put on trucks and many ended up back out at Jay Creek. They were forcibly taken there – they had no choice. Our people needed food and were rationed to get them to move. Families were also picked up from the fringe camps and threatened with having their kids removed or being locked up unless they relocated.

The Amoonguna assimilation dream was to integrate Aboriginal people into towns through teaching them work and living skills. We were even taught 'proper' white ways of bringing up kids. We were to go to school, get a little bit educated and learn to speak better English. We would be trained to go to work. Most of the jobs would be in the trades for the men and domestic service areas for us women. We would also be introduced to the 'civilising' influences of Christianity and European cultural traditions.

It was not too much different from the dreams of many of our elders for our children. Not much different from my own hopes for my kids and grandkids. But the families weren't running it ourselves. It wasn't done from within our own cultural ways of doing things. Assimilation became a nightmare. Many of the bosses were cruel and uncaring. Everyone likes to have some control of their choices and what we do with their lives. This is especially strong in Aboriginal culture. Nobody likes jobs that mean working away from home and that are leading us nowhere.

The new Amoonguna Reserve stretched south-east along the sandy banks of the Todd River. White supervisors were employed to make the rules. But the construction of buildings lagged behind. Most of the people taken there set up their own wiltjas or built new humpies to sit down together in their family groups. By 1960 when the new reserve officially opened, Amoonguna had some big sheds, smaller houses and offices.

The buildings were mostly from surplus recycled building materials moved out from town. There were even old aircraft hangars and ex-army Sidney Williams sheds from the Second World War like our girl's dormitory. The government completed communal kitchen areas, communal eating places, and communal toilets, showers and laundries. A few houses were being built but these didn't have kitchens, bathrooms or verandas. Over time some families got the option of living in sheds with hard dirt floors.

The plan had been to not leave many of the Aboriginal campers behind within the town boundary area. The dog tag permits were enforced by local police and only Aboriginals who were workers were to be allowed in town. There was a new wave of anger. We were again refugees in our own country. A younger, less traditional Aboriginal leadership grew up that was tougher, stronger and better organised. They had more support and an awareness of 'legal' rights. There were also protest marches, especially from Christian groups, the unions and the Communist Party. Lots of white people thought Aboriginal people should have equal rights and opportunities. They came to help us organise.

·········

Amoonguna grew into this big, mixed-up place. When there was trouble or fighting, the government and town bosses said it was all being stirred up by a bunch of white troublemakers. The government made lots of promises that Amoonguna and the new Aboriginal compound would be a good place. They told us that we would have houses, schools, training centres, jobs and a good life. Not many of our people believed much of this. But we weren't given any real choices.

It was the Amoonguna supervisors who decided which people were the 'troublemakers'. They would kick people out and have them charged by the police, whether they were Aboriginal or white. The court would mostly find people guilty and lock them up. Lots of our white helpers were punished and stopped from going into Amoonguna. My family used to tell the story of the Little Sisters nuns moving with them to Amoonguna. When the white bosses tried to stop them, Bill Gorey and Mompy argued for the nuns to stay.

The older mob had grown up knowing it was better to keep smiling, keep walking. If some white boss asked why you were smiling, you started walking even faster. Always it was a good idea not to make eye contact. We sometimes let the white missionaries and union bosses have their arguments with these bully boys. They were less likely to be locked up, less likely to be taken out, bashed up, or even shot and buried somewhere hard to find. We knew what had happened to big talking Aboriginal leaders, and they didn't want to be killed or imprisoned by cheeky white fellows.

Families were terrified about having their kids and grandkids taken away and sent a long way from their family and homelands either. So our grandfathers and grandmothers, fathers and mothers, and even us younger ones knew we had to be very careful. At least when the bully boys were looking straight at you. We could only get smart among ourselves and behind their backs. Else you were going to draw attention. And the police had long memories. Everyone would get into trouble.

The white supervisors at Amoonguna were given a lot of powers. If white visitors were labelled 'dangerous' or 'misguided', they could be stopped from visiting our families. But the new reserve was a big paddock surrounded by our own country. So people just stepped over or cut through the fences, or went around them. Plus there was vacant Crown land all around. Emily Creek and the Todd River were nearby if people needed a private place to come together.

Some of our senior men started talking ceremony up again even though we were forbidden from doing any traditional ceremonies and dances in Amoonguna. And the women's circles grew. Talking up culture business became more active again out at Amoonguna and in the nearby camps. Amoonguna was supposed to train our mob so we could be integrated and assimilated. But a more political leadership was also being trained. There were plans for an assimilation that included equal rights, regaining control of our own lands and a more accountable system where we made our own decisions. These battles continue today.

·········

The weather remained dry meanwhile and cattle prices were low. Sheep prices were so bad that entire flocks were sold up and sheep replaced by cattle that didn't need so many workers. The stations now used bikes to muster their cattle and mobile yards to put them on trucks. They didn't need many stockmen on horseback, even in the good years. The managers had more cars now to run themselves into town to pick up shopping. They didn't rely on their gardens. They had bores and water pumps so they didn't need their Aboriginal shepherds looking after the waterholes and soakage points. They didn't need skilled stockmen to fix their windmills. They had new barbed wire fences so they didn't need big muster camps. Station bosses didn't even need good stock horses. The horses were forced out to 'the long grass' for a long rest, or rounded up and taken to the abattoirs.

The homesteads got radio transmitters, refrigerators, washing machines, vacuum cleaners and new kitchen gadgets. They didn't need the Aboriginal cooks or cleaners. On the close-to-town stations, the bosses and their families started living in their town houses. Further out, employed managers replaced the bosses. The stations started the push of local Aboriginal people off the stations and into new fringe camps. It was like the camels; the white bosses saw them too as old fashioned and largely useless. Our families now needed permission to visit our own places. Our custodial duties to our sacred sites and our ceremonies had to be left behind.

In town, welfare officers and the police visited our old camps and the newer fringe ones, telling people to pack up all their belongings, all their dogs, pots, pans and billycans, and get on the trucks to be taken back out to Amoonguna or Jay Creek. They gave them an offer 'too good to refuse'. They tore down campsites and took people's blankets.

The new hidden camps in the Sadadeen and Coolabah swamp areas were created. They closed down camps where the Western Arrernte stockmen and painters had stopped near Morris Soak. They closed down all the families that had camped in the St Johns Valley near where the casino is today. They closed the camps along Chinaman's Creek and even the family groups hanging around near the Little Sisters of the Poor Mission just south of town. Even the Finke River Lutheran Church mission was told to send everyone who wasn't sick off to Jay Creek or back to Hermannsburg.

Old canteen at Amoonguna.
Courtesy of Frances Coughlan

CHAPTER 15

Working at Amoonguna

One time when I couldn't get work at Santa Teresa I drifted back to Amoonguna to stay. My family got me a job working in the kitchens soon after I arrived. The workers there were older women that I knew from my Middle Camp days. Some of us working were friends from the Bungalows or the girls' dormitory school days. It felt a bit like that old women's circle coming together again. I had just turned twenty-one when I arrived; I was real shy at first, but keen. It was great fun, lots of teasy talk and gossip. So many funny stories told of people coming for food. Sometimes I couldn't work for laughing so much.

All us kitchen and canteen women would get up very early every morning before sunrise. We had to make everyone's breakfast so they could start work, go to school or just get on with their day. It was like my mother getting up before all of us to go to the mission bakery for work. But my mother wasn't there. That was still a great sadness.

As one of the workers, I had a proper bed and room to sleep in. Once at work, us women just stayed busy in the kitchens all day. As soon as we finished breakfast we'd start making the lunches. Later there was the evening meals. And always there was cups of tea, baking cakes and cleaning up. At night we would sit together around our campfire with family or friends. The next day it all started up again. But even though we were all tired, I loved everything about it. We all did. The busyness, the energy and the laughter of working as a team. I often thought of my mother at the mission bakery. We both liked being busy. It was the same busyness that made me happy in my dormitory days, and gets me out of bed today.

My uncle Huckitta was staying in Amoonguna too. He had recently got married up to Marjory and was staying with his mother Nelly, his other mother Jenny and his big sister Mompy. Marjorie got work in the kitchen. It was there that I learnt how to cook properly. Amoonguna houses and humpies didn't have kitchens so we were feeding everyone. They'd all come in when the food bells rang three times a day. They'd pick up a plate and line up. We'd be behind a counter serving them up. Then they'd pick up their knives and forks and sit along big rows of tables to eat.

People would eat in families or with their mates. After they finished they had to scrape their plates into a big bucket and stick everything in big tubs. Later we'd wash it all up, stacking everything into piles. Then we would eat together before starting to cook the next meal.

·········

By the time I got my job in the Amoonguna kitchens a lot of the Heffernans, Goreys, Lynches and other Northern Arrernte and Southern Anmatyerr family groups were coming and going out of Amoonguna. My father often stayed at Amoonguna, a senior man now visiting all our families around town. He became part of the bigger leadership groups, trying to sort things out. He liked this role, and it helped him heal after the sadness of my mum's death. He loved working for his family, and was passionate about building this better Aboriginal world.

Leadership was always really hard work. There were lots of different families, lots of jealousies. As Dad grew older he was sometimes a bit sadder when they couldn't get more shared ideas in our own Aboriginal groups. Like lots of his brothers-in-law, he felt powerless to change things when it came to white fellow business.

Amoonguna became the new gathering place for lots of senior men. They were wanting changes that often included going back to the way they had thought life had been, when they were young themselves. They wanted a world where Aboriginal law, culture and language remained strong. They wanted control of their own lives. The trouble sometimes began when they wanted power and control over us women and kids. Not like in the old days when we had the powerful circles of senior women, and only a few senior men and young boys in camp. The old cycle of life where men were away from camp teaching their younger men, or working, had changed. Now there were too many men living close up everywhere. The men wanted to take over running the family business. Even if part of it was 'proper way' years ago, none of us younger people or many of the women really shared this part of this plan. We had always liked our freedom from being bossed around, no matter much who was doing the bossing.

Not all the senior women thought much of the new culture if it was going to be led by often angry, sometimes drunk men who seemed to want to punish their own women and kids. Us young women had new ideas. Like every new generation before us, we wanted to be more powerful in a better world. There was a lot of new things coming out of the white fellow ways of being in the world. Culture was changing and we wanted more freedom from some of the old rules that wouldn't work anymore. We liked the new music, films, shopping places and fridges. We liked the cars, the bikes, and being able to dress up and move about in a bigger world away from our parents. Our parents liked most of these things too. Many of our older people also liked the cars, the new cowboy outfits and dresses they could wear about the place. They liked the parties and they liked their grog. We were happy for them to lead; but only if the senior people had control, listened to us and behaved respectfully in the circles of their own family.

Many of our senior people worried about us kids learning these new ideas, having lots of white fellow schooling, and thinking we were safe in this new white fellow world. Today I'm a bit like that myself. It is better if our older people are treated as the clever ones, helping to stop the kids from getting into trouble. Young people still need to listen and understand their own family history, and culture, before they think they can change the world.

....

Looking back today on Amoonguna is painful. It was a hard, bossy place, run by tough bosses. It wasn't our way to live all together across tribal and family groups. Family fighting was often a problem. The white supervisors thought they could just tell us what to do. There was no sitting down listening and working things out. They thought they knew best, and they wanted to be the bosses. They could decide whether you worked or not. They decided the housing. In fact, they decided just about everything. And they made some terrible mistakes.

When families first camped in their humpies and wiltjas at Amoonguna people separated off into their different tribal areas. The camps were set up traditional way, with single men's places outside the married couples' ones surrounding the circle of senior women, single women and young children. This kept families reasonably safe, even in the overcrowding.

But the government had ordered the supervisors to start living in proper white fellow houses. So they forced families who wanted to work to move into their tin sheds without fireplaces. Instead of sitting around campfires, people had to use the communal kitchens. There were no bathrooms inside any of the tin houses either. Instead, everyone had to use the communal showers and toilet areas.

The bosses regularly came around and inspected families' progress. If you failed their tests they could take away your kids. And they could kick you out if they didn't like you, for 'causing trouble'. Families had to look like they were changing if they wanted to stay. If we were 'good', we might get a better house. Then our family was looked after, our men and women got some paid work. But many families chose to still live away from these houses in their own groups of humpies and wiltjas, especially the older and more senior family members. These families got punished.

Later on, the Amoonguna bosses got money to build some bigger houses for their 'good' families. These were offered when you passed the 'cleanness and goodliness' tests. You had to scrub everything and do what they were told. But some people were never going to change quickly. We were a stubborn lot; especially if it wasn't our own ideas.

Other people did slowly change how they lived after a while, just like at Santa Teresa mission. Some families adapted their ideas of 'old traditional' culture to fit the new policies and rules. Especially the young people changed. But the bad side of this for the senior people was that lots of the kids stopped respecting the old cultural values. They didn't listen to our senior leadership.

These kids got all mixed up. Some tried to fit into the white fellow roles that the supervisors expected of them. They thought they were going to get ahead in the beautiful new world being promised. But the education, jobs and money never really happened. The best positions still went to the white kids. So a lot of them got angry and just floated around as a wild bunch, forming their own gangs. And they lost respect for everything.

Because kids were kids, they'd be given food and places to stay. But they didn't always have some adult around to listen to and talk things out with. They weren't always loved, and held close. Some of the kids started getting out of our family control. There was a big mix-up of all our kids at the schools, and in the training areas and sports. These kids from different families hung together for safety and fun. If they wanted something, they might just go out and take it. Especially if they'd been taken away by welfare for a while.

·········

When I was there, the simplest houses were made from sheets of iron and had a single steel- or wood-framed room with an ant-bed dirt floor. The builders would smash up old termite mounds, mix in water, sand or dirt and cement, other things too if you wanted, until you had enough for the floor. Then you'd pour the mix into a solid wooden frame the size of the floor you wanted, filling the frame. Then you waited till the floor dried, scraping it smooth and flattening it with a big roller or something heavy. Ant-bed floors dried nearly as hard as concrete. Some of these little houses also had 'lean-to' verandas as well. After that it was mostly steel posts and tin walls.

There were never any dormitories in Amoonguna. Husbands and wives weren't split up. But there were rules about how many people could live in the houses. These houses were built along straight roads. Alwekkere, our women's gathering places, weren't allowed. Extended families couldn't live all together. Families from different tribal groups were close together. This created conflict. Over time, the humpies were pushed further towards the reserve fences to make room for the new houses.

Lots of welfare people visited, making sure we cleaned our houses and swept the floors. Some of the younger people started work in town. The men got jobs as railway fettlers, on the road gangs, as night-can workers emptying the back lane toilets, or in the hygiene teams picking up the garbage bins and cleaning the streets. Some got jobs spraying the DDT to kill the mosquitoes. And some young women got contract work cleaning and cooking in the laundry and kitchens at the hospital. Others worked in private houses looking after white people's kids, cleaning up, and doing the laundry and cooking.

·········

In the old days, the different family groups mostly lived a long way away from each other. This avoided a lot of trouble. The senior men would meet up quietly to sort things out. Long-time gaps between catching up would heal a lot of the wounds. But now everyone was living close by. Everything had to be sorted out together. It was complicated and messy. It soon tired everybody. Kids would get into little silly fights and old disputes across family groups and different language speakers would explode into crazy violence. Families could be easily triggered. The bossiness of the white managers and the amount of grog creeping into the camp only added fuel to the fire. There was a lot of angry and displaced people.

I would sometimes see my father and the other senior men sitting down in the middle of fighting, trying to make decisions in line with our own laws and culture. But each tribal family's leaders would stick close together to their own story, for the fear that bigger families would double-bank them and take something away. Families had to stick up for each other, right or wrong. This meant that family leaders had to be careful not to give away things that their own families wanted held on to. Being a senior leader could get a bit dangerous very quickly.

If there was trouble some families would send messages out to other family members, telling them they had to come to Amoonguna quickly. These outside people would turn up with big sticks expecting a fight. But weapons never helped 'settle' these family disputes. The other side would get their own reinforcements to come in too. And the fighting and ambushes would grow into bigger, harder problems.

Fighting could flare up quickly. If someone or some group felt disrespected or left out of a decision, then the fighting sticks, spears and boomerangs would come out quickly. The shouting and growling became explosive. It could be really scary. Us kitchen workers might have to close the doors and hide away. And once the fighting started it could take a long time to slow down. Whole families might have to pack up and go. Even without the white bosses, some families were told by the senior leaders that they had to leave or be punished.

·········

We were still being treated like wards of the state by the police and Native Affairs. These government men had powers to order us around and tell us what to do. But we remained defiant. They could punish us if we didn't say yes to whatever they wanted, but behind their backs we remained free. Welfare still decided whether it would feed us at the new government settlements out of town. But they couldn't make us agree with them.

Meanwhile the grog stuff got much worse. The granting of alcohol rights in 1962 to Aboriginal people opened the doors for white people coming around selling grog. Later on it was often 'metho', or other made-up stuff. Over time there were lots of our people lost to the grog on the fringes of town. My uncles tell me that one day a white man came in and sat down with them where they were camping in the Coolabah Swamp in Alice Springs. This fellow had some grog with him, a large bottle of sweet wine. He talked up the grog saying, 'It's nice, taste it, try it. Good sweet water like honey ant syrup.'

That's what happened to our parents. Some white men started giving wine to our dads and mum who were sitting down under gum trees. They got them drunk and stole away our parents' power to protect and feed their kids. People got mad on the grog, and were just handing over their money to pay for it. People got sick. Some died in grog violence. And the welfare people were always taking 'sad' kids away from their heavy-drinking families.

Lots of our people liked the magic of the grog. It made them feel stronger and better in the world. But those feelings didn't last long and the price they had to pay was terrible. We didn't have any dreaming stories for the alcohol. Families stopped looking after each other and started hunting grog instead of food for their families. People became sadder and more lost. Sometimes kids were taken away a long way from home. Culture and family responsibilities fell away. I grew into an adult in this quickly changing world.

It became harder to organise traditional tribal gatherings as some of our young men were becoming grog sick. Our leadership was swamped with people that couldn't think beyond their next drink. Some were even senior men. All the sadness and losses within families became an excuse to drink grog and behave badly. These people could talk up their ideas but they didn't follow through. They had lost their strength.

Despite all these problems, there was a lot of good things that happened at Amoonguna. For the first time lots of people lived in weatherproof houses with safe beds for their family. There was food and work opportunities. Many people that had only known camping on the ground got the comfort of a bed. They were able to lock a door on the outside world to get some rest from the troubles. Schooling, training and better health services got some funding. These changes inspired our families about what might be possible. Dreams of land rights, building Aboriginal community-controlled organisations and owning their own houses became much bigger issues. Things started to feel much more possible and our young leaders gave us more hope.

All the time though there were more police and welfare workers in town. You had to be very careful if you were young and black and out on the street. Being older and black was tough too. In 1963, the Alice Springs council even tried to extend the Aboriginal permit zone to three miles around the town. But this new rule was seen as being too much and got blocked. This was the first Aboriginal win in a long fight for Aboriginal rights.

....

I met my husband at Amoonguna. Tommy Dixon was a good-looking Anmatyerr man from Napperby Station. Like my father, he was a proud stockman and wore the cowboy uniform with style. I always liked that proud stockmen look. I had grown up seeing my fathers and uncles riding around on their big horses. Tommy Dixon had that horseman's way of walking and being in a space. I still love that sort of thing.

I soon found out Tommy's story. I only had to look up twice and the other women started cracking jokes. They pouted their lips at each other, pointing him out. Then one of my cousins started on his story. They were cheeky and rude stories too; rolling eyes and moving their hips. Difficult to keep a straight face. I blushed and the heat rose in my head. Over time I'd heard so many different stories in the kitchen that it could be difficult to make eye contact when serving some people. Now it was my turn. Anyway, the consensus was that Tommy would be a good catch and I might have a chance if I wasn't too shy. Else they might beat me to him themselves.

Tommy had got work on lots of stations around Napperby and east along the Plenty Highway. He was a good horseman and worker. But the long drought, and then the political backlash by the cattle station bosses against union pressure to pay Aboriginal stockmen equal wages, had seen him out of work. Tommy, like my dad and lots of the stockmen, was now mostly between jobs. He'd ended up at Amoonguna unemployed with his mates. It was 1965.

Right from the start I noticed him. We seemed to choose each other. Luckily he wasn't 'wrong way' for me. My family would have been very angry then. He was a Peltharre man, the skin of a second choice partner for me as a Pengarte woman. It could have been worse. But it was good enough for town, and it helped that my father's country and Tommy's mother's country lay next door to one another, only a small range separating them. So we had neighbouring country. That made it seem right for us to marry later on. By the time I talked to Tommy, he already knew lots about me. And he knew my father.

The women in the kitchen watched everything. Especially the young men and women making eyes at each other across the kitchen benches. And they talked about it if they needed to. So Tommy and I started going out together secretly. We had a secret messenger. I'd go into Alice Springs with other young women to the football. Tommy and me would meet up and walk around together. We might have been thinking my family didn't know, but of course Alice Springs and Amoonguna are small places. The kitchen already knew. Keeping a secret was impossible.

Someone told Aunt Mompy. It would have been better if it had been Aunty Nancy who had her gentle side. Soon everybody in my family got to know. I got 'growled' by Aunt Mompy, and my grandmothers and aunts sat me down. Then my father came over. Dad said he was very angry, but he didn't seem that upset. He said I wasn't following the 'proper way' rules. I should have asked and got permission. I dropped my head stubbornly, not saying anything. Everyone rolled their eyes. I thought Mompy might slap me. But Dad and my grandmother took charge and I was asked to leave again.

You couldn't have a quiet chat with the family when Mompy was growling someone. People liked to talk really loudly and used their hands for emphasis when they wanted to make a point. A big space was cleared by this time. Other families moved further away. Everyone knew. Soon Tommy was hanging about; him and his mates. A bigger family meeting was pulled together without me. The older ones started talking about me with each other.

Afterwards I was called back in. They were sitting down in a circle, waiting for me to give them my entire story. I shook in fright when they asked what I wanted with Tommy. They already knew, but they wanted me to tell them. They started by asking me where he was from, what skin he was, who were his parents, which country they were from, which way did they go, what was their family dreaming. Lots of questions I hadn't really worried about as I was holding onto Tommy's hand on the way back from town. And they already knew the answers anyway.

My father asked Tommy's mate Bruce Stirling to come over and talk to them. When Bruce was finished he had to bring Tommy over for some further questions. After that we stood together answering their questions. Then they sent us a bit away while they talked some more among themselves. Eventually, after a bit of time, and when other representatives of the families settled a few things out among themselves, my side of the family decided not to flog me for sneaking about, and not going through the 'proper' way. We got their permission to walk out together. They let us both go.

Later the two of us got approved to being treated as married in the Aboriginal way. Our families could be very strict about Aboriginal law and culture. But we hadn't been back to talk to Tommy's family in Napperby yet. And we didn't get married in the church at this time. We stayed living in our own separate places; me in the women's circle and Tommy in the single men's camp. We could meet in town.

I got offered work in town a bit later on. Some white couple wanted to train a small group of us young women to work as cleaners in white people's houses. I didn't really want to leave the canteen. But none of us could say no to being trained. My Amoonguna supervisor had already agreed. I felt really uncomfortable in these strange big white houses. They had so many things. Big beds and blankets everywhere. Tables and chairs. Fridges and washing machines. The kitchen and bathroom had all sorts of things I'd never seen before. They had everything. I didn't like it much. We didn't have nothing much. It didn't seem fair. And the white people all seemed a bit nervous too. Always watching and worrying. It was always a relief to finish every day and get out of there.

Then, after some long overdue rain, Tommy heard from Brian Stirling that there might be work coming up at Yambah Station. And Tommy wanted me to move there with him. I heard from my father that Uncle Charlie and Aunt Ruby were staying at Yambah. Before I left Dad, Mompy and the family talked to me about Napperby and Tommy's family. Nice family, but the hard old rules for the women. Dad had worked at the stock camps at Napperby for a while. So he knew Tommy's dad and family. He knew Tommy. They told me how it could be a hard place, much stricter than in Amoonguna or the mission. They were all a little bit worried and scared for me. Reminded me to be a bit quieter, or I'd get flogged.

They all had a bit of a laugh when they said this, looking at me shyly and with great love. Even Mompy was a bit sad and worried. I said I'd practise sitting quietly at the back. This amused everyone. My sister Sandra pretended to be me, trying to sit quietly. This cracked everyone up. And I got the message.

With it coming up for the muster season, Tommy was itching to be on the road and working from the back of a horse. He was good at this. Nothing much else made him feel so good. He was good at sport. But it didn't make you money. And Amoonguna was making him restless. Not enough for him to do. He didn't want to be trained for a town job. He was a stockman. So we packed up a few clothes, blankets and things. I said goodbye to my family and friends. I would miss my friends at the kitchen big time. I had done a lot of growing up there. But I didn't want to stop holding Tommy's hand. No-one knew of a lift going past Yambah so we wandered into town and up the north highway, to try to get a lift.

Country around Ilewerre.
Courtesy of Frances Coughlan

CHAPTER 16

Walking out with Tommy

It was a hot day and a long walk from Amoonguna into Alice Springs. From there we headed up towards the Anmatyerr camp near the old Bungalows where some family still sometimes camped. We sat down on the highway, past the old racecourse, hoping for a station truck to pass by that might be driven by someone we knew. But no-one came by. So before it got too dark we found a small camping place in the Anmatyerr area.

We waited many days for family heading to Yambah to come by. It was quiet time on the station, and there weren't many cars or trucks on the road. Not like today where family are in and out all the time. Finally, Tommy talked to an old fellow at the Anmatyerr camp and they worked out where to sleep, and the best places to find water and food along the way. It was full summer by then and there was the vague promise of a bit more rain about.

The walk to Yambah rolled out as a big adventure. That first day we walked a long way, up and down through the MacDonnell Ranges north of Alice Springs, following the track along the old Overland Telegraph Line north. I don't remember all the little stops we had but I remember it was a hot day. I wasn't the athlete I once was, that was for sure. And the path we were following got a bit windy and abstract fairly often. After a fair few hours, when the sun was high in the sky, we waited at Collyer Creek in the shade of some trees for the coolness of the late afternoon before continuing.

We walked till it was getting near dark before camping. My mind and body was screaming to me, and I was very relieved when we finally stopped at that first bore on the left just before Bond Springs homestead turnoff. All we had were two blankets, one pillow, a small billycan, one small cup, a packet of tea, a packet of sugar, a packet of bread and some matches. But it felt heavy enough. I was so tired and could have fallen asleep straightaway. But Tommy was pretty buoyant that he'd found the bore. He filled up the billy, made a small fire and we had some tea with a fair bit of sugar in. I must have fallen asleep because when I woke up it was just before dawn. I had all of the pillow and the other blanket around me. Tommy was stirring the fire, getting the billy going. It seemed perfect except for my leg muscles and I dozed off back asleep. Tommy woke me up again soon after with our one cup filled with sweet tea.

We set off walking beside the old Telegraph Line again in the early morning coolness, getting to Sixteen Mile Creek, McGrath Creek and then Harry Creek. It was flatter country now, and Tommy showed me everything on our way. He talked of how to live out on the land. Some places we stopped to rest and would eat berries from bushes nearby. Then we walked again till it got late, stopping to sleep at a place called Burt Creek. Here Tommy set up a sleeping spot in the dry creek bed, making a little windbreak shelter, while I boiled the last of the water for tea. We felt excited to be nearly getting there.

Next morning Tommy got up to look around for some water to boil up for our tea but the place must have missed the recent rain. There was no ground water in the creek. He searched everywhere up the creek until he dug a little hole in a likely spot and got a little water for us to drink. Tommy knew all about how Aboriginal people could find underground water in creeks. He showed me where to look and how to dig for the small soakage points that slowly filled with water. That knowledge probably saved our lives that day.

We walked all through the morning before resting our weary feet and our aching muscles. We knew that it would be our last day. In the afternoon we headed off again. Tommy said Yambah Station was close by, just over the horizon almost. It was only a couple of kilometres before we saw all the buildings standing in our sight. Thank goodness. What a relief. And I thought to myself I never really wanted to go walkabout like that again. For me that was the start and end of choosing long walking holidays. I suspect that over the years I had become too much of the soft mission girl.

·········

I hadn't been back to Yambah since escaping my arranged marriage years before. It was not like last time when I was worried and frightened. This time I was really happy and excited. I knew that 'promised man' had long since headed back home. We ended up staying at Yambah Station for the muster season. We camped near my uncle Charlie Heffernan and Ruby Perrule. Charlie still had his donkeys and a few horses as well. There was lots of my family around: Aunt Mary and her husband Lesley Tilmouth and their children, and even some other Anmatyerr family from Napperby Station that Tommy knew.

Tommy's mate, Bruce Stirling kept working, as one of the stockman. For the next few months all the stockmen went out to the bores, moving the cattle to where there was water and a bit of green grass to feed on. The bit of rain had helped, but the country was still dry. While Tommy was away with the men, I stayed at the Alwekkere with the old women, helping them with the cooking and carting water from the bore. Each day we would wander out with the young kids to collect wood and hunt a bit of bush food.

After the cattle muster they took the ones for sale into town. Later the station found Tommy some other jobs to do. Some rain had fallen by then to save the countryside. Come mid-1966, I was thinking I was pregnant. Tommy decided we should go to Napperby where his father and mother lived, to meet everyone. He wanted to take me home. This was important, but also very scary for me.

·········

It was a big walk out to Napperby, about 140 kilometres, much longer than the trip from Alice Springs to Yambah. Tommy asked my uncle Charlie if we could borrow his horses. The station owners, the Gorey brothers, had given Charlie the two riding horses as part of his payment for working there. And the mare had since had a young colt. Uncle Charlie said we could take all three horses, even though he would miss the colt because he had the makings of a useful stock horse. Tommy said he could drop the horses back off when he or someone else was coming in.

When I heard about the horses I felt much happier. All I could think was God bless old Uncle Charlie for lending us them for our journey. Even though

I knew nothing much about riding I knew I never wanted to do anything like walk too far ever again.

In the days before we left Uncle Charlie found me some old riding boots and some slacks to have a bit of practice in the saddle. He and Tommy explained how I needed to be the boss for that horse or it wouldn't obey me. Tommy was to ride the colt while I would be on the old mare. They had me in front of the old mare, holding the reins tight, looking her in the eye and telling her I was the boss. Then I got to walk her around. After a while Tommy showed me how to hold the reins tight, get my foot in the stirrup and pull myself up into the saddle. They all had a bit of a laugh at this. The mare walked around in circles, teasing me, until Uncle Charlie held the reins tight. Finally, with a helpful push from Charlie, I got myself sitting up in that saddle.

I got led around for a while, learning swaying back and forth as the horse moved. Then Charlie handed me back the reins, telling me to tie them into my hands tight and never drop them. Tommy rode his young horse just ahead while I sat on the mare, reins loose following along behind. He made me pull on the reins to stop the horse, then start it up again and turn it this way and that by pulling the reins. Nobody, especially the mare or me, thought I was the boss, but the mare was old and well trained. We both agreed to the pretending and I gave her a big hug.

After a bit of this walking Tommy broke into a trot. That had me nervously bumping along faster and holding on much harder. But I got used to it after a while. Then Tommy broke into a canter. This was faster and smoother, and a bit terrifying. Once he saw my face, he decided not to worry about galloping yet. When he slowed and stopped, my horse pulled in beautifully behind his. Both the horse and I was glad she was really good at following. There was an agreement that she would basically follow the leader. I gave her another hug. Tommy smiled at Charlie. Charlie signed okay. Everyone was smiling happily. I'd be alright, they thought, on that old mare anyway.

·········

That last night in Yambah was a very restless one and I couldn't hardly get to sleep. It was all a bit much leaving the safety of family to be going into Tommy's country. Of course it was also my father's and grandfather's country, and I'd heard some of the old stories about my grandfather and the families out there. I must have fallen asleep because Tommy had to work hard to wake me early the next day.

He set out on foot before the sun was up to bring the horses into the yard for saddling up. I rolled up all our things. We had added a few more possessions now that we had the horses. I packed up tea, sugar, flour, meat, matches and bush tucker given to us from the station kitchen. Soon enough we were both in the saddle, with the other horse carrying our packs, proper swags and some water. I was still a bit flustered and scared at first. I had on some old ladies slacks and a scarf. That made me very proud. Uncle Charlie and Ruby and all the camp watched us set out, waving, telling us to pass on messages for their family members if we saw them. It was one of the few times in my life that I got to ride a horse. The men always tended to ride the horses.

This time, with horses, our journey was no real trouble. We started out early so we could get all the way to Aileron Station by nightfall. Tommy stopped to rest the horses at Ten Mile Bore. My legs were rubbed raw from the riding. We had ourselves a couple of hours to rest and something to eat. Then we got going again and into the big Aboriginal camp around Aileron Station. We met up with Stanley and Lucy, and Lonny and June, and lots of other Anmatyerr family living there. They were mainly Ti Tree Station families who had been forced off stations. Decades later, after they won their Land Rights claims for a living area, they all moved back to their own new community near Ti Tree at the Six Mile.

When we visited this time, the Aboriginal camp had their own clean water source. We camped with family, ending up staying a couple of days. Tommy learnt some of the gossip of what was happening out Napperby way. On the last morning, the families gave us some bush food in a big package to take for families at Napperby. We had something to eat, packed up our camp and, after a bit of a struggle getting myself back in the saddle, off we rode. The families blessed us, telling us to travel safe. 'Aretyeneng,' they said.

It was spring time and there had been plenty of rain around so we had no water troubles travelling. There was bush foods everywhere and fat goanna tracks meandering across our path. The rockholes in the close-by hills had fresh water. There were even deep waterholes in the creeks along the way. Tommy showed me this country for the first time and I was very excited. That day we had a few extra stops to look around, rest our horses and eat up big. In the end we were running late and for the first time Tommy put me into a bit of a canter as we rode into Twenty Mile Creek just before nightfall.

Next day we were up early. Napperby was not too far away. I was excited but nervous to be meeting all the families who were waiting for us at the camp. I decided that before we came to the camp, I would get off my horse and walk in, leading my horse. I thought a woman riding in might have been seen as a bit bold. We both knew that these Laramba families were much stricter than the mob at Amoonguna. Much stricter than the Yambah mob too. In those days old people living in their own country away from town still used the very hard laws and culture. It is not like what the young people face these days. These old people expected respect as bosses of their country.

·········

You can never slip quietly into an Aboriginal camp. Not without magic anyway. From a fair way out dogs were barking madly and sniffing and growling suspiciously at the horses and me. Tommy got off his horse, kicking one of the big dogs, silencing them all briefly. He took off his hat and took hold my hand, helping me down.

I looked around, seeing straightaway I was well overdressed in my shirt and riding slacks. Tommy was looking flashed up too. As well as the dogs there was the start of a gathering of kids, all looking our way. So Tommy tied up his horse and the colt, then mine, before he headed straight up to his father's and mother's house, me following behind. They weren't expecting us, but everyone had heard the dogs. And everyone came out from every tin house and humpy and wind break to greet us.

Laramba community on Napperby station,
Courtesy of Frances Coughlan

CHAPTER 17
Napperby Station

Tommy went ahead waving to everyone. I tried to practise being quieter. But walking into his family camp made me nervous. I was nearly walking past Tommy before I pulled myself up and dropped back behind him, consciously trying to walk slower. It felt like going to first confession; or when I was performing in the dormitory Christmas play. I was sick with fear, but excited too. This was a test. I always did good at tests. But there was always the possibility of failure. I was real worried that I might say something wrong.

All the families were out and I saw that I knew some of these people. There was the Tilmouth family. I smiled nervously and nodded polite way. We'd met at Amoonguna and Yambah Station. And over there was Valerie Ross. We'd played as kids in the Bungalows school. I tried to relax. I recognised Tommy's family by the descriptions my father and others had given me, trying hard not to remember some of the funny things Mompy had told me. Hopefully nobody knew any of my thoughts.

'Keep quiet, keep smiling, keep walking,' I was saying to myself, as I concentrated on following Tommy like the old mare had followed the colt. As we came closer, his father walked towards us with a welcome smile, causing Tommy to stop. I nearly walked straight into his back. His father took my hand softly, moving family about, guiding us both to places to sit down in the circle around the campfire. I sat down and looked towards the ground, trying to make my head quieter. But my brain was still talking to me all the time.

Tommy was asked to tell them what he had been doing. He introduced me and started to tell them who I was and who my family were. Which country we were from and what skin I was. My parents' dreaming paths. People were nodding. I kept my lowered head still as they looked at me. Tommy wasn't telling much about our life together. He was careful like that. It was both our story to tell or not to tell.

But he told them all the important things about my father's and mother's sides of my family. Everyone was able to place me from their lines. The senior people knew my grandfather's and grandmother's country, all of them much better than me. Many also knew my grandmother's side from Ti Tree, and my mother's side at Yambah Station. Some of the men had worked there at Ti Tree or Yambah. Some knew my father from stockyards and the men's gatherings. Or from living in town.

Tommy's father kept asking questions and Tommy answered them for both of us. The talking had a formality to it, like in church. Tommy smiled at me. It would be alright. He went off with some men to unsaddle our horses and turn them out. Our gear was brought near to the campfire.

Later, after tea and some food, and without me answering even one question, I was invited by Tommy's mother to sit down with her at the women's camp. As I got up I heard his father asking other family men to join him. We were greeted by the senior women and Tommy's sisters and sister-cousins. The women made me a cup of tea and the talking started. They wanted to know everything about town and what was happening. They asked about my family, my clothes and the horse ride. We discovered lots of people we all knew. They looked at my stomach and smiled a little. My mind slowed down a little. It would be alright.

Not long after we all sat together I had seen the senior people sitting together, talking softly among themselves. When everyone was back settled into the gathering, Tommy's father said it was alright for Tommy and me to live together at Napperby. There were smiles, a bit of a welcome story and more cups of tea. More food was brought out and cooked. I had my formal blessing for the relationship and was welcomed into the Dixon family. I could stay and share their campfires, country and stories.

I felt quieter after the family meeting had worked things out. My family connections made it easier for everyone to place me. Tommy's dad had worked with my father. It was always going to be alright. But what would Tommy's family think of me after a while? I was a flashed-up, mission-taught young woman, and they were very traditional in their dress, language, culture and ways of seeing their world.

Tommy's father had two Nungala wives, Rosie and May. They all lived together around a Sidney Williams hut. Tommy and I were given our own tin shed next to their place. His mother Rosie and his two sisters, Liddy and Lisa Pultara, helped us move our few things in there. And the family settled around the fire talking to us both. Other families came and went, saying hello and introducing themselves and their families. Everyone was real pleased Tommy was home again. They asked more about the horses, and later Tommy's father took him up to see Mr and Mrs Chisholm at their homestead.

·········

We spent about two years all up out there at Napperby. Tommy's sisters and their sister-cousins made friends with me and helped me learn what I had to do. They took me hunting and looked after me. I was welcomed into the circle of women, especially when the men were away with the cattle. It was mostly a peaceful and quiet time. They were very friendly and wanted to hear my stories of the mission dormitory and life in town. But I still got a little worried and lonely sometimes. I was still learning more of this language, and the correct ways of being in this country. There were lots of different rules.

The Aboriginal camp stretched between the trees along Napperby Creek, close up to the station homestead. A windmill dragged water from a soakage hole into tanks. This was fed into the homestead. We even had a tap in our camp. The Chisholms had bought the station in 1948 and made a lot of improvements. They had put up seven small, Sidney Williams steel-framed sheds, well built, not from scrap metal like on some stations. And the Chisholms weren't mean or cheeky. There were some trucks but the men mostly still used horses to check water and fences. No movies or radios to listen to. No books. It was more like our lives when I was young. You had to make your own fun.

Like at Yambah, the old people and many families preferred to sleep and hang around under the trees next to the creek in their humpies rather than in the sheds. There they could look out at their country and watch out for everything, and the water was sweet and clean.

The camp was an easy walk to the homestead and the Chisholms shared a lot of their things with us. The station store room was a shop for buying or booking up food and other goods. Cattle were still killed and some rations still given out. The Chisholm kids had a teacher who helped out schooling the camp kids. The classroom was a big demountable shed. Mrs Chisholm helped out with medicines. If she knew someone was ill she would visit and use the station radio to talk to the hospital in town. She had boxes of medicines that she would give out. And if someone was really sick they would call the doctor in town to work something out; get the Flying Doctor to come out, or arrange for an ambulance or truck to take sick people into town.

Napperby was an old-fashioned station. They didn't always make much money, and they didn't always pay much cash, especially to the local Aboriginal workers. But families could book up food, clothes and other things at the shop when they were really struggling. The Chisholms usually worked something out, especially in dry times when bush tucker was hard to find. It would still be hard though when you had to pay back for the book-up later, but people swapped having enough now instead of worrying too much about down the track. But Tommy wasn't getting a lot of work. It took a long time and better follow-up rain to build up the Napperby grassland and the herd after the drought. All the local stations were struggling.

·········

The Anmatyerr elders still followed the old ways. The senior men were still the bosses of the law. The women spent a lot of time in their own circles. The Alwekkere operated under the eyes of the senior women. Men's ceremony still happened during the times when the station management didn't need all their stockmen around. And the cycles of renewal continued on as before.

But the Aboriginal camp was often pretty empty. Some of the young stockmen would get restless. They might get a lift on the station truck into town to visit people. Or might go to live in town on the fringe camps or at Amoonguna, wanting something more to do. Their family would be worried and sad for these young people leaving. They knew that traditional culture and law was struggling to be heard in town. They knew about the partying. Young people from Napperby might get in trouble in town.

I was happiest when I got out of the camp walking into country. After rain, Tommy sometimes took me to show me his special places. Usually we'd just carry swags and some water. We would hunt for bush tucker along the way. Tommy would tell me all the names and help me understand this place.

Old George, who travelled the countryside with his three camels, would sometimes turn up to take everyone out visiting local sacred sites when the station didn't need him, or us. He might have presents too. Other times he stopped at one of the bores, looking after cattle, just walked the countryside by himself or with the senior men. He always had a lot of hunting dogs for company. His camels carried water in big canteens that stretched over their backs. The camels carried our skinny swags we made up from a few blankets, with some spare clothes tucked in the middle, and all our food. Old George had a gun too, sometimes used for hunting. But mostly it was the big dogs and our men with spears that chased down the kangaroos, emus, bush turkeys and perenties. The gun might only be used for shooting a dingo for its scalp. Everybody walked behind the old people singing the country. The younger ones would be collecting bush tucker and looking after the kids.

On the first big family trip I went on we walked all the way around Lake Lewis, camping out for weeks. We would clean up the waterholes and sacred places, sometimes teaching the kids to dance these stories. I learnt my own family dances out there on my grandfather's country. I was told the old traditional names for this creek, that tree or this hill. These old dreaming storylines were repeated within our circles of women.

·········

Ilewerra is the story of the two arlantye lizards. Today they're called bicycle lizards. They stand up on their back legs and rotate them as they run away. I have permission to tell this story.

In the Dreamtime, there were two arlantye, father and son or anyenhenge atherre. These lizards lived there at Ilewerra and made the patches across the grey saltpan places. They went running around and dug these big holes in the rocks to make their home. After they had made this place they made a home in the big rock called Mwetyeke, the arlantye sacred site, the low red hill you can see from the side of the road as you are passing Ilewerra. It's an important place.

Later the two lizards decided to go west. They went around to where Karrinyarre is, past Papunya. There the arlantye changed into two men; they called themselves Angale and Mpetyane. They had boomerangs, fighting sticks, and fighting spears or urrempere.

From there they came back to Ilewerra, travelling north-east. They gave their shields to one another at a place in the hills nearby the western side of alhere altywepe or Napperby Creek. Because of that, the place is named Apmere Arlkwerte-arle Antherreke, the place where they gave their shields to one another. You see that they laid their shields and fighting sticks down on the ground at this place. It is there that the two bicycle lizard men disappeared. I can't tell you more of this story.

Ilewerra is also a place for bush onions, called yalke. They grow wild and very big. The area around Ilewerra is full of red sandhills. It has the green of the trees, the grey of the saltpans, the light browns of the bush onions, the white sand and the dark brown of the hills. Penangke and Pengarte. My father was Penangke and so I'm Pengarte in the skin names given for our Ilewerra place. That is why I must worry for our Napperby country. It is my job as Pengarte, to be the caretaker looking after that land. My father as a Penangke, is a traditional owner.

......

Another time we travelled south to Narwitooma Station towards Glen Helen Station. It was special country for all the families at Napperby Station because of the waterholes. I really felt alive on these trips. The women and kids might go for longer hunting walks into country for a few days. These were fun. You would go as a group because of fears of bad spirits and maybe running into other trouble. Plus groups could be good if there might be jealousy stuff happening. We would go to close-by waterholes and rockholes, cleaning up these places.

But sometimes I had no real jobs to do on the station and found life pretty quiet and boring. It was mostly my sisters and cousins that cooked and looked after the old people. I was living out there when I was pregnant with my first child. It was a special time. But the birth came too quickly, and it got really painful. Tommy and his family midwives couldn't help me.

Mrs Chisholm had to call the doctor in town. They sent the hospital ambulance out to meet the station car halfway between Alice Springs and Napperby, at the Aileron turnoff on the highway. The car trip was really painful. Rita Dixon, Tommy's mother's young sister, came with me to meet the ambulance at the turnoff. When the ambulance arrived Rita had to go back to Napperby in the car. So there was no-one in the ambulance I knew. Only the white hospital men. I was alone and didn't have my mother or any old women of my family around me to keep me calm. The ambulance bringing me to Alice Springs hospital travelled as fast as it could. But my baby couldn't wait. In the end my son was born in the back of the ambulance on the way. It was 20 November 1966.

That birth was very hard, all by myself. But then the baby was born and I was holding a little boy. Blood and mess everywhere. The men stopped the ambulance to help me clean up. They cut the cord and tied it so I could easily hold my little baby for the trip. That was how we arrived at the hospital. Once inside, the doctors and nurses gave us a big look-over and took us straight up to the maternity ward. It took me a long time to get over the shock. Gilbert and I had nearly a month in the hospital till both of us were strong again. Then I had to wait until Tommy could get a lift into town to be with me.

I wanted a new name for my son that was different from all my family names. I had heard the name Gilbert from a white woman and her husband. I was working with them in town doing housework and cleaning after I stopped working at the Amoonguna canteen. I had liked the sound of that name ever after that. So when Tommy finally got into town on the station truck, he was okay about Gilbert. And that was what we called our baby.

Gilbert was a very sweet boy. When Tommy came, I got out of the hospital straightaway, ready to go back to Napperby to show off our first baby son to all the family there. We left the hospital to camp with some of Tommy's family near where we'd waited for a lift two years before. The station truck had to wait for the train to arrive from down south. It took a little while. When they loaded the truck they came to get us.

Luckily my father was around in town to see my little Gilbert, coming to join us out at the Anmatyerr camp before we left. He walked in and I was so happy to see him. My father was very proud for me. He squeezed and hugged my baby as all grandfathers do, and shed a few tears of happiness. Gilbert was too young to remember this, but it was a very happy memory for me.

I was really pleased Dad spent that special time meeting my baby. He was staying at Amoonguna at that time. My sister was still at Santa Teresa, and Malcolm and David were living down at Ernabella. So seeing Dad was really an important reconnection after being away so long. I wanted my own family around, and asked Tommy about coming to live at the mission. But we agreed we needed to take the baby to Napperby first.

·········

Back at Napperby everyone was really happy. They'd worried when I'd gone to hospital. People didn't always come back after going to hospital. But I had come back with Gilbert. He was passed around and squeezed joyfully. I got to grow up Gilbert in the Anmatyerr circles of women. But Tommy still couldn't find much work at Napperby. This was when all the Aboriginal stockmen and us families were talking about Wave Hill and the walk-off by their stockmen. Everywhere our people were thinking maybe we would start getting paid better, and that we might even start getting our land back.

Not long after Gilbert was born there was the 1967 Referendum where Aboriginal people won becoming Australian citizens. Native Affairs couldn't tell us what to do, how to live or where to live after that. We got to vote like everyone else. This became part of a bigger fight with a lot of the cattle stations that started pulling down their camps and kicking people off. We didn't have a fight like that with Napperby. Those bosses were alright. But we still wanted things to change for the better.

We stayed there for another year but Napperby was becoming hard for me, especially when Tommy was away so much. Lots of people started moving to town. Our culture tells us that the father should spend time in the mother's country after the first baby is born. It was proper way. A man gets respect for sitting down with his wife's family once the child is born. The baby needs to learn the mother's side's stories, and the mother needs the support of her family.

I talked to Tommy about needing my sister and family around to help me with the baby. Finally he agreed to come to Arrernte country out at the mission. So when Gilbert was big enough to travel we got a lift with the station truck into Alice Springs. Once in town we went to the presbytery and they gave us a lift out to mission. I was so happy.

Margaret as a young mother at Santa Teresa.
Courtesy of Lesley Riley

CHAPTER 18

Back in Santa Teresa

I did not realise how much I'd missed being out at Napperby until I got back to Santa Teresa. Napperby was just a long way away, and a very different place. The mission felt like coming home. It was like a little dark storm cloud had lifted off me as we turned the corner of the Santa Teresa road and I saw the big white cross painted on the hill above the church. I couldn't stop smiling.

As we pulled into the old village, my grandparents, Brandy and Dorrie, greeted us at their new house. We climbed off the truck to be hugged by my sister Sandra and her partner, Thomas Stevens. Gilbert was smothered in kisses. With them was Malcolm, now twelve, still shy, but a much bigger, smiley kid. He had been stopping at Santa Teresa since him and his town gangers had been caught by the police for camping above some shops near the picture show place. The woman at the welfare had lost patience, and the courts ordered him to stay with his grandparents or get sent away down to school in Adelaide. Dorrie and Brandy were both looking older and frailer, but with a playful twinkle in their eyes. I was so happy, I was almost crying.

Family came from everywhere, hugging us and checking out Gilbert. Aunty

Hilda and Uncle Alex, Uncle Paul and the whole McMillan family came out of their houses to welcome us and show off their own new babies and houses. Tommy was greeted. Gilbert was grabbed and squeezed. My fat stomach was patted and commented on. There were my old friends crying out and coming over. Lots of babies I didn't know.

Sandra said we could stay with them when they got their house. Meanwhile our stuff was piled onto my grandparents' veranda, away from skinny hunting dogs and the wandering, always-hungry horses.

It was my first time back at the mission since going away from Amoonguna. Some hadn't even met Tommy. None of them had seen Gilbert who was toddling around, babbling away. Napperby was only a car drive away. But people didn't have cars back then, and if it was someone else's country they never went. Not like today where people visit each other all the time, call on their mobile phones or even send photos through their phones or computer.

I was twenty-five when I came back to Santa Teresa. Life in Napperby quickly became a long time ago and a thousand miles away. It was wonderful being back. Now I was a mother I had a more grown-up space within my own family. And my own happiness made it easier for Tommy who'd left his own country and family.

It was 1968. The times were a-changing. In Central Australia things started to seem more possible after the 1967 Referendum. We started to feel more included in this idea of Australia. The racism of the white people slowed down a bit. We even had our local new black leadership talking up getting back control of our own land again. We had hope.

·········

Sandra had married up with Thomas Stevens, my skinny, always smiling, old playground friend, from Middle Camp days. They were nearly the same age, and knew each other from being little kids at the Bungalows and then mission school days. Thomas was the very clever kid, always poking fun at the world. He could get his own way with his big smile, bad jokes and natural charm, even with the bosses. His father was a traditional owner in Mparntwe country. Thomas's mother's country was from just north of Alice Springs, at Sixteen Mile camp. It was good to be sharing Sandra and Thomas's tin shed and yard.

In the next five years Tommy and I had four more kids. My first daughter, Pamela, was born in 1968, a few months after we arrived, an easy birth this time. I got pregnant again soon enough and my second son, Trevor, was born in 1969. My second daughter, Karen, came along in 1971, and my last daughter, Joylene, in 1973.

Sandra and Thomas started having children too. Their first son, Johnny, was born about the same time as my Pamela. They went on to have one daughter and four more sons. Those years Sandra and I were always pregnant or had a small baby in our arms. These kids all grew up healthy and strong, playing together 'proper way' as one big happy family. Maybe a few loud arguments, but it was a good sweet life.

The rain kept falling regularly enough. Tommy was going off doing jobs with the other men. More times it was as a gardener, rather than stockwork. There was only a little bit of local stockwork happening. My sister and I had plenty of our own jobs with cooking, cleaning, washing and looking after our kids. Family and visitors were always around. Those early years back at Santa Teresa with my growing family saw me and Tommy really happy.

After a time Sandra and I both moved into new tin houses, next to each other. There was Commonwealth government money for new housing coming through. This was in a new area of the mission called Eastside, nearer the school, and past the church. Tommy and Thomas were able to join our two homes together, using some steel posts and sheets of iron, to make a middle veranda. After that we spent all our time out there on the ground under that veranda, sharing the cooking fires and sitting down all together.

In the hot summer months the tin houses got very hot, sometimes more than forty-five degrees during the day, often with a hot, dry wind. On those nights, everyone took their beds outside at night and hoped for a cool breeze passing by. Later on in the cooler times family and neighbours might gather for a chat or game of cards. Sometimes there might be a car and a group of men going off shooting. On those nights there would be houses with kangaroos cooking on open fire-pits. There'd be lots of kids and dogs hanging around, hoping for a late night feed.

Sometimes you might hear someone playing a guitar off in the distance, and people might be singing an old cowboy song or a new pop song. Thomas's brothers, Basil and Frankie Stevens, were both great musicians. All those Stevens family, and the Rice families, were like that. Nearby there might be women organising church matters. Not far off the old men might be talking about culture and ceremony, or just gossiping.

The mission always came alive for an hour or two in the cool of the early evenings. Around the fires life was organised and arguments sorted out. The older kids would wander around trying to find some excitement. They were always hungry for a bigger life. Just like when we were teenagers. Except by this time they were with their own families instead of in the dormitories with the sisters and sister-cousins. Everyone's little kids would fall asleep around the women at the fire-pit, listening to the gossip and stories.

Later, one of mothers would scoop them up and bed them down all together on mattresses and swags. Puppies and playthings would be cuddled in close. Sometime later, the adults and older kids would fall asleep as an outer circle of protection. The old ladies who had scared us as kids still made us all hang close together to escape the clutches of wild bush women, hairy men and the evil spirits wanting to suck people's souls away. Now we re-told these stories to keep our own kids close. And we truly believed them. The whole mission was usually in bed a couple of hours after sunset.

In the colder months families would huddle around windbreaks with small fires, cooking food and trying to keep warm. There was usually plenty of wood. The men would take a truck, bringing in good wood and cutting it up for all the camps. But even with a bit more wood on the fire most nights we'd settle in early and the kids would sleep close to the warmth of the fires. If there was a cold wind blowing, the whole place, including the dogs, would crawl into their blankets and find shelter behind a windbreak.

·········

One afternoon in the late summer, Thomas Stevens came back home and saw a big snake track going into my tin house. Me and Sandra were sitting outside on beds under her veranda. Thomas called out for us to come see the snake tracks. We looked. It really was a big snake. Sandra told Thomas to go in and kill it. But it took a lot of persuading, and a bit of pushing, to get him into that tin shed. And when he didn't come back out quickly, we started to feel guilty. Sandra had a quick look through the door. Thomas was standing deadly still on top of a bed in the furtherest corner. There was the really big snake curled up in the opposite corner. With his mouth, Thomas made it absolutely clear he wasn't going to move another inch.

Sandra and I had to find some long sticks. With them, we lifted and moved the table and cupboard so we could whack the snake. But he got spooked and managed to slide and disappear away outside. Quickly we grabbed the kids and got them inside and onto the beds next to Thomas.

Thomas wouldn't leave the sanctuary of his bed. He wasn't much of the warrior type and was shaking with fear. Me and my sister and all the kids might have been up on the beds next to him, but we teased him non-stop. Finally he took a long look around and got down slowly. Then he spent the longest time picking around for the biggest stick he could find and giving us a brave heroic smile he walked outside, stick in hand.

Unluckily for Thomas, he nearly stepped on the snake. Back-pedalling fast, he managed to hit it hard enough with the stick to at least stun it. We found out later that it was only a carpet snake and not even poisonous. But for a while Thomas was feted by everyone, with much amusement, as the big hero of the family. Never one to be shy, Thomas took to acting out the heroic scene for anyone who couldn't escape. He was very dramatic and very funny. Even the dogs would fall about and howl.

·········

I had Gilbert and Pammy by then and was helping out at the mission school. Malcolm was mostly stopping with us. He often worked, helping out Alfie Gorey, who was a plumber, cleaner, gardener and mission odd jobs man. My Tommy had a job with Brother Bush, watering the plants at the community garden we called the Bottom End. It had a big fence to keep the horses and any goats wandering around out of the vegetables. It slowed the kids down too. There was a big windmill close up to where the big dam used to be. It pulled the water from Yam Bore into big tanks that allowed you to use a hose. The big stockyard was nearby. But it was dry times, and little horse or stock work happening. The horses were turned loose to fend for themselves.

Me and Sandra were both offered new block houses back at the old village. These were closer to our Northern Arrernte families – the McMillan, Stevens, Rice, Gorey and Golder mobs from around Yambah. We all lived in this one group of houses, and our children all went to the local mission school together. The school had changed a lot, with bigger and better classrooms than when I was a young girl. And they had a lot of good things inside them. The kids had more books, pencils and play things. There was no taking turns milking goats in the morning. We all had tins of powdered milk from the shop now. And the goats were left to go feral.

My oldest boy Gilbert grew up a quiet, shy boy. In the early days he often just played quietly with his toy cars. His great uncle Paul showed him how to make them from powdered milk cans. Later Gilbert developed a close friendship with Matthew Ferber. They became best mates. Together they made hand-held wires to steer the cans around. A lot of the other boys made these toy cars too. Like in the old days, they also made their own playgrounds in nearby bush; they'd build toy cattle stations and make low fences with strong sticks. The big camp pie tins became water tanks on top of sticks. They built their own trucking yards too, to hold the cattle.

Each day after school, Gilbert and Trevor would come home, pick up their toys and join their friends out in the nearby scrubby area. If some of the men were working they might go to the workshops or cattle yards to watch them fix things or help push up the cattle onto the road trains, or break in horses ready for a trip. Like boys forever, Gilbert and Trevor learnt from watching their fathers. Their grandfathers and fathers taught them how to fix their own stuff and make their bush toys.

Santa Teresa and Central Australia was still cowboy dreaming country for our boys and their fathers. They even owned their own horses to ride around on. But there was less stock work, fewer muster camps. The stations were using their motor bikes and helicopters. The mission year wasn't any longer split up around the cattle station seasons. Now it was all school terms and church festivities. The men stayed around home more, or would hang around the offices talking and looking at the girls. Sometimes there might be a bit of work for them. There was still the Santa Teresa racing days.

My daughter Pammy always needed me close by when she was little. She followed me around like a shadow when I went out to sit with the other women. Not that she didn't like to play with the other kids her own age. Pammy and her friends would make their own playgrounds and cubbies using flour bags, old blankets and sheets, just like we did. Like my mother had done, we showed them how to roll up towels and pretend they were babies to be nursed. We told them about using old bottles or something else to pretend feed their babies too. They learnt how to play at making cups of tea with an old billycan and jam tins for cups. Just like we did.

It was the same with all my three daughters. My mother would have been so pleased for me. It was proper way that mothers and grandmothers led their own young girls into the world. It was a way of teaching them the old ways, like we had learnt ourselves. Santa Teresa wasn't rich. We didn't always have spare money for shop-bought toys. We made toys for our kids or they made their own.

Our kids would fight and argue with each other at home. But they would stick up for each other too and stood together when strangers were about. And even when we were out visiting other people. They were taught that if there was fighting, the older ones had to stand up for their younger sisters and brothers and fight back for them. They were taught that family had to stick together, right or wrong. Old Mompy would have been proud of them.

As parents in those days we separated them, sometimes smacked them hard too. Not much, just when we were scared for them. We knew the kids needed to learn discipline. The nuns would have said I was too soft with the kids. Old Mompy too. They had to do what they were told. And it was mostly to stop them hurting themselves or each other that we might hit them. Especially the older ones that might be too bullying. But we were also proud when they could stand up and fight for things that were important. We wanted our kids to be strong and passionate.

....

When I was at the Bungalows or Santa Teresa mission school I got the cane or a ruler on my hand when some teacher got a bit angry with me. But I can't remember seeing my kids ever get the cane. And I was never at the school when anyone else's kid got hit. Sometimes the kids might hide themselves when it was school time, pretending they were sick or had sores that were hurting. But this was usually more about being told off for no homework, not about getting hit too much. We weren't perfect parents, and nor were the kids little angels. But I think our kids liked each other. Our family was a big one. Everybody, all family together.

When there was any trouble in the school with our kids fighting, all the families of kids involved, we'd all go to the school to settle it down. We would talk with the other parents and call all the kids who were fighting together to shake hands and be friends again. Sometimes my kids were the good ones and sometimes they were the cheeky ones. But when the families met together they sorted out things properly. That is the proper way. Me and Sandra we'd sort it out later at home. These days the kids are bosses of their mothers too much. And some mothers, usually those who don't properly look after their kids anyway, are the ones that keep the fights going at school saying their kids are always right. Nobody's always right. Not kids especially. It's hard when parents are worse than their own kids and families get dragged into arguments. Really their parents need to sort things out properly, sitting down together as adults.

At Santa Teresa, my kids all liked going to school and playing sports. The girls played basketball and softball, and the boys played football, sometimes cricket, basketball and hockey. Like me, my kids all liked winning. Even today they are pretty competitive though they aren't playing much sport themselves. Instead they might be watching their own kids playing. When they lose the fathers can get pretty cranky too.

The school took the kids on excursions. One time all the older boys went to another Catholic mission in New Guinea. Gilbert very bravely went on that trip. They met the tribal elders and their families. Our mission boys had a great time seeing this new country. Gilbert couldn't stop talking about the place.

After mid-year there were kids' sport days at school. Later the whole school would go into town for the community schools events at Traegar Park, same as when I was a girl. All my kids would be super excited and go in all the events they could. They'd bring back all their ribbons. Santa Teresa had good athletes and my kids were determined to be champions. Sometimes Santa Teresa beat all the other schools. Just like in my day.

Once a year there would be the Santa Teresa sports weekend for kids and adults. This still happens today. Teams from other nearby communities would turn up. Malcolm was a good runner, and he'd go in the individual sprint and relay events. Thomas Stevens was a good high jumper, often winning. The Aussie Rules competition would start down at the oval near the old village. Malcolm played Aussie Rules too. Later he went on to play with the Amoonguna team in the town competition.

The women and girls would play softball, fought out very competitively. Lots of bragging rights involved. Being the umpire, whether it was in football or softball, was really tough. If you lived at the mission, the local teams always had to do well. The umpires sometimes needed protection to get out of town if Santa Teresa lost. Later in the year the community teams would end up playing against each other, and the town teams, in town.

Teams of men also competed in some of the events, sometimes against each other, sometimes against the younger men. In one competition you had four team captains and anyone could nominate to play. The teams would get points in relay running, spear throwing, boomerangs, tug-a-war, tunnel ball and athletics. The captains would toss a coin and pick in rotation from the pool of people wanting to be picked. The best people got picked first.

My Tommy was always one of the first men picked. He was a great athlete, especially good at spear throwing. A cardboard kangaroo target would be placed towards the end of the sports ground and people would throw their spears at it, with the closest getting the points. Then the target might be moved to different spots. Closest to all the targets would win. Then the teams would move onto the next event, maybe relay races or jumping. The team with the most points overall would be the champions.

Santa Teresa had a weekend for horse racing too, usually in October. Most family had their own horses, and it was a showdown for the local horsemen and rodeo riders. Sometimes there might be a few horses from the nearby stations or outstations and even other communities. Everyone would camp out at the racetrack with big family campfires.

Saturday was the big racing day. Sunday after mass was more of a kids' and picnic day. There was lots of singing, guitars and dancing during the evenings, especially when the McMillan, Hayes, Palmer or Wallace families had done well. All you could see was a mob of dancers flashing around, kicking up the red dust through the flashes of light from the fires.

In July 1969, my father died. He had been sick in hospital but we hadn't known about it. When his mother, sisters and other family couldn't find him they thought he might have gone out bush. He was often doing this, travelling to visit people. But later when he still wasn't heard from, his sisters checked with the hospital and were told that he had died there. The hospital hadn't known who to tell. When the family didn't come to collect my father's body, he'd been buried without ceremony in a pauper's grave. It was a terrible business for us all. His grave is in the old Alice Springs cemetery near Araluen.

News spread fast. David and his family came up from Ernabella. Sandra, Malcolm and I came in from the mission. Malcolm was thirteen years old and staying at the old village in Santa Theresa. We gathered in Amoonguna. It was a simple affair with lots of close family gathered. We were all so shocked. My father was a stockman and tough like that. He never showed any pain, so we hadn't even known he'd been sick in hospital.

All his friends were really sad, and we all went away with this terrible anger, not knowing what we could do. Later, sorry business moved out to Willowra but David, Sandra and I couldn't go. We were needed back home again with our kids. After the funeral we all felt older and more tired. All orphans now. My father wasn't going to be around to look after us and sort things out. He wouldn't be there to look after his grandkids and help them make sense of the world. We were all going to miss his toughness and wildness.

My father's family took Malcolm to sorry camp at Willowra. Our father's mothers, brothers and sisters all went too. Malcolm stayed with our father's brother, Willy Williams, who was called Salty Willy. He took Malcolm back out towards Yuendumu where he stayed with his uncle and the men out that way. Much later he came back into town and stayed at the old village in Santa Teresa. He was a young man now.

In 1970, David picked Malcolm up in an old second-hand Holden he'd bought and away they went back to Ernabella. By this time at Ernabella there were no more sheep herding, just cattle everywhere. The mission and government had money and were moving people back out to their homelands. They had created a new town called Fregon. Malcolm was there when the families started to move in. People were still living in their humpies then. It was only later that they started making bricks and building houses. My cousin Johnny Leo was doing that work. David was working at the Ernabella store, running the shop with the store manager, an Irish guy called Trevor Lewis. Malcolm was doing odd jobs and working with his brother sweeping, filling the shop shelves and doing odd jobs.

My mother's parents, Brandy and Dorrie, both passed away when Malcolm was down at Ernabella. They are buried at Santa Teresa. Dorrie died first. As a Luritja woman from out near Mt Zeil, sorry business moved west to her family place. Because both Sandra and I were looking after small kids we couldn't get out there. But there was a big gathering for her funeral. All of the mission families were there, even the priests and nuns. Dorrie was farewelled with great sadness and love.

Brandy passed away soon after. Sorry business for Brandy happened at Yambah. It was a big gathering of all the Northern Arrernte and Anmatyerr families. He had been a very well respected leader and head stockman. It was the ending of an era with my grandparents passing. They had looked after us with great determination all through their lives, especially after my mother's passing. I still can see their faces smiling and loving us all.

·········

The Catholic church was big at Santa Teresa during the late 1960s and early 1970s. Nearly everyone was baptised and went to mass every Sunday. There were big confirmation ceremonies, with the bishop from Darwin coming down each year. Weddings and funerals were held at the church. There was even an Aboriginal Parish Council. The priests and nuns would come around to people's houses if they needed to talk with them. Brick houses were being built. Life was feeling pretty good.

The 'Outside World' changed a lot while I was growing my family in Santa Teresa at this time. All the Christian churches were talking up social justice for Aboriginal people everywhere. Especially in 1972, when the Federal Labor Party was elected. Aboriginal Land Rights was one of its promises. The Catholic church joined other churches in handing back their mission lands and houses into Aboriginal community ownership. Beside the church and its gardens, Santa Teresa mission only held on to its schools, staff houses and buildings.

In the early 1970s there was the first election for a Santa Teresa Aboriginal Community Council. Mr Kernan was elected chairperson. At the same time Alice Springs saw new Aboriginal community-controlled organisations starting up. Everywhere our people were becoming more political. Lots of things had started to get better for us all. We had many promises.

The Methodists, Presbyterians and some of the other Protestant churches had all became part of the new Uniting Church. This mob gave the land in town for the Institute for Aboriginal Development (IAD) and gave ownership of some church land to Aboriginal people. The Methodist church had built houses and training rooms, and now the Uniting Church handed them back. IAD became the first local community-controlled Aboriginal organisation in 1969, and got its first government funding in 1971.

....

Before the 1970s there was still pretty much no proper Aboriginal housing on our Aboriginal camps in Alice Springs. People had no ownership, so people could be pushed out and moved whatever the town authorities wanted. Some of the mixed descent mob, many who had grown up in town, had been given public housing in the Gap Estate area. But more traditional families still had to squat on the hard ground in a raggedy mix of humpies, tents, old cars and hand-built tin shacks. There was no taps, electricity or council services. In the rain the camps became swamps. In summer they were sweat boxes full of diseases. In winter you needed to cuddle up to the mangy dogs just to keep warm.

In the early 1970s the churches helped host meetings of our senior leadership from all over Central Australia. They negotiated with funding bodies for money for community-controlled legal services, Aboriginal housing and better health services for the Aboriginal community. By 1974 the Aboriginal leadership decided to incorporate as the Central Australian Aboriginal Congress (CAAC). It was based on the Indian Congress political movement and the African National Congress. It started the fight against oppressive colonialism.

The new Whitlam Labor government funded the Central Australian Aboriginal Legal Aid Service in 1973 to help us fight in court for better protection of our rights. That same year a Royal Commission into Land Rights was started under Justice Woodward. It helped get start-up funding for our new Aboriginal Land Council. The government finally gave Aboriginal owners the rights back to camp on vacant Crown land. In 1973 a lease granted Aboriginal ownership of the Little Sisters town camp and soon other groups established their own claims for traditional camping areas in town. Even the name of the Native Welfare Department changed to the Department of Aboriginal Affairs. A local Arrernte man, Charlie Perkins, later became its boss.

In 1984 Congress got funding to run a community-controlled Aboriginal health service and became the organising force for other similar community-controlled health services across Central Australia. Congress was important too in the setting up of the Central Land Council (CLC), covering two-thirds of the Northern Territory. Aboriginal Land Rights legislation was finally passed by the Fraser government in 1976.

Other things like Aboriginal employment and better education started to be talked up in the new political environment. A trickle of funding came for training programs through the new Aboriginal colleges like IAD in Alice Springs and Batchelor College in the Top End, which gave a lot of hope to all our families and children. We thought we could run our communities and our own lives again. Our people started to be trained as builders and construction workers. We had management training to have our own people running our own organisations, housing associations and land trusts. Best of all, we were told by our new leaders that we were allowed to be proud of being Aboriginal.

....

I couldn't see feminism happening anytime soon in Napperby, but in Santa Teresa things were changing more quickly. Us women became more powerful. Even the nuns were cheekier to the priests. There was also plenty of strong white women coming into Central Australia talking up a more equal power sharing between men and women. It might be us mothers who were kept busy popping out our babies, looking after the house and kids. But some of our sister-cousins and friends were getting the new jobs created at the Santa Teresa clinic and schools. So a lot more of the young women and mothers started looking around for something more to do outside of looking after everyone.

The paid women's jobs came with the church getting a lot more money from the government to run the school and clinic. Gough Whitlam did this. Me and Sandra had a lot of years where there was always babies, at home as well as kids in school. If we worked, we still needed someone there for the babies. So I talked of one of us getting a bit of work and one staying home.

It was me really. I was much keener to get out there than Sandra. I was older and more restless in spirit.

I wasn't much good at looking after sick people; I didn't have a lot of patience. But I always knew I'd make a good teacher. Just ask anyone. I'd been a 'best girl' in the dormitory. And I liked teaching people how to do things better. Since there wasn't as many nuns coming into the church anymore, the school teachers weren't always nuns. I made friends with the new white women teachers who came to work at the mission. It started in the kindergarten classes with my kids. I'd stay around and help out. One teacher in particular, Nancy Archdeacon, I liked watching. She looked after all of our little children. She reminded me of Sister Marie Therese reading to us. And as a mother I really liked how Ms Archdeacon always made sure the young kids had a good rest before they went home.

One day when I was helping at the kindergarten, Nancy Archdeacon asked me, 'Margie, do you have any Dreamtime stories to tell the children?'

'I sure do,' I said to her.

From the next day onwards, I started my storytelling in classrooms.

CHAPTER 19

Working at the Santa Teresa school

I loved having a job telling stories, and being back in the classroom. Stories were always magic for me, from when I was a little girl listening to my grandmothers telling their stories around the campfires. I was always hanging on every word. My mind and body would follow every twist and turn. I would laugh and cry with the people in the stories. Sandra was like this too.

I couldn't sleep after Nancy said I could tell some stories in class. Me and Sandra had the loveliest evening remembering stories from our childhood. Thomas Stevens helped me write some of them down. He sure could spin out a storyline. The next day in the classroom the kids were following every word. Nancy was really happy.

Later Nancy told Sister Robyn about me, so I soon got to know Sister Robyn Reynolds who had come to Santa Teresa wanting to tape our traditional stories in Arrernte. Mr Kernan, our council chairman, had given permission for the project, but the elders told Sister Robyn that she needed to start by talking to us women. So I got the job of working with her.

I was really excited to be working with Nancy Archdeacon and Sister

Robyn. It was the start of a bigger life for me, as a worker and educator. Every lesson I'd rehearse with Sandra and Thomas at night, practising the lines and the way to move my hands and body. Tommy and the kids would listen in too. I would hear them, they were listening so hard. I loved the idea of being a storyteller for my family.

I would get up each morning feeling full of life, almost dragging the kids into their clothes and getting them something to eat, so I could rush down to school. Sandra would be left with the babies and the job of taking them to school. I was the 'best girl' again as I gathered my stories and headed to the classroom. Sister Robyn and Nancy had to slow me down. I wanted to do sand drawings like my grandmothers had, and include them in the lessons. I was full up with ideas. I'd have my hands dancing, the kids' eyes following every movement. Just like in the old days with our storytellers, sometimes whispering the words, sometimes dramatic and fearful, using their hands to make a strong point as us kids lay in our blankets with the stars above and the music from campfire songs off in the distance coming through on the wind.

The stories I was telling were the ones handed down from my grandparents in the Alwekkere. Sister Robyn wrote these stories in both Arrernte and English words. I would use them in Nancy's classroom. Some kids didn't know a lot of their own language. Others kids needed to learn more English. Later we also used these same stories and tapes to help white teachers to learn Arrernte and Arrernte teachers to learn better English. It was bi-lingual education. Even Father Dixon got better at Arrernte and started to use it in our masses.

Our stories were mostly to help the kids in our classroom. But I was also proud to be helping white teachers and everyone else to understand more about our own language and culture. This classroom storytelling was the start of my love for teaching, and my first try at getting stories written down to help people understand. It was very good fun. I was nearly thirty years old at the time, with a good husband and father for my kids. I was living a good life.

In those days two friends of mine, Catherine Young and Theodora Johnson, were already working at the mission as Aboriginal health workers. Some of the nuns and the new white staff had the job of helping our people go into the new training courses, either in Alice Springs or even further away. When people came back after finishing their training, they got jobs in the school and clinic. I was now one of them.

But a lot of these new jobs were in the women's world. This was a hard thing for our husbands and the senior men. They weren't happy that women were getting paid more. There were lots of men's discussions about the roles of women in culture. But my Tommy and Thomas Stevens didn't seem to mind us women working. Tommy thought teaching kids was women's work anyway, and he was okay about me earning some money. Thomas and the men in his family just got on with their own stuff. But some of the other men were really angry and stopped their wives working. They said it wasn't proper way. They worried like they had always worried about the white fellow ways. They were scared they'd lose their wives to these new ideas. And often they did.

But lots of us women were dreaming of working in proper jobs within our own communities. So when I was asked to tell stories to kids, I thought 'now it's my turn' and my mind started galloping. No-one could have stopped me following along this path of becoming a teacher. Not even the senior men and women. I just knew that this was the right thing. And bi-lingual education became my passion.

·········

The new Aboriginal leadership in Alice Springs was also supporting training and jobs for our people. Many of them had been 'taken away' themselves to be educated far away from Central Australia in the cities. They had got a proper white fellow education and they valued the ideas around 'two-way learning'. It was part of talking up a stronger Aboriginal culture and identity. They spoke of us being the bosses of our own lives. We were told that we needed to become better than the white fellows. To do this we not only needed to keep our own language strong, but also understand good English, so we could argue and persuade the government. I wanted to become not only a teacher but as well an interpreter and translator for my community.

And I wanted to work across the two cultures to train white fellows how to work better with our Aboriginal leadership. My own thinking was about the importance of our kids learning two ways. They needed English to know about the modern world. But they needed to understand their own language and traditions too, following the old ideas taught to me by grandparents and parents. They had worked hard to survive this white fellow invasion of our homelands. If we didn't know the white fellow words and stories it would be harder to control our own futures. We knew the power of stories and songs. We needed our kids and grandkids to be able to shape this magic power for themselves. Our children needed to be able to compete in the circles where decisions were being made.

To show our children the right way we needed to be trained up and employed ourselves, and teach our own kids in our own communities. We needed them to learn English. And we needed them to have a way of writing down their own Aboriginal cultural traditions in our own language. The ancient Arrernte words and sounds are at the centre of our systems of understanding. Keeping language strong is the backbone of keeping Aboriginal identity and pride strong. The white linguists and educators knew that teaching our kids literacy in their own language first made it easier for them to become literate in English. They had this knowledge from studies of indigenous communities all across the world.

Getting our own kids to learn Arrernte had always been the dream of our senior people. It was central to their system for holding our children and grandchildren strong and with love. Our children needed to learn so they could have 'big lives' on their own land. They needed to have their language to continue, in their own way, the ancient Aboriginal rituals of death and renewal.

Many of the Santa Teresa families started to talk up keeping their languages and sacred knowledge alive. Language held everything that was important in our culture. And our senior language speakers now needed to be telling and writing down their own stories.

………

In the early 1970s bi-lingual schools started up in Maningrida and on Bathurst Island in the Top End. I thought the school at Santa Teresa should become bi-lingual too. Mr Kernan, our chairperson, had lived for many years away from Arrernte country before coming back home with his family. He had seen a lot of the white fellow world and knew that education was very important for everyone. He became a big supporter of bi-lingual education.

It was Mr Kernan that went to the NT Education Department, telling them that Santa Teresa wanted to start its own bi-lingual school. The government mob were okay about helping to fund our program, and I was chosen by Sister Robyn to go with her to the Summer Institute of Linguistics in Sydney. We would then be able to start teaching our children how to read and write in Arrernte.

It was really hard to leave the mission and go to Sydney. But Sister Robyn taught me a lot about being brave. You had to know how to face up and talk up in the classroom, she told me. So I did it. I knew I had to go away to study and learn how to write down our Arrernte language. Sister Robyn believed that teaching was my vocation. I saw myself being like her and Sister Marie

Therese. I was re-living my dormitory daydreams of coming back a hero to share my wisdom as a leader in my own community.

So after Christmas, in 1972 my kids all stayed home with Sandra helping Tommy when I flew down to Sydney. I felt really funny leaving them behind and being driven off to the airport. I tried to be brave in front of everybody, but that whole trip I stuck so close to Sister Robyn that people must have thought I was her shadow. I had to breathe slowly and I held on tight to her hand all the way.

The big scary airplane clunked its way high into the sky. I looked out the window and was terrified. Most of the time my eyes were shut tight and I was whispering my Hail Marys. The landing in Sydney was even more scary. I had a peek. We were flying over the ocean and then big lots of houses. But Mother Mary, the blessed virgin, managed to get us all back on the ground. Being around Sister Robyn made everything turn out okay. She knew how to make it safe for me, even when I had my eyes shut tight. She was so funny and tough.

I learnt a lot while we were away at the University of New South Wales. We both worked really hard. The discussions were very complicated and really difficult for me. Eastern and Central Arrernte as a language hadn't been written down much at all, and this made it much harder for me. I had to imagine Arrernte as a piece of writing to learn how to write it down. If I was to be able to write our language, then I could teach others. Me and Sister Robyn would become dictionary missionaries and bring all the words back to share with everyone.

After we got back home, Sister Robyn took me into town to spend three weeks with her and Jim Wafer, the senior linguist working at IAD. He let us have a little room there and a lot of recording equipment. We made lots of tapes in Mparntwe Arrernte. These were written up as word lists. This was the start of recording our language and turning our school into a bi-lingual one. With Sister Robyn's help I started sounding out Arrernte words and working out how you might spell them.

But after all our work at IAD, we got stopped by some members of the school council. Someone had stirred up the families, telling them that not teaching in English was a really bad thing for their kids. A lot of the parents said to the school, 'No, don't push it. We don't want to do that. You'll get the kids mixed up.' They had a vote and a lot of the families said no to bi-lingual education. They told the school that we shouldn't do it and the school council told us we couldn't do bi-lingual classes if the parents didn't agree. Sister Robyn and I were really disappointed. We had to wait until we were able to change their minds.

But I still got the job of teaching Arrernte to the white staff. We used the word lists and expanded them. Senior Arrernte speakers came into the classrooms sometimes to help explain new words. That was a lot of fun. Every week I'd have a lesson one night for the white teachers and anyone else who wanted to turn up to talk Mparntwe Arrernte. We would use the tapes and the writings to practise and straighten things up. The senior leaders often challenged us and we had a lot of laughs and arguments. It was hard work getting everyone to agree.

Later Sister Robyn and I quietly started to do a little bit of teaching the kids, but just with the older ones, talking to them about the reading and writing of Arrernte. It was an upside down way from how we'd been taught to start. The people in Sydney reckoned it would be easier starting with the young kids. Anyway we settled into a routine, building more and more tapes and written resources. When the school council changed its mind, we were going to be ready.

········

In the middle of this, I had a few tough years. It started with Tommy feeling restless and sad. I was busy and there wasn't much work or anything happening for him. During this time the grog started to flow more out at Santa Teresa. So far as I can remember, from when I was a little girl in the 1950s, there was not much of a grog problem. None of the Aboriginal people I knew had ever drunk any grog. They didn't know how to drink. There was no grog in our riverside camps. Family and culture kept everyone busy, and we were still hunting most days for our own food from the bush. Besides, there was no spare money for grog. And families were trying to live in peace. If anyone was drinking they were doing it a long way away from the camps. We might sometimes see the men looking sick and sneaking back home.

Up until 1962, under the Aboriginal Ordinances, the law had mostly stopped the sale of grog to any Aboriginal person. It was illegal for my people to be drinking any grog at all. You needed an 'exemption permit' to be drinking any alcohol. These were the 'dog collar' tags. People getting the exemptions weren't treated by government as being Aboriginal. Albert Namatjira got exempted, but there wasn't many other traditional people who did. And he got locked up for buying grog for drinking with his own family. So it was mainly just the white people and some of the mixed Aboriginal descent families who were drinking in the pubs or buying any grog back then.

Once the law changed in 1962, it was legal for all Aboriginal mob to buy grog and drink it. By the late 1960s, instead of there being just a few drinkers hanging around in town, maybe hiding out in the Sadadeen swamps or in one of the shanty town camps with their cheap wine or methylated spirits, it became more common to see Aboriginal people sitting along the river or in the parks drinking whenever they had a bit of money. By the end of the decade some heavy drinkers stopped coming back home much at all. They became the 'circle of drinkers', sharing their money and lives. And sometimes things turned nasty when the grog ran out or the police started chasing them. People might be locked up for a while.

I remember being with my father's family drinking once in town. It was the mid-1960s, after my mother died. We were catching up with family when my brother David and his family were visiting. It was a family gathering, down towards Charles Creek. Everyone was catching up and a few people were drinking a bit. Sandra was a young teenager and Malcolm maybe about seven. David was visiting from the Ernabella.

A welfare car came by the park and somehow Sandra and Malcolm ended up in the car. They were driven away and taken to this house in Eastside that welfare had. I had to walk down with my father and David to get them back. The welfare mob gave Sandra and Malcolm back, but my father was told off. The lady said he couldn't be drinking with young children around. It scared everyone a lot. My father was really angry too, but in a quiet way in front of them. We went back to Amoonguna quickly.

I didn't drink much when my own kids were little. Santa Teresa didn't have much grog. But other communities started 'wet canteens' where they'd get a licence to sell grog. Around 1971, after we became an Aboriginal community council, people voted to have a 'wet canteen' at Santa Teresa.

'It's alright now,' some of our people said. 'Now our family can stay home and get their grog here, instead of drinking in town and getting in trouble.' They thought we could look after the drinkers better at home. They argued it wasn't illegal anymore. 'It's our right to drink like everybody else.'

Some families argued that many of the younger people, and especially the young men, couldn't stop their drinking in town, but they'd be okay at home where the senior people could control everything. So the leaders of the drinking group formed the Santa Teresa Social Club. They promised to build up money for a new big hall for everyone to use. The money from selling beer would also go to having a sports and music place near the club. They argued the place would provide a good playground where the children could hang around after school. And the senior people could drop in to see their kids and look after their grandkids. The social club promised that everything would be 'good, good, good'.

The discussion about selling alcohol caused lots of family arguments. One day the mission priest spoke to the community council about calling a meeting with our elders to talk about the social club. At this meeting the council decided to set up this club. The rule started off that people could only drink a few beers after work at the end of the week.

The club started in 1972. Lots of family and friends told me about beer. 'You will feel good and happy. Go get some,' they said.

So I did. I drank a few with Tommy and our friends. Soon we were all having a few beers. For the first year the limit was three cans of beer for each person once a week. And the social club made a lot of money. People got jobs there. A basketball court was built. Dances and parties were held there. It became a meeting place for families.

But then the social club wanted to sell more cans to everybody. Next year it went to six cans. Another year later and they wanted 'take away' on the Friday afternoon after work so people could enjoy themselves at home. A few years later the club decided to make take away one carton per person. After a while the community 'wet canteen' idea had a lot of enemies. Not just the church mob, but a lot of the old women too. Our men would come home drunk and angry all the time.

....

There were lots of good times. Thomas's brother Basil started playing country music on the electric guitar and yodelling his way through the old songs. Thomas joined him with another guitar. They started a rock-and-roll band. Even the priests started to ask them to play and sing in the church. Folk masses, they were called. But they'd soon drift away from the hymns into their own rock songs. Everyone would turn around to look. The kids just smiled and started secretly practising their cheeky dance moves. And this was in church! Sandra would get wild and tell them off. She had a sharp tongue on her. But Basil and Thomas didn't miss a beat. Better to apologise later was their usual style.

At night you would hear guitar music and the sounds of parties from the social club on the weekend. Later Frankie Stevens joined his brothers in the music making. Some of the Hayes family liked their music too. Gibson John was always up for a song. Everyone started their own bands, usually a mix of country and rock. Even my brother David's oldest boy had a guitar.

I loved the dancing from when I was a baby. Chanting and moving with the old women. I was shy, but once we got started I wouldn't want to stop. After leaving school it had been the music and dancing that had got me in trouble. Later, when me and Tommy were sneaking out of Amoonguna, we would go to the picture shows and the dances. So again, when the music and dancing started up at the social club I thought it was a lot of fun. There were weekend dances as well as after work family nights. But later on when there was more drinking it got rougher and nastier. Sometimes the party didn't stop after the weekend.

A lot of the heavy drinkers thought they should be able to drink as much grog as they wanted because they were entitled to it. They thought if they weren't drinking they were missing out on something special. And if a little bit of grog was good, then a whole lot of grog was even better. When the social club closed some of them got into cars and went to town. And the party was even wilder in town because grog was cheaper. So often they'd get stuck in town.

It was hard to control the grog once it was 'legal' on the communities. Our mob weren't used to playing the 'white boss' roles within our culture. Even our senior men on the community councils couldn't really tell some initiated men that they were drinking too much. They couldn't say no to family wanting you to get grog for them, even if you didn't drink. Nobody wanted to say no. It got you into trouble. People couldn't say no, even to drunks wanting to borrow your car. It wasn't really in our culture at that time to be able to say no to family.

In some houses there was no money left over for food. But it was still hard to stop people. Nobody wanted to be the one to tell a drunk angry man that he couldn't get any more grog. But in the end lots of us didn't wanted the violence and constant humbug. Nobody wanted the family fighting, people getting hurt, even if there was paid work for some people in the social club. It was often our kids that suffered the most. And because our senior people couldn't easily say no when the 'wet canteen' was legal, they had to shut down alcohol across the mission altogether.

It was the strong senior Christian women who stood up as a group and ran this campaign. Soon everywhere 'out bush' became 'dry communities' again. People couldn't even bring grog into their own homes. The councils made the rule that people could only drink outside the community boundaries. A lot of our men, including my Tommy, had started to have problems with the grog, especially when they weren't working. And it took some drinkers a long time to become sober people again. A lot of the problem drinkers went back to town, or else every night were out at the boundary fence.

Many people died of the grog. People got killed or killed other people 'on the grog'. Many more got bashed up by some angry drunk. Others got smashed up in car accidents. All the big drinkers got sick. They ended up dying young or not able to look after themselves. Some women drinking too much had their kids being born with foetal alcohol syndrome. These kids couldn't think straight or sometimes walk properly. Then ganja started making a lot of young people act even sillier. Later still there was young kids sniffing petrol, and all these new scary drugs. Not just in our small Aboriginal communities in Central Australia. Everywhere had the same problems.

·········

In 1974, Tommy left me and our family. He said he needed to spend more time in town looking for work. Anyway, even though Tommy was in Alice Springs and I'd heard he was drinking a lot, I thought everything was still alright between him and me. Then one day it all changed forever. Joylene was still a small baby when Tommy told me he found it too hard living at the mission away from his own families and country. He said it was just like I had felt when we were at Napperby. He said he was leaving so he could catch up with his family and old friends. Then he got a lift into town. We both knew he wasn't coming back.

I heard his life had become one long party. Even in Santa Teresa, I knew about his women. He was picking up a little work and then drinking all his money with whoever turned up. I was left with all our children to care for. Sandra and Thomas helped out, but it was a very sad time for me and my children. Eventually, many years later, Tommy stopped partying and went back to live at Napperby Station, getting work around there. Later he worked at Jinka out along the Plenty Highway towards Jervois. He had married Winnie Ross by then. I stayed sad and angry with him, and it took a long time for me to forgive him.

After Tommy left me, I moved with our kids into Sandra and Thomas's house. I couldn't stand stopping in our old house. Too many bad memories and spirits of the past were there. Sandra and Thomas had their own mob of children but they invited us in and we lived all together. They said sharing our children was alright. They would be 'company' for me during this sad time.

I still give thanks that I had Sandra and Thomas to turn to at this time of great need. It was this blessing that saved me. And Sandra and I still had our good time growing up our kids together. Thomas was good with all the kids. Those years of sharing with Sandra and him were some of the best times I can remember.

Around this time Land Rights consultations were being held in town. Thomas followed his father into town, taking Sandra and their kids when the Ward hearings to talk to senior Aboriginal family leaders were happening in 1974. They stayed with family in Wiltshire Street. The Stevens family were traditional owners for Mparntwe country, and could tell all the dreaming stories. Lots of these families moved back onto their own land in town. This was when the claim for land behind the old Sadadeen swamps was granted and gazetted as a town lease. It became the traditional Mparntwe–Arrernte camping area and was called Ewyenper Atwatye or Hidden Valley. It became the home for lots of our families. But out at Santa Teresa it was quiet and lonely for me and my kids.

CHAPTER 20
Going to Batchelor College

Some years later, Sister Robyn told me that an American linguist, Barry Alpher, was coming to Central Australia. He was working at the School of Australian Linguistics in Darwin, and his visit was to talk up bi-lingual education. It included a new meeting with senior Arrernte elders on our school council. We were both excited about our dream being reborn.

Mr Alpher talked at the big community meeting about writing down our language and getting help to train local Arrernte teachers for our school children. He had Commonwealth government money to fund the training of Aboriginal bi-lingual teachers at Batchelor College, a new community-controlled Aboriginal and Islander education institution in the Top End. After this meeting Sister Robyn brought Barry to meet me privately. We sat down together and I excitedly told him of coming into the pre-school and being asked by Nancy Archdeacon to tell the little kids my old Dreamtime stories in class. We talked of going to Sydney to learn linguistics, and of all the work we had done with the mission school and IAD.

Barry asked if I wanted to become a bi-lingual teacher. I was bubbling with enthusiasm, and said 'yes' straightaway. I told him that I loved working in schools and said I'd find a way to go to Batchelor College to study. Barry was very pleased. Before he left he said, 'Alright, you're in. If you want, you can take all of your kids up with you. Bring your family too if you need to. We'll pay all your fares.'

This meeting was the turning point. It led to parents trusting in the bi-lingual teaching ideas. Nearly all the families said they were happy for their kids to be taught Arrernte part of the time. Barry and the mission school arranged for me to go to Batchelor College. I was so pleased and proud. I was thirty-two years old, a single mum with five kids and I was selected to become the school's bi-lingual teacher. It was better than winning the long jump as a kid. It was all a bit scary, but I was busting to give it a go.

In the end Batchelor College took a bit longer to sort out the money, tickets and everything. My young cousin sister, Geraldine Ryan, had agreed to come with me to look after two-year-old Joylene but a month went by before I got a letter with the tickets for me, Geraldine and my little baby. Sandra was back at the mission by now and happy to look after the older kids so they could continue school. So I didn't have any excuses. I was going to be a bit late for the start of the winter term but I was soon on my way.

Except for the trip to Sydney years before with Sister Robyn, I'd never strayed far away from my own country. This time Sister Robyn couldn't be with me to lend me her courage. People kept on saying the Top End was full of crocodiles and we had to be careful. All of the rest of my family had never been very far out of their own country either, or on an aeroplane. I had to pretend I was the expert. But when I saw the TAA jet at Alice Springs Airport, I was still wondering 'Will I go or will I stay?' My family got very frightened for us at the airport. By the time we walked across to the airplane, Geraldine looked terrified so I had to keep myself calm. Geraldine and I walked up the steps onto the plane, me carrying Joylene and holding my rosary beads and mumbling my Hail Marys. None of us saw much during the trip. Geraldine closed her eyes. I held onto Joylene tightly. When we landed at the airport in Darwin, I said a prayer of thanks.

Even though it was a bit dark in Darwin it was still hot and sticky. We were both shaky as we walked into the terminal but there was this friendly white man waving at us, called Erwin. He had been sent by Batchelor College to take us to where we would be staying. What a huge relief. He knew exactly what to do. He found all our bags and we followed him out to where his bus was parked. The place seemed very green and there were traffic lights in the streets. As we travelled our headlights showed these strange big trees covered in leaves and there was grass everywhere. Everything seemed much bigger than at home.

Once out of Darwin the highway felt a little spooky. It was a couple of hours before we turned off into Batchelor and its campus. Barry Alpher was there to give us a big smile of welcome. It was getting late by this time so Barry organised some snacks for us and showed us to our rooms. The place seemed new and shiny. He said goodnight and that we'd meet everyone in the morning at breakfast.

Me and Geraldine fell onto our beds, tired and excited at the same time. Joylene quickly fell fast asleep. We talked for a bit and then I had a quick scout around the place. Geraldine watched me from the doorway. The place was really big and spooky. I didn't run into any crocodiles, but I got worried someone would see me and get us in trouble. So at the corner I went scurrying back to our room.

Next morning Joylene got up early. Neither of us had slept much. There was the noise of other people moving about, so we got Joylene ready and wandered off along the path, following the other students to the cafeteria. Inside were lots of students sitting down eating. It was a much flasher place than our old Amoonguna canteen. The food seemed good and plentiful. More fruit than I'd ever seen. I was tempted to just hang around the cafeteria with Geraldine and my baby that first day. But Barry came into the cafeteria and I went nervously with him to our classrooms to be introduced while Geraldine and Joylene were taken off by another person to see the childcare place.

·········

In the classroom I met students from many other Aboriginal communities. They had started term a few weeks before. Everyone seemed happy. They were all there to study in these new language training courses. Barry introduced me to my teacher, Karen Courtenay. She had an American accent, but I understood her well enough. Later he introduced me to an Indian man called Gnani Perinpanayagam. He was my main lecturer. That was a difficult name and I struggled with it all term. It made Arrernte seem easy. After these introductions I had to fill in paperwork and got the day off.

We soon met everyone at the cafeteria and in the garden areas. It gave me an idea of who would be working with me. We met lots of mothers and their children. Everyone was coming from smaller communities. Everyone seemed very friendly. We were still spooked by all the warnings of crocodiles and wild buffalos. And there were giant fat snake stories too. The previous night when there was some noises we had hid away inside. But we could see they were just teasing us too. All the same we didn't go for any bush walks, staying close to the buildings.

The second day we got up feeling more comfortable. Geraldine and Joylene were more relaxed. Batchelor College was a happy little hideaway from the world. After breakfast, I watched Geraldine and Joylene walk away before I went off for the start of my first full-time day of classes with all the other students.

Mrs Courtenay was teaching about all the sounds in our different languages; and how we use our tongues, throats and lungs to make the sounds. We did something I'd never done before in my life. She gave us all small mirrors to look in our own mouth as we said words. I could see the movements of my tongue, from front to back. She showed us this so we could learn how to move our tongues to make the sounds when we needed to say a new word. This was the same whether it was in our own language or in the language of some other mob. I never realised how I made these sounds to make words until I did this exercise that first day.

Later on one of the other students teamed up with me so we all had someone sitting in front of us and watching our mouth and tongue movements as we were talking. At first I felt very shamed. Then, when I got to know what I was supposed to be doing, I did it to other people. I had always enjoyed learning these new things. After practising how we make these sounds, Karen sat with me to help me write down one of my own stories in a book. I called the story 'The Crawling Baby'. Together we started working it up and fixing up any mistakes. Many years later when our Yipirinya School was looking to get more Arrernte language books in the school, the council decided to publish my crawling baby story.[5]

I had a really busy and interesting time studying. After classes Geraldine and I made some good friendships with the other students and mothers. We would all sit around together practising our language lessons and having a bit of a laugh. Our kids would run around us in the playground while we talked about our families and our life at home. Geraldine, Joylene and I lived in one of the student flats. The studying was really hard but I loved it.

Then the term finished and we all went back to our own little communities again. I was sad in a way. And not just that I had to face getting back on another plane to fly to Alice Springs. The first months of study had made me stronger in my understanding of my job as a linguist. We had some really interesting discussions. I left at the end of that first term feeling that I could succeed in my studies to become a teacher. But it had also been a long time since seeing my other kids. I was really looking forward to catching up with them and getting back into my life at Santa Teresa.

·········

My second trip to Batchelor College was a month later in September 1976. I was to be away longer this time and decided to bring all my kids with me. Gilbert was nine, Pamela was becoming a big girl of seven, Trevor was five, Karen was four and Joylene had just turned two. An older sister-cousin, Nancy Lynch, came up to help look after them all.

The kids were laughing and excited to be flying in a jet plane. That was until we had to walk up the stairs and the engine started up. I can still remember the plane taking off. I had Karen and Joylene sitting on my lap, holding onto me really tight, with their scared little faces. When I looked around I saw Nancy sitting behind me holding onto the very silent and scared Gilbert, Pamela and Trevor. They had all stopped laughing and were hanging onto their seats with clenched fists. Their eyes were full of fears and tears. I tried to make eye contact with them. When we got into the air they got brave again and all wanted to look out the window in wonder. Flying is a magical thing.

When we were coming into Darwin they were all worried we were falling out of the sky. But they were very impressed when the plane levelled out down low and landed safely. I never really got used to flying that much. The kids and grandkids are better. But me, I'd still drive a long, long way over dusty corrugated dirt roads to avoid having to take a plane anywhere.

Back at Batchelor, I was really getting strong about learning to write my own language better and teach it. Why should our people know how to write English but not our own language? This time I met Gavan Breen who had been specially brought up to work with me to develop a writing system for Eastern and Central Arrernte. The mission at Santa Teresa had been asking for one. On top of my studies, Gavan and me worked together two hours every day for eight weeks. Gavan helped me to learn to think through the spelling of my own mother's language from Yambah and Mparntwe. It was different from Western Arrernte which had been written down before.

First Gavan showed me how we had to develop orthography or a spelling system for Eastern Arrernte. No-one had written this down before either. We had a good time working together, and we became very good friends. I was learning how to write a language, but I also learnt how to be a teacher as well. Gavan showed me how to teach him about my language. We both did teaching and learning in our work. We called it helping and sharing. This 'two-way learning' was a good thing for both of us to do.

It took time for us to learn how to write up an Arrernte word. We had to think through the sounds of the word. At the start it was slow and I was often unsure. One day you'd spell something one way and the next day you'd want to spell it another. There were many words which I'm still not sure of. Because I couldn't read the words in other books, it was left to me and Gavan to start writing the language down. It took a while to get an idea of what the words and sounds should look like on paper.

Gavan would get me to think of how the words sounded by telling me to say them over and over to myself. I had to think about how the words broke into individual sounds, and then work out what letters go with these slightly different sounds I was hearing in my head. Then I had to find a way to write it down.

Gavan was a lot faster than I was. Those linguists really made me think. I grew to like learning about how all these sounds were made, and how to write my own language for the first time. It was so good to see all these people working on our Aboriginal languages and to understand how they worked. And it was important for us as a group of Aboriginal linguists from very different tribes and languages. I really worked hard to earn that Certificate of Literacy Work, and I was very happy to finally get it.

My kids seemed to enjoy themselves living up there at Batchelor for ten weeks. We stayed in one of some new houses built for the language students. My older kids went to the little school there. They had a tuckshop for them to get food at. After Nancy dropped them off she would take Joylene to the playground. Sometimes after classes we would take them all to gather the red seeds that had fallen from the trees on the oval. On the way back home, we also picked up some mangoes that had fallen on the ground. On Saturdays we sometimes took the bus into Darwin for shopping and treats for the kids.

One time Trevor got boils and stayed home from school. I went off to my classes and he stayed in his bed. Nancy was busy with Joylene and cleaning the house up and hadn't heard a sound from Trevor. He got this idea to wear his toy vampire teeth and hide behind one of the doors. He peeped his head out, waiting to catch her. When Nancy turned to go and suddenly saw him looking at her, she got a big fright and screamed. Then he ran away outside laughing. When I came home from my work Nancy was waiting to tell me. And when I heard what had happened, I asked her, 'Why you never smack him for doing that?' But she laughed, saying he had been too quick for her.

Another time Nancy and I sat together under the shade of the house and started to play card games. Trevor joined us, asking, 'Can I play with you too?'

He sat down in the middle and started to play. The name of the game was kangurt. Everyone in the towns and communities around Central Australia plays it. I told Trevor when you got your first two cards, pick them up to see the numbers. Then you know whether you need to add or take away cards, like sums in school. But he got up and went around the corner. Me and Nancy sat there waiting for him to come back and sit down again. But he was nowhere to be seen. Then he turned up with his vampire gear on. He started to sneak up to look at the numbers on his cards. He could be a very strange boy sometimes.

One day Gavan told me about a wild buffalo that he had met in the bush after work when he was out walking by himself. We'd all been warned about this. Buffalos can go wild and chase after you. They could kill you.

'You really frightened?' I asked him.

'Oh no,' he said. 'The buffalo was so scared it took off into the bushes. I got home safe.'

We sat and laughed together. But for me, I never did go out for a walk in the bush at Batchelor. Nor did my sister-cousins or our kids. Our old people always told us, 'Don't ever go out walking in strange country.' We needed permission from the owners to do this. But it is just common sense really. Especially if there is something big that might eat you or kill your children. It was better to stay away from them.

········

I came back home with my certificate of completion at the start of the Christmas school holidays in 1975. The school told me they had a full-time job waiting for me next year. The council had decided to support teaching Arrernte to all the students, from the bigger secondary kids to the smaller ones. My job would also be to continue teaching all the white teachers who worked at the school. The school also let me go up to Batchelor College for more teaching blocks over the next couple of years. These times, the kids stayed home and Sandra looked after them.

During the school holidays that first year my friend Sister Robyn helped me to prepare the new Arrernte lesson plans we would need. We made word cards, simple sentence cards and spelling lists, all in Arrernte. Later, after each school term had finished, we would put away those lessons and start making the next term's lessons. This was how we grew up our own library. Sometimes we got all the kids playing bingo games with Arrernte word cards, teaching them to recognise words and read. I was teaching the Aboriginal staff to read Arrernte too by now, as well as any white staff who wanted to be trained.

Sister Robyn was a wonderful help to me. I especially liked that she was teaching me the skills to learn in a white man's way. For my part, I was helping her to understand about our ways of learning. Altogether I had three or more full years as the school's bi-lingual teacher and I felt very proud that I even had white teachers as students. Together, Sister Robyn and I made a lot of lesson plans and language books. This helped us do the two-way teaching in the classroom.

Eventually a new group of Aboriginal teachers that had followed me through the Batchelor College training came to the school. There was Rosie Ferber, Carmel Ryan and Imelda Palmer, among others. We were all good friends but I became especially close to Rosie. She was my sister-cousin Rosie Rice, who had married Maxie Ferber. She started working with me all the time. We had grown up together as children in Middle Camp, at Yambah and at the mission. Our children were close together in age. She was always very brave, and we both liked a bit of fun. It was always an unpredictable time working together. We made a lot of mistakes and had lots of laughs.

But the school days in the mission was where I really learnt to be a classroom teacher. I learnt important things, like how to be the boss in the teaching and how to prepare interesting lesson plans every day. How to think through ways that words could be written down and translated from English into our own language. As a teacher you needed things to help the students to practise their lessons. All teachers need to plan ahead and run a proper program for all their courses.

I also learned to sit down to work out aims, ideas and themes, and to organise what you might be needing every day. Our classes started going out on bush trips looking for bush foods, wild animals, wild foods and honey, as a way of grounding the students in what the words we were teaching them meant. We would go on our trips with senior language speakers to teach our kids all the proper words for relationships, Dreamtime stories, skin names, and all the names for different plants and animals. You needed to watch carefully to make sure the kids were learning everything properly. If they didn't know something, you had to go back to straighten things up for them or else they might fall behind and start to lose interest.

I got to teach a lot of the younger Aboriginal teachers who are important in the school in Ltyente Apurte still today. I taught some of them when they were just young girls in the classrooms. And I taught some of them as adults. Over the years the mission school has built up a great bi-lingual program. I was proud to be part of its development. Kids should learn to read in their own language. And they should learn their own Altyerrekenhe (Dreaming-belonging) way and their Altyerriperre (Dreaming-after) stories. It's good nowadays because you can see Central Arrernte words in lots of places: on signs, on shirts and on buildings.

Back in the early days you'd just see lots of English words. And I'd be thinking: 'Why can't we see the language of our own country?' But there wasn't really much to read in language, only little bits in the Western Arrernte dialect. That's why I was really proud later on to make books for Santa Teresa School, IAD and our Yipirinya School in Alice Springs.

Sometimes I go into the schools and listen happily to our kids reading our Arrernte books. A lot of us worked really hard to make an Eastern and Central Arrernte dictionary too. All us bi-lingual teachers can feel proud about that. It helped to spread that writing and make it important. People like Sister Robyn Reynolds, Gavan Breen, John Henderson, Rosie Ferber, and all the other Aboriginal and white linguists, we worked really hard for a long time. It was a terrific job we all did. Hopefully it will continue to grow as a dictionary as new words are added and understandings change.

But there's still not enough to read in Arrernte yet. There was only just what we were writing down ourselves. I have read English. When I was younger I read newspapers. And I have read a lot of comics. Anything really. I wasn't much interested in reading big books at the time. But our own kids, more than ever, need to know what is happening in their world. It is important to read it in our own language. I'm hoping a translation of this book into Arrernte can happen later on. My people need to grow up a whole library.

·········

Malcolm stayed at Ernabella until 1975, so he missed his grandparents' funerals. But he came back to live in Alice Springs after Cyclone Tracy hit Darwin. He was eighteen and married up with Yaritji by then, and Christopher was born in Ernabella in 1975. Malcolm's family stopped with Sandra and

Thomas in Wiltshire Street when they were helping Thomas's father's brother, Howard Stevens, who was involved in the traditional owners' meetings about the proposed town camps. This was part of Justice Ward's Land Hearings and part of CLC and CAALAS applying for the Special Purpose Leases for the town camp communities to set up a new Aboriginal Housing Association to be called Tangentyere Council.

Later, when David and Malpiya came visiting Alice Springs, Malcolm and Yaritji moved in with them in Old May's Guest House. Malpiya started working with Father Jim Downing, the head of the Methodist Aboriginal Inland Mission and the chairperson for IAD. Lots of people from Ernabella used to stay at Old May's when in town. Malcolm told me he remembered going there as a kid to visit the police tracker Larry Jabaltjari and his wife. It was also the place that Mompy used to take him when he had to see the welfare lady after Mum died and he got into trouble. The guest house had been bought by IAD and was where IAD Press started working from.

After a while, Malcolm and Yaritji moved back out to Santa Teresa and got a house there. Their other two children were both born at the mission, Joseph in 1976 and Sally-Ann in 1978. Around this time, Sandra and Thomas decided to move into Alice Springs to be part of the setting up of Hidden Valley town camp. And I found out I was pregnant again. This was a big surprise for me. A new chapter for us all was about to begin.

CHAPTER 21
The Institute for Aboriginal Development

I'd been working hard at the mission school when Sister Robyn got a let-ter from Dr Jim Wafer at IAD. They had funds to start developing ways for writing up spelling and meaning across all the words of the Central Australian Aboriginal languages. They wanted to save the richness of these languages and get dictionaries written while the languages were still in everyday usage. Jim was organising meetings with family groups across all the different Aboriginal language groups in Central Australia. We all knew that in other parts of Aus-tralia a lot of Aboriginal languages had been lost, or had shrunk from people's memory, once English became the main language of the kids. The project was about getting a good dictionary finished while we still had so many senior Arrernte language speakers using it every day.

Jim asked whether Sister Robyn and me would help him work on the Mparntwe Arrernte Dictionary Project. IAD wanted us to be part of writing down Mparntwe Arrernte words in ways that would help to teach our own language. We could build on our existing word lists. They would fund and support us to sit down with our senior language speakers to record, spell and write down the meanings as the Arrernte language had been spoken around Alice Springs from traditional times.

This was exciting. We were both trained and ready for this challenge. And it was an acknowledgement of what we'd achieved so far to be asked to work on this project. It was arranged with the mission school that we came into town once a week to start the work. IAD set up workplaces where we could interview our senior people to grow our word lists. It was hard but really important work, and I continued on these language dictionary projects for the next twenty years. It became my vocation. I still like to correct and extend the words of my friends. During this time, like before, my family and friends helped me look after my kids when I had to go away with this work.

Then in 1977 Sandra, Thomas and their kids moved into Alice Springs to be part of Ewyenper Atwatye, or Hidden Valley as it was called. It was on the eastern boundary of the Coolabah Swamp, about a kilometre short of the river. It went right back into the valley country behind Annie Meyers Hill. This was after their son Bernard was born in Alice Springs Hospital. The camp became the main Eastern and Central Arrernte place, and the Stevens, Rice and Golder families all came back to town. Through one really wet winter Congress started a tent program on the town camps. They would give away a tent for families to live in on their town camp. But humpies were still the main shelter. Eventually some money was found and some tin sheds were built. At least they were good places to keep stuff dry.

·········

Tommy rang me up around this time. We decided that I would ask our older children about going on holidays to stay with him and his new wife, Winnie. She was my cousin-sister, an Anmatyerr woman from Napperby, who also had a young daughter Topsy. Tommy was working out at Jinka Station, north-east of Alice Springs, at the time. I talked to the older kids, who all said they wanted to spend time with their father.

Tommy came out to the mission to pick up Gilbert, Pamela, Trevor and Karen. Joylene was a bit little and wanted to stay with me. It felt good to see Tommy again, sober and back in his cowboy uniform. That was the start of me really getting over Tommy. I was ready for something new in my life. Gilbert was about ten by now and as an older boy he was starting to leave the circles of women for the company of men.

This was the kids' only time out bush at Jinka Station. Gilbert and Trevor both got a chance to learn stock work with their father. The girls spent time caring for the cows and calves in the station yards as well as with Winnie and the women. It was nice break for me. During all this time I was working at school I was still studying my linguistics.

Trevor later told me the story of how his father had arranged for them to meet the head stockman. He asked Tommy, 'Would your kids like to do a little work for me and I'll pay them for their time until they return to school?'

The kids were really excited. The boss gave work to each one of them. Gilbert had to go out with his father with the cattle. Trevor would help feed the bulls and the boss's race horses. And Pamela, Karen, Topsy and Joylene would all get paid to clean around the barnyard every day.

One day, when Gilbert was coming back from checking a bore, he saw some wild oranges near the track. They were ready to eat. He got down from his horse to pick them, tying his horse with the reins knotted over a branch of a nearby tree. While he was getting the wild oranges his horse got spooked and broke free of the tree, taking off home. Gilbert had to walk all the way back to the homestead, getting there just before sunset. The other stockmen teased him about not tying his horse up properly. Lucky he wasn't further away from home on a really hot day. But if it had been hotter they would have been straight out to find him after the horse turned up without him.

The kids all came back with money and presents. Gilbert went back to school with a new bag, and a cowboy hat, shirt, trousers and boots that his father had bought him with his pay. He was a real proud boy. Like every cowboy, he had dreams of becoming a big-time rodeo star. Years later, in 1990 and 1991, Tangentyere Council organised rodeos, and Tommy came in to take the kids to this. They would go see the show and catch up with all of Tommy's family in town for the event.

·········

My sixth pregnancy was blessing from God but I was sort of 'in denial' about it for a long time. Then on 21 June 1978 my last child, Lloyd Heffernan, was born. I came into Alice Springs Hospital for this. It was a good birth. He was a beautiful baby and we all loved him.

I had to stop working in the school for a while and look after my own young family. This was the time when I started to think about moving back from the mission into town. But I was worried for my kids. Gilbert was only eleven, Pamela nine, Trevor eight, Karen six and Joylene four. They were happy at Santa Teresa. Alice Springs schools would be very different for them. They would miss their friends too much. I remembered how happy I was growing up, settled into Santa Teresa and the dormitory, after all the years of moving around. The kids had a nice house and family around them. I had a good job. So I didn't move yet.

In 1979, I went with Sister Robyn to the Yuendumu community that had a long history of bi-lingual studies and Aboriginal teachers using Warlpiri and Anmatyerr. We wanted to borrow a few ideas of what they were doing in their school with their language teaching. I had Lloyd with me on this trip. He was just a little baby. We drove out the 300 kilometres and the language teachers welcomed us, putting out their worksheets for us to look at. We got some really powerful ideas of how they were teaching and what was working well in their school. They showed us how we could make our flash cards better and how to build up easier readers with pictures for young kids.

We had been out there two days when it started raining really heavily. The community bosses decided we needed to leave quickly before the road got cut off. Sometimes when the Tanami Highway became flooded and boggy, the road could be cut off for weeks. But by the time we were organised, it was already too late to drive out. So they arranged for us to fly out in a little plane going back to town.

I looked at the plane and thought I'd take my chances waiting. But brave Sister Robyn talked me into flying again. The plane scraped along the dirt landing strip, threatening to get bogged until it finally hit a dry spot, accelerated and managed to get into the air. Up in the storm clouds we were bouncing up and down even worse. The lightning was terrific. Sister Robyn was sitting behind me holding Lloydie on her lap. I was doing the praying, promising to be a good girl devoting the rest of my life to prayers so long as we got home safely.

I could see the pilot trying to hold the airplane straight. He had his teeth gritted and arms strained. The plane groaned its way slowly upward into the clouds, hitting pockets of wind that dragged us down or threw us around, struggling to get above the storm. Then Lloydie vomited, the smell making everyone feel sick. Vomit ended up being everywhere over the seats and down the aisles before we saw the hills of Alice Springs. I was so relieved when we got down safely on the tarmac that I could have kissed the ground. It was the scariest ride in my life. I said a big thank you to Mother Mary, and to the pilot. But keeping those promises to God was a challenge, with real life temptations and the forgetfulness that makes keeping those promises very hard.

....

The late 1970s was when lots of the Central Arrernte families at Santa Teresa moved back home to Alice Springs. Rosie Ferber, her kids and her parents, Willy and Hilda Rice, had gone to town even earlier than my sister Sandra. They were among the first families from the mission to settle back into town when the lease claims were being negotiated. But a lot of my McMillan family stuck it out with the Catholics. We were the first mob baptised in the 1930s, and among the true believers. Even today we continue in the church community, and have many family still living at Santa Teresa.

Between 1976 and 1988 the Commonwealth and NT governments agreed to fifteen special purpose leases for town campers around Alice Springs. The NT government was not keen on this and often held up the leases for years. In 1978 town campers formed their own organisation, Tangentyere Council to advocate for their land, look after the houses and worry for all the other things town campers were concerned about like education and employment for their kids.

Geoff Shaw became the first manager of Tangentyere. Like me he was born in the river bed and his family were still living there just north of the Bungalow at Mount Nancy camp. A young activist from NSW, Bob Durnan, was employed to help with setting up the management structures and services for the council at 16 Kidman St, across the railway line, in the industrial area just west of the main part of town. Eventually Tangentyere Council built a central administration at its present site in Elder Street.

Mr Shaw had been a soldier in Malaysia and the Vietnam War in the late 1960s and early 1970s. When he came back home he was shocked that his families were still living in humpies in camps around the town. The white town bosses were still saying the camps were illegal and trying to shut them down. He couldn't get a job in Alice Springs. He had to go off to find work in the mines in Tennant Creek and Mt Isa.

In 1976 he became the welfare officer at Congress and, like a lot of those old camp leaders he was passionate about the right of Aboriginal people to have their own living areas in town. Not just be pushed out whenever white fellas wanted that bit of land or wanted them out of sight. This fight for Aboriginal living areas in Alice Springs, controlled by the 'proper' families who should be living there, still goes on. Mr Shaw's vision for family leadership making their own decisions and organising their own places as more self-supporting village structures was an attempt to rebuild the protectiveness of families like in the old days.

Each of the camps was linked to different language and family groups that had always lived in or had visiting rights to Alice Springs. It was hoped these

new leases might stop the harassment by town councils, police and welfare officers. And stop the tourist sticky beaks. Now we could grow up our own families
and look after our own kids with our own cultural leadership. We would build
our own places and work in with our own organisations.

But it was never really like that. Funding was slow and hard to control. If
you take government money they get to make a lot of the decisions. And the
housing associations needed to answer to government bodies that didn't really
understand. Basic houses and support took a long time to come. And people
needed a lot of help making these houses work for them when they hadn't had
houses before and keeping them in a good healthy state for everyone

Most of all there was still not much real work happening that paid our
young men any money after the station jobs dried up in the early 1970s. So
a lot of families had young kids with not much money and too much time
on their hands. The drunken party scene grew up within many of the town
camps. Geoff Shaw tried to get trainers and training money so that young
people got work skills alongside tradesmen. But local businesses wanted the
work themselves and had the ear of the politicians. Little paid work made
everything harder.

It took years for the funding for new houses to come trickling in. First,
each town camp building needed plans approved. Plus Tangentyere itself and
all the housing associations needed to be legally set up with proper gover-
nance and administrative systems. The Commonwealth government and the
new self-governing Northern Territory Legislative Assembly needed to sign
off on all the plans, before Tangentyere Council got the go-ahead to start any
building.

A lot of time was taken to talk to and question the right people in the
proper way on each town camp about what type of houses they might want,
the design, where they should be placed and what might be fundable. It was
also slow work getting young workers trained up to help with everything that
needed to happen. Lots of people were also needed to look after the town
camp toilets and clean up.

A lot of my relatives, the Rices and Stevens men worked on the first Tangentyere building project in 1978, building the seven community facilities at
Charles Creek, Anthepe, Warlpiri Camp, Morris Soak and Trucking Yards
under the guidance of a local builder, Vince Agosta. All these new things people had to think about if they were going to make good housing happen for
their families. The traditional owners and custodians wanted to do all this the
right way. There were lots of discussions with the various family and language
groups who were setting up on town lease land around Alice Springs. Many

had been living here a long time, some since the army training and working days in the Second World War, but for some it wasn't traditionally their proper place.

·········

I got lonelier out at the mission when my sister and some of the other families started leaving. But I was still working in the mission school and doing work with Sister Robyn at IAD one day a week. I would take Lloyd with me or my McMillan family would look after him when I was working. But it was hard on all my kids and I decided it might be time for me and my kids to follow Sandra and Thomas into town. So in mid-1979 I told Sister Robyn and the school that at the end of the Christmas term I was heading into Hidden Valley. I started dropping things off with Sandra in town, and in December me and the kids packed everything up, all our clothes, blankets and toys, and took it all into Alice Springs.

We joined Sandra, Thomas and their kids at Hidden Valley. Thomas's father, his two brothers were all stopping in humpies nearby. The camp was in the north eastern corner of the lease. Everyone was living in tents and humpies, and sometime around 1978 Tangentyere got some money to build tin sheds. Tangentyere carted water for us. There were no taps or showers or toilets. It was not very flash after Santa Teresa.

We came back in the summer time and it was really hot with a young toddler living back in a tent. During winter it was often really cold, with the winds blowing straight through the flimsy canvas. Everyone struggled, especially the old people and the young babies. But we were happy enough. There were teams of men going out getting firewood and shooting kangaroos. People were working together. Everywhere families were waiting for plans and proper funding to come through. By the end of 1980 Tangentyere had started building the first nine houses at Ewyenper Atwatye and all the water and power and sewerage got put through.

We were living in hope, all sharing the same story. Like in the early days of the mission, it was all a bit desperate. But there was the excitement of everyone sharing a big dream again. We were all Arrernte people working together, getting control and ownership of our lives again.

·········

David's kids had grown up by now. He had his car and was visiting town more often with Malpiya who was still doing work sometimes with IAD. She also got work doing the translation of the Bible into Pitjantjatjara. When they were in town we could catch up more often as a family. My brother then decided to leave Ernabella to help build his own Alice Springs homeland dreams. My other brother Malcolm was also helping out, back and forth from Santa Teresa with his wife and young family. Then in 1978 they too moved back in town for good. David got work with Tangentyere Council building houses. He taught Malcolm how to build and got him a job too. We all lived close by at Hidden Valley.

The political mood was still mostly helpful. There was a combined Aboriginal organisations leadership group still meeting and fighting for our rights. IAD got more funding for education and training. Congress got extra health moneys for their clinic. Central Australian Aboriginal Legal Aid had lawyers working hard in the courts. The Central Land Council was talking to claimants and lodging the land rights claims, every one of them opposed by the NT government. And now Tangentyere Council was doing the Aboriginal town camp housing. We were all building good homes to grow up our kids into this new world that was going to look after them. Each camp was going to become a cultural hub for the different Aboriginal mobs.

All this was before some families and organisations started fighting about who should run what and who was the boss. Back then, all the different mobs from around Central Australia were mostly all together. It even included a lot of groups from South Australia and into the Western Australian border country, in the Ngaanyatjarra, Pitjantjatjara and Yankunytjatjara (NPY) homelands.

Both Congress and the Central Land Council were part of forming Tangentyere Council and Land Council pushed hard for getting the town leases. They pushed hard for funding to help set up proper housing and build community centres. There were some strong leaders in those days like Wenten Rubuntja who helped to bring all the people together to argue strongly.

The Tangentyere Council meetings were big, with everyone turning up. Often big groups attended from all the town camps. New program money employed a lot of new staff, mostly people living on the camps.

The Stevens family were important, talking up the needs of our Hidden Valley villages at these meetings. Like a lot of our senior men, Thomas Stevens could circle talk until he knew exactly what people wanted to hear. His cultural knowledge and charm was also useful when dealing with the government men. He could talk things around till he got what he wanted. He had ways of speaking about the sacred traditions of the Mparntwe that saw his opinions carefully listened to when decisions were being made.

Anyway I was there when Hidden Valley finally got some houses and their community centre. And we got one of the first houses to be built.

Margaret's sister Sandra, James Ryan, Thomas Stevens and two Steven's children.
Courtesy of Yipirinya Yeye, December 1985

CHAPTER 22

Changing schools, changing jobs

School for the kids was a problem in Alice Springs. The public schools were struggling with numbers. I went with Sandra looking for a new school for our children. Rosie Ferber also came along. We all wanted a Catholic education, so we asked the priest and nuns who were in charge of the Our Lady of the Sacred Heart School (OLSH) on Bath Street for an interview. It was decided that a lot of us parents from Santa Teresa would meet together with the Catholic School Council to discuss our children's education. Thomas came along and did a lot of the talking. His gift of never asking a question where the bosses might be able to say no saw our kids soon start at OLSH.

All the town schools had a majority of white kids who didn't like having raggedy Aboriginal kids coming into their classes from the town camps. OLSH helped make our kids' education happen. But there were the same overcrowding problems, and it was hardest for the older kids, especially Gilbert and Pamela who were nearly teenagers and used to their own group of friends. Change wasn't easy for them. They found it really hard living in the tents at Hidden Valley too, where we didn't have bathrooms and laundries to keep our kids and their school clothes clean.

In the public schools our kids had felt out of place and were silenced. They got teased for their language, their colour, their cleanliness and for being stupid. When they got angry or fought back, they got smashed around and sometimes got into trouble as well. Some teachers didn't always help much, or want the extra work of looking after our kids. It was just more trouble as far as they were concerned. Soon enough our kids stopped wanting to go to school at all.

Like the other schools, OLSH couldn't seem to stop the teasing and rough handling of our kids in the playground and classrooms at the hands of the white kids. Even some of the teachers ended up targeting our kids as the problem. We went to meetings, but it didn't change much. We started looking around again. Some families even sent their kids back to grandparents or other family who were still out at the mission or at Amoonguna. But it was our land we were living on and us Heffernan and Stevens families decided to stay.

Gilbert ended up starting at the new Aboriginal High School just south of town called Yirara College. Pamela started there too, but found herself getting pregnant and then married when she was just a kid. Trevor got tougher and harder, hanging around with the big kids, fighting their own battles. Karen shut herself away. And Joylene became a tough-talking young girl. And they all got angrier. It was a really big price they paid for me deciding to come into town. We are all still paying for this.

....

Thomas, and his two brothers, Basil and Frankie, soon got jobs working with the new Tangentyere Council. Rosie and I both hunted around for jobs too. The bosses at IAD said that if we came to town they would be happy to find work for us. Sandra again said she was happy staying home to look after our younger kids. IAD said we could be interviewed for new jobs as bi-lingual language teachers and work in a new cross-cultural orientation program. Part of this was teaching Arrernte language courses for white fellows. We were interviewed by local Arrernte community members of IAD and they picked both me and Rosie to be their Central Arrernte teachers in Alice Springs. We were very pleased.

Every day Rosie and I would walk to IAD from Hidden Valley. We started by using the programs I had helped develop with Sister Robyn for the Santa Teresa teachers: flash cards, word lists and teaching the basic grammar structures. Our classes were mostly for the white staff working in town or the communities who wanted to speak Central Arrernte or who had an interest in

Aboriginal culture and linguistics. They included the doctors, nurses, religious sisters, police and teachers who were working out in the communities. Knowing some language and culture was part of these workers' better understanding of our Aboriginal mob's way of being in the landscape. We were helping them explain what they were seeing and thinking when Aboriginal clients came to see them.

Arrernte is a very complex language for English speakers. The grammar and positioning of nouns and verbs followed different rules. The different sounds also required people to learn new ways of getting their tongue in the right place. My role was as the main teaching programmer. But it was Rosie who could make the classroom fun for everyone and keep them coming back. I was the one who kept things straight. We both had to be representatives of our culture, educating our students in bi-lingual ways of working.

First we would teach them words like the ones for 'man', 'woman', 'boy' and 'girl', and very short sentences. Second we would tell them to say the word for us to hear whether they pronounced it right. We got them saying the words onto tapes. We would sit at the teacher's table with earphones on and use the switchboard to listen to each one of them and give individual feedback. Then they would have a break and start again. There were also written lessons. The first few days of these classes were usually very hard for both us and the students. But then they would start making some sense of things and the lessons would get easier.

Traditional Aboriginal communities had always been multi-lingual mobs. In old times the different groups met together in trade and ceremony gatherings. They might meet to trade or talk important sacred business. But everyone would talk in their own first language because in our culture it was very important to say things correctly. Usually the listeners could understand exactly. If they couldn't, they'd ask questions or talk to someone nearby.

It was different for many of the white fellows we had to teach back at IAD. They had only ever really known English. They thought and saw everything in English. They dreamt in English. It was much harder for their brain to learn a new language. So sometimes we had to have a bit of fun with them in their efforts to speak Arrernte otherwise they could get too frustrated and leave. They might have been smart people with big salaries and qualifications, but they could feel pretty silly in our classrooms. We made it a lot of fun so they enjoyed our classes, and felt okay about taking a few risks and making lots of mistakes.

I met lots of white people through my teaching Arrernte at IAD. Many became good friends over the years. We gave lots of them their first language lessons when they came to town. It was the days when people and organisations took it seriously that new white workers had to learn a bit of language and cultural frameworks if they wanted to work with us. It was a good idea then; and it is still a good idea. Plus it sometimes teaches the white bosses a bit more respect.

I was never formally qualified to be a classroom teacher. Rosie went all the way through that training, but I was linguist trained with teaching experience. It was sometimes harder for me when I found myself in the classroom in front of all these white strangers. At the start it made me really nervous. Luckily Rosie was much bolder and more confident with everyone. She was good at explaining words that everyone tried to say and got wrong. We sat together facing everyone and at first I would closely watch her. She was a good teacher for me too; I learned a lot from her. It was a real blessing for me.

In our IAD classroom we started to build up new programs for all our courses. I was the one good at working out new lesson plans and handing out the word lists so that everyone could follow a pattern of learning. Luckily our students were mostly an obedient lot. In Aboriginal classrooms it was natural for people to ask lots of questions and wander around. We didn't run a time-table that said we would finish a lesson in one hour. Us Aboriginal mob could talk for days without anyone having to agree on anything. White fellows had a more 'boss' thing about time. Schedules were the boss. I got better at under-standing this. I even got to like it.

The other thing different was the way that white people respected teachers. They didn't talk over you. If you were the 'boss' person then others were re-spectful, at least in front of you. As teachers we got this respect and obedience. This was good for us. In the early days it would have been pretty easy to spook Rosie and me. We weren't used to being the bosses. But we got to like it more and more. Especially me. It suited some of my inclinations and needs. I liked being in control of the classes. It was much harder to get that obedience at home.

Sometimes Rosie and I couldn't help ourselves from laughing when our students tried to say some Arrernte words with a lot of 'kngw' or other com-plicated tongue combinations. Even the words for dog, goanna or big can be difficult until you know the sounds. So Arrernte was very, very hard to teach new people to speak confidently in, unless you learnt the sounds at a young age. We would try to laugh behind our hands or under the table. But Rosie would say something to me in Arrernte, and I would be laughing my head off again. She was very funny.

We kept the teaching and the jokes flowing, proper Aboriginal way. But one day Russell Goldflam, a new IAD lecturer at the time, was watching Rosie and me giggling at his efforts. He started talking to us in French. We looked at each other, wondering what on earth he was saying. He said he was paying us back for being cheeky. We tried to keep it a bit more respectful after that. For a little while anyway. Getting people more comfortable at being laughed at was good for them. We all get laughed at bit, and we all have to get used to it.

I'd like to take this opportunity to apologise to some of my old students who we taught. I just didn't have that much experience teaching back then and so was often giggling under the table at their mispronunciations. It was often very funny some of the things people accidentally said. Sometimes you just had to burst out laughing. But I do apologise.

·········

Sister Robyn kept coming into IAD to help us out with developing our coursework programs. And Gavan Breen was always there helping if we got stuck with writing our own language or with the teaching. I want to say a big thank you to all of those linguists that I worked with: Jim Wafer, Jenny Green, John Henderson, David Wilkins, Gavin Breen and lots of others who helped. Many of you are still keeping on the good work you started in recording our languages and supporting our family groups to hang onto our language.

So the teaching work Rosie and I were doing grew and grew. We were asked to start teaching Arrernte at Alice Springs High School for a while. Later on we did the same at the Catholic high school. And we got involved with the Yip-irinya School from its earliest days. But most of our own kids were struggling.

At one time IAD gave me a place to stay in one of the small units they had on their campus. This made life a bit easier. But there was still always a lot of work for us to fit in. And there was plenty of humbug from people wanting things from you. I bought a second-hand car at one stage to drive family out to the mission on the weekends. But a cousin stole it and it was wrecked before I got it back. So I ended up moving back to Hidden Valley.

After work Rosie and I often caught up with family along the riverside. One time we were having a couple of drinks in the river after pay day, sitting around with some friends. When it was time for us to go home, we picked up our bags to walk back into Eastside. I saw someone behind a tree hiding there, looking at us, waiting for us. When we got closer I saw it was a white man. He had a long coat on and was trying to get our attention. Then I saw he was opening and shutting his coat, showing us he had no trousers on.

I was a bit scared, but not Rosie. She stopped dead in the middle of the track and finished her beer, staring straight back at him. Standing there with her hands on her hips she said, 'What you think you're doing? You don't scare me. What you want? We're not your colour?'

She was always so brave. Then she pulled me along and we got going. I started walking fast but Rosie caught up in a couple of strides. Once we got a bit further away, we both started giggling and laughing. Then I got spooked again and grabbed her hand, pushing her along to keep on walking. Rosie was stopping in a house over in Sadadeen at the time. I was worrying the man might have a car or some bad friends.

Rosie was always a lot bolder than me, especially when it came to men. She had studied and learnt those really powerful love songs, called the 'irlpentye'. These songs would carry the enchantment magic from our country. Any man would come straightaway when he was sung with these songs. I don't know anything about those irlpentye. I heard them but I didn't learn them. I'm not sorry I didn't learn them. I already had too much man trouble in my life.

Rosie and I worked together for a long time. Not just here in Alice; sometimes we worked together on trips down in Adelaide and up in Darwin. We made a good team and built a really strong friendship, caring and sharing over many years. I was so sad when she became very sick. It was terrible. She was still only young, only 56 years old. And I still remember her with so much love. I still remember all the stories we shared over the years.

Sometimes I catch up and talk about Rosie to my family and to her own children. Now her children are grown and have kids and grandkids of their own. They often sit down with me and my brother Malcolm to talk about their troubles. Rosie and me shared lots of good times together. Today I sometimes go to the Desert Park and hear her voice on the old recordings that she did, telling the stories for our country here in Central Australia. She recorded the voice-overs for a lot of radio and video clips over the years.

·········

After a while, Alice Springs started to feel like home again with my family and friends now living in town or visiting all the time. And town was always busy. I started to like that more. But the kids still didn't really settle down much. They missed Santa Teresa a lot. But in the 1980s and 1990s places like Santa Teresa and other strong communities became full of old people looking after their grandkids and single mothers looking after their children. There were only a few working men. Most of the single and young men were off drinking in town.

After a while these men started filling the new jails being built in town. They were getting drunk, causing fights and behaving really badly. There was an Aboriginal idea in town that saw everywhere as a drinking space. They thought they could drink as much as they wanted. Circles of men would be drinking every day. This caused a lot of sadness in our circles of women. It wasn't just me that got left behind by their partners. Some women even joined their men and became drinkers themselves just so they could keep their families together. But it didn't work out very well for them, or their kids. Everyone got smashed up. This was one of the big problems in town. There was no story in culture about how to manage grog. This one of the things we are still needing to fix.

Yipirinya teachers in Sydney – Margaret, Fiona McLoughlin, Nanette Sharpe, Louise Sharpe, Dulcie Raggett.
Courtesy of Fiona McLoughlin

CHAPTER 23

Dreams of our own school

When I was a girl going to the Bungalows and later the mission school, the teachers might be cruel, but all us Aboriginal kids were in it together. It was the same in all the Aboriginal community schools. A lot us didn't speak much English, and we all came out of our family camps and humpies. No-one had shower blocks or even running water. We were all raggedy kids. They gave us showers and clothes when we went to school. We had to take them off when school finished.

So we didn't notice any differences between each other. We might fight with other kids. But it wasn't racist or cruel. Just stuff about some of us mobs being better than the others. Same as in sport. We just took the opportunity to set them straight on a few things. Visa versa. It was another game that was played out. There were rules. If we got too cheeky and caught out, we risked getting a bit of a flogging. Some group would organise to double bank us. But it was mostly okay once things settled down. Our family would try to make sure everything was 'paid back' between us all. Because of this, kids' fights didn't seem to spark up in the old days like they do today.

Back then, all of us Aboriginal kids left school by fourteen or fifteen. And a lot of us started late as well. Nearly everyone across Australia finished about that age. Everywhere, the boys mostly left earlier. Aboriginal boys didn't like coming to school after they had become initiated men. There was too much boss stuff for them and they made trouble in school. Instead of staying at school they went into stock camps and away on culture business with their brother-boys and uncles. The teachers were mostly happy to see them go.

We weren't thinking of 'going to university' or 'getting a profession' in those days. Working was about going with your mother and grandmother to learn how they do things. Learning how to look after old people and kids. For the boys it was hanging around with their fathers and grandfathers learning how to ride horses, follow cattle and do stock work. Nobody thought you needed to read a lot of books to be able to go to work.

No-one in government was going to fund remote Aboriginal communities to have high schools then, so us kids got educated to a fairly basic primary school level. We thought we were pretty flash being able to read and write a bit of English. Often we were much better than our parents at this. There was no electricity at home. No books, computers, TVs or even radios. Everyone just told stories in language and joked around; we made our own fun. Life wasn't so serious then.

But the reality was that lots of our kids out bush didn't get any real education at all. They couldn't read or write. We all knew our own culture: its rules, relationships and ceremony. All of this was in our own languages. Our parents had little or no school education. They got by without all those words and numbers. Many senior people in remote families worried that white fellow schools would steal their kids away from our old culture.

Some of our old Aboriginal leadership knew that school education was the future. They wanted their kids and grandkids to be able to work in the new jobs that would grow up in our communities. Our culture taught us that 'knowledge is power'. That's why cultural knowledge was held sacred. And in the new world our kids needed to be educated so they could sit at the big table where decisions were being made. We wanted these things for our kids. That is why the McMillan and other families sent their kids to the mission school and dormitories in the first place. The boys could grow up to be builders and mechanics. They could cut stone, fix cars, even climb up and repair windmills. Their daughters were trained to work in schools and clinics.

My cousin Carmel Ryan was one of the first kids at the mission who went straight on to high school in Alice Springs. Carmel became a teacher and worked with me. Gabriella Wallace, as a teenager, was also able to go to high school by staying in town with her big sister, Veronica. Gabriella became an artist; Veronica became an author, writer and educator. This was the new world. Earlier, the government built ANZAC High School and Alice Springs High. Yirara College was built a bit later. But not many of the girls in my year at the mission came out of school prepared for much more than getting married or working as cleaners or domestics. I had been lucky getting picked by the nuns for linguistics training. But the rest of our community was still catching up.

More and more it became clear that getting a job meant us Aboriginal people needed to be able to read and write, have a trade, or at least be able to do lots of things white fellow way. This was why Tangentyere Council meetings happened every second Tuesday; to get our people talking, and to explain things like government money and planning. We needed to have people that understood and took responsibility for these things. The meetings were also social events where people from every town camp could talk about what was happening. They brought all the family groups together, so they could get organised together. Taking back power was only going to happen if all our people stayed strong.

It was the Raggatt family from Nyewente camp, known as the old 'Trucking Yards' camp, that first talked up having our own Aboriginal school. Mothers and fathers everywhere talked about the trouble their kids were having going to the town school. So Eli Rubuntja and other Tangentyere Council leaders decided to call a special meeting to listen to all the families about what was happening and what was important for our children.

Over the years welfare had tried to send some kids away to school, like they tried to send my brother Malcolm to Darwin, to the new Aboriginal boarding school starting up called Kormilda College. But Malcolm didn't want to go to Darwin. He had family here and knew caves and hiding spots everywhere. He was good at disappearing when he didn't like something. So going to school in Darwin didn't happen. He ended up just scraping through primary school like the rest of us, even though we were all real smart kids. Some boys and girls did go away and came back with their qualifications. But lots failed too; they got too homesick and just wouldn't go back.

Despite the problems, lots of us thought that schooling needed to be pushed. But it should be proper Aboriginal schools in our own communities. So at the special meeting Louise Raggatt and her young sister Nanette talked this up. The Raggatt kids were having big trouble at their white schools and wouldn't get on the school buses. In the school yard some of the white kids mocked them for not having clean clothes, saying they were dirty. How could our families keep our kids clean? Our struggling town camps had no showers or running water.

We all knew the story. In the town schools our kids were mixing it with the biggest mob of white kids. They were outnumbered and we couldn't protect them. Even the teachers and white parents were sometimes saying nasty things. Every family told the same stories. We hated those schools as much as our kids did. There were good people but there was racism and cruelty, like in most parts of the town. We decided to push for government money for our own school where our kids could be taught our way. It was to be bi-lingual.

I was there at that first meeting with my brother-in-law Thomas Stevens and his brother Basil. Rosie Ferber came along with the Rice and Ferber families. The meeting decided to form a new education council. Thomas suggested it should be called the Yipirinya School Council, after the caterpillar dreaming story running through Alice Springs. Thomas and Basil went out to Santa Teresa to speak with the bosses for that story. 'Proper way', we needed to know we could use that name. They came back with the right permissions and the Yipirinya School Council was started. As well as me, it included Eli and Wenten Rubuntja, Louise Raggatt, Nannette Sharpe, Basil and Thomas Stevens, Rosie Ferber, Augustine and Michael Rice, Sylvester Renkaraka, maybe Peggy Branson, Phyllis Whistle and others I might have forgotten.

We got together to talk about what we would need for our new school. We had no money yet; it existed only as an idea. And it wasn't really going to be bi-lingual, but multi-lingual. We needed to cover at least four language groups. And we wanted our children to learn two ways, in English as well. We started with donations from parents, other Aboriginal organisations and some white supporters. The NT government never offered any money. I was asked by Thomas Stevens to represent the Central Arrernte families on the Yipirinya School Council and from then on I got really busy with the setting up of this school.

The school council got Helen McCann to come and work as the coordinator and she was able to get some philanthropic funding through the churches, and also from a Christian group connected to a local fellow, Ian Yule. Some big donations from charities in Holland and Germany, one called 'Bread for the World' helped out, enough to make a start with the teaching. But it took many more years to build a proper new school. The NT and Commonwealth governments kept saying we had to prove we could educate our kids properly, even though they knew there was nothing really being offered to our kids at the government schools. But how could Yipirinya evaluate our school if we didn't have one, or any money to even run our programs?

....

Right from the start, in the late 1970s the school council decided we would start teaching. We didn't have classrooms, or any way of carting everyone into school and then carting them all home again. So the schools had to be in the camps themselves, with Aboriginal teachers from the community. They would be supported to provide the Aboriginal programs first and then repeat these exercises in our own languages. The kids' parents would be encouraged to be involved.

We decided to train our new teachers in a demountable building in the Tangentyere yards. Teaching the kids in English was a secondary teaching plan that us teachers needed to adapt as we went along. Luckily, Rosie and I had a lot of experience setting resources up to run teaching programs. White teachers were employed to coordinate the office space at Tangentyere.

Under this arrangement, family needed to be responsible for their kids' education. This helped to satisfy the government requirement for compulsory education. It was a struggle at the start. We concentrated on the younger kids, between five and ten years old. Getting them into school was the priority. The intention was morning and afternoon classes. But as a teacher I knew it could be hard to hold our kids' attention past lunchtime unless we did stories and games to keep them engaged.

We also did lots of excursions and had sleepovers out bush. Usually this was out Yambah way or at Sixteen Mile or out Amoonguna way. Thomas and Basil came, Davy Hayes, Old Howard Stevens, sometimes Willy and Hilda Rice. We had access to a few vehicles, including a Coaster bus. We spent lots of these trips talking to the kids about where families had lived and telling dreaming stories. If it was hot we might go to a local waterhole, Wigley's or Standley Chasm, for swimming.

The camp-based teachers were supported by any parents and volunteers that turned up. We looked at ways of supporting the camp teachers in delivering the programs. The white staff assisted with organising materials to support the English language sessions. Four days, Mondays to Thursdays, seemed vaguely possible. Fridays had to be spent at the office making up our next week's program. We would photocopy and drop off all our teaching materials on Mondays. Our office meetings were also for mentoring and writing things up. Helen told the story of our school to government and anyone else who might give us some money. She did the evaluations and some ongoing training support. And she helped provide ideas and practical assistance to the less experienced teachers so that the programs could be delivered as best as possible.

School council members asked around the camps and found Aboriginal teachers to help get things started. Louise and Nanette Raggatt were employed to teach for the Western Arrernte families at Trucking Yards. At first the classes happened under a canvas roof. Later, a community centre was built. Sylvester Renkaraka and a family member were teaching at Anthepe Camp. Peggy Branson and Phyllis Whistle were the teachers at Little Sisters. Rosie and I worked with kids at Ewyenper Atwatye.

It took a while to figure out how to use everyone's knowledge and ideas. Even finding a way for me to use all the stuff I had learnt at the Santa Teresa mission school and at IAD took a bit of thinking about. But with help from our friends and supporters, we were able to develop some good lesson plans. I tried my best to be a really good teacher. Every day I reminded myself I had to have the courage to become a good teacher for the sake of our children.

········

I knew how schools could work. So we followed Santa Teresa and I got permission from the Yipirinya School Council for the kids to go on bush trips as part of learning words. They said this was good. The bush trips were a way for the Aboriginal teachers to meet with families, so we started meeting every month to talk about bush trips and the different ways to teach our kids about our culture. The teachers had to visit the place first. Then go on a walk around to find exciting things to do.

Most times on bush trips we would go with family and elders. When everyone came we always had a shared meal on country. It might be sausages, kangaroo or perentie. Then we had a list of things the kids went to collect to bring back for the lessons back at our camp class.

One week it was teaching the kids about all the trees: where they grow and what wild foods could be found at different times of the year. The next week it would be the names of places and getting the kids to know about the country: whose place it was and what dreaming tracks went through it. It might be to Emily Gap, where the kids could find plants from their list, get some samples ready to take back to school, draw a map of where they'd found it, and complete worksheets with their teachers and parents. Then when the kids came back to class they had learning exercises to do. We had to evaluate each bush trip, white fellow way. Otherwise the government would say the bush trips weren't proper teaching, just a way to have a free barbecue.

Later, after the bush trips were happening, we adapted some of our other bi-lingual teaching programs to bring in more of the teaching of English, Maths and Science. Some linguists and teachers from IAD and different schools got involved in this. We got Mparntwe Arrernte, Warlpiri, Western Arrernte and Pitjantjatjara programs started, and found Aboriginal teachers and parents to help to run these different programs. Some grandmothers came along as well.

One time when my brother David was in town he saw how busy I was and offered to take Lloydie back down to Ernabella for a couple of weeks with him and Malpiya. Lloyd must have been about four at the time. We were both happy for him to go. Later David told me of how one day Lloyd was at the Ernabella store where David was working. Somehow Lloydie managed to end up on a truck that had pulled into the shop. Lots of people and their kids were on the back of this truck, which was heading a couple of hundred kilometres across the mountain tracks and sandy country, back to Amata. About 10 kilometres out of Ernabella someone finally noticed Lloydie.

'Who is this young one here? This little pale one? Who owns this kid?'

Nobody knew. So they turned around and came back. Malpiya was so pleased. She'd been running around looking everywhere, getting more and more worried.

Anyway, Lloydie being away meant I could get on with some writing work. My job now included writing down new stories for our Central Arrernte language program. These had Central Arrernte words on one side of the page and an English translation next to it. Some of my earlier writings were the old traditional tales I told in the Santa Teresa kindergarten. Two got published by IAD Press; and I also wrote and helped write dozens of new Arrernte–English classroom readers based on traditional stories. Other teachers wrote their own traditional stories

One of my favourite readers was about a little girl who snuck away from her grandmother and danced with a boy kangaroo. But she couldn't escape or run away. He trapped her there. When they grew up she still had to stay with the kangaroo man. In the end the kangaroo ate the young woman. Gabriel Turner illustrated this reader. There were beautiful pictures of the kangaroo holding the young woman by the neck and sprinkling salt on her head before eating her. Another favourite was about a boy and a dingo. It didn't go well for the silly boy in that story.

The storylines were all taken from traditional stories told to us as young kids, teaching them to listen to and obey their elders. Most of the kids in our stories who didn't listen had horrible things happen to them. Some of the lazy or silly mothers and young girls did too. Bad boys and fathers got into big trouble too. This was our traditional way.

I also wrote up and copied lots of lesson sets, like crossword puzzles, in Arrernte and spelling lists and search-for-the-word grids. We had games and quizzes to teach the language of maths and science. Me and Rosie also adapted them to teach Arrernte and English ways of counting numbers and doing science stuff. We always followed the 'two ways' rule of doing the subjects first in Arrernte and then the same work in English. Same material.

We also helped to train up our younger bi-lingual teachers like Carmel Ryan and Rosalie Riley. Sometimes Rosie and I got paid to travel to talk about our schools on communities and teach the linguistic training approaches. Different teachers were sent to speak at National Curriculum conferences. I went to Canberra and Sydney twice, speaking about bi-lingual teaching, linguistics and keeping Aboriginal languages alive.

·········

We were finally given another demountable space in the Tangentyere Council yards. This became where we prepared all our lessons and had our school meetings with all the language teachers across the camps. We would pick up our teaching materials each morning and go out on different days to teach the camp kids under trees or in the tin sheds built on the four main camps in which Yipirinya operated. To the east it was Hidden Valley; west we were at Trucking Yards; north it was Warlpiri; and south on Anthepe town camps. We would have liked a central classroom but the demountable was too small for the number of kids wanting to go to school. And we thought it was really important for the kids to have their family helping out in the classrooms.

CHAPTER 24

Living the dream

All through the early 1980s we tried hard to get accreditation so we could get proper school funding. I even travelled with other teachers to Darwin and Canberra trying to do this. A group of us even started giving private language lessons in Robert Hoogenraad's house to keep the school going.

Then in 1984 we got funding for some linguistic support for our work and David Wilkins was employed. He was completing his university studies in linguistics, and we grabbed him to help us with our programs and accreditation. He was a wonderful young man. Perfect for all the jobs we could find. And he laughed at all Rosie's great jokes, and even smiled at all the really clever ideas I had. He was always telling us how intelligent and creative we were. We held onto him for as long as we could, then talked him into coming back. He's been a great friend ever since.

The first day David started we began to teach him Mparntwe Arrernte and the other languages. He had to sit in our classes with all the kids. We taught him to sit up straight, open his ears and listen hard. He learnt how to play the teaching games with the kids. After work, Rosie would teach David all the parts of the language that weren't used at school, including the rude stuff. She argued that we had to teach him how to understand and say these things just in case. He needed to know when he was being sworn at. She also taught him which lucky charms to wear, and what new charms he might need when he was out on the town looking for a good time. We taught him how to play his cards close to his chest. He was a funny young man.

The school never had any money for teaching equipment and little things that helped in the classroom. At the start, we just sat outside under trees on the good weather days. But the kids would still get bored and wander off. We had one bicycle that the kids could take turns riding on at lunchtime; but no toys, library or sports stuff. We begged and borrowed things, but only really had things we could lock up or carry out each day. So we programmed a lot of language games and rhyming songs to teach the young kids their own language and culture, and other easy learning stuff. The kids loved these stories and games in the afternoons.

I also started using hand dancing and sand drawings because we didn't have a blackboard. The kids would gather around me. Some of the stories and games were based on kinship relationships. I might ask questions like if I'm a Pengarte woman and you are my sister's daughter, what is your skin-name, doing the drawings to explain. What is your grandmother's skin-name? And on it would go around the circle of kinship relationships. If you got it wrong, everyone helped out.

Other games we made up included pretending to shoot kids in parts of their body. You would point a stick as the gun at their eyes and they had to name which direction you were shooting from when you pulled the trigger. My baby Lloydie was often the first that got shot. He was very dramatic, falling down with his hand on chest, trying to play dead. Last one not shot dead was the winner, and we might have a small prize. There were other games with body parts too. Like the 'head, shoulders, knees and toes' song. The kids had to say the Arrernte word and the English one.

We also played games like North-South-East-West, teaching the kids their language and English, plus how to follow complicated instructions. It might be directions as part of Easter egg hunts, or reading maps and other tracking games. The kids might be broken into small groups, helping each other to beat the other groups. Sometimes they had to work out where they were in relation to another child, and what direction they were away from them. We used traditional hand signs and pictures for some of these games, old ways of storytelling.

Lloyd and Joylene were a part of our Hidden Valley school. And there were some of my sister Sandra's young kids, Malcolm's kids, James and Pamela Ryan's young kids, Maureen and Rosina, as well as McMillans, Johnsons and others. Usually it was about ten regular kids with others coming in and out. And they loved it when our games were played. Rosie taught them how to sing. She especially liked love songs. Sandra would help out, and sometimes David or Malpiya. If Malcolm was in town he would come down to school leaving Christopher, Joseph and Sallyanne in the classroom with us.

Sometimes when I was teaching I had a bit of a song going in my head. An idea for a story would start from there. I really loved making up sand drawings as I was telling stories. The hand swirling was a dance to the music in my head. Each session would start with me waving my hand dramatically, smoothing down a sandy space before starting the drawing. The kids would cuddle up close, following every line. I would be flattening out and redrawing in the sand as the story grew in my head. The kids had to interpret and repeat the storyline in language, then in English. Then we'd get them to practise their own hand signing and sand drawing.

....

In 1985 we got to go to Canberra and meet with Prime Minister Hawke. His Education Minister, Susan Ryan, visited and saw us at work. Funding was increased. It allowed us to start the search for a permanent home for our school. We still kept travelling from our small demountable, where we had to pick up our programs every day, then head out to the town camps. But with the new funding we could base ourselves in proper classrooms.

My kids were growing up in this time. Gilbert was at Yirara. Sometimes Pammie was home and acted as my assistant. But then Tommy and the Gibson family organised a 'promised' marriage for her to Alec Gibson. Tommy had taken Gilbert and Trevor up to men's camp with Alec and other Gibson family. I said she was too young. She was only thirteen. But when she met him she agreed and the marriage happened anyway. A year later she had her first baby, Shawn. He was beautiful, and I was a very proud and happy grandmother.

Karen too was often by my side helping with the kids when she wasn't at school. All my girls went to OLSH or Ross Park. But they didn't like it much, and often got in trouble. Later I couldn't get any of them to go. Trevor was like that too. After men's camp he didn't ever go back to school. The place was too hard and bullying for them. So we tried to include these older kids as helpers where we could. Train them up and keep them learning.

Houses had been built at Hidden Valley by this time. We got a house near the Stevens and McMillan families. Later when the community centre was built we held School classes there using a room, the veranda and the open spaces under trees. The old people often sat in, joining in the games. We started having classes where everyone could learn together. It was much easier for our kids to just come over the road to the community centre.

After a few years talks with government funding bodies heated up. Doug White and his colleague Marta were employed to observe the curriculum, write it up and develop a formal evaluation process with the idea of the school being accredited and registered. I was pulled out of the Hidden Valley classes to become part of the interpreting team and worked with Doug. We put our programs into more structured curriculum frameworks. We wrote up our workshops in science and maths. Our school programs were finally registered in the late 1980s.

·········

Things sped up once we had funding approval. I was worried that the school was turning too much away from our bi-lingual approach. Our new managers found it easier to bring in other materials from other places rather than developing our own. I thought it got too fast and was well ahead of working with our own family leadership. We needed them to understand the development of good cultural and language programs.

The government had agreed to give us money for our own school buildings. People searched about and located a place out near Morris Soak camp on Lovegrove Drive, not far from where the Scout Hall was and fairly close to Tangentyere and some of the town camps. The School Council had a meeting and agreed to this place, and the government granted us this land. Just like that, they signed it over. The School Council and Tangentyere architects continued to work hard to get the building planned and built.

The School Council decided to hold a big meeting to decide our future. All the elders from the Tangentyere Council and traditional owners from Mparntwe country and all life members of the School Council met with parents and families. The final decision was to separate the school from the rest of the Tangentyere Council management and set up an incorporated community-controlled association to run the school. But we were to keep on calling it the Yipirinya School because it is a good 'proper' Aboriginal name for our school in Mparntwe country. A new management structure was set up. The School Council and Tangentyere continued to work hard to get the building planned and built.

Now that it had proper funding the School Council had an election for its Board of Management. Most of the old members continued on this new body. Wenten and Eli Rubuntja were on the Board. Tangentyere Council continued to help out with buses, recruitment and everything else. The school recruited Ian Yule as the first white fellow school principal. He had been a big supporter of getting the school started. They recruited an Aboriginal deputy principal. Together with the School Council they searched to employ the best qualified and experienced white and Aboriginal teachers.

I was still doing some of the classes with Rosie at IAD, but less and less. Me and Carmel Ryan were supposed to be the main teachers with the Hidden Valley kids. But I started to get really exhausted. One day it was hard to get up and the doctor came. He said I'd become sick again with diabetes, and had to be hospitalised. This was in 1986. The doctors told me that I had to change my life and start taking insulin injections. I had to eat better and different foods. I had to rest up and take it easy.

When the school became registered, the funding body made it condition-al on having qualified teachers in the classrooms. It was hard to push back against the funding bodies about proper bi-lingual ways of working. We wor-ried we would lose our control as the Yipirinya School Council, and as a group of Aboriginal teachers and parents. As teachers we weren't given equal status any more. The Government kept changing the qualification requirements for Aboriginal teachers to get registered. They are still doing it. The qualified teachers were white teachers and gradually they have become the bosses of the classrooms.

Many of the teachers supported the push for Aboriginal teachers running the classrooms. Maggie Wallace and Inge Kral were strong about this. But the classroom lost its bi-lingual balance. Lessons on bush medicines or birds in country with senior people like Davy Hayes and Veronica Wallace, were changed to white teachers in classrooms using books from the library and vid-eos. Everything was done in English first; then maybe we got to work with the kids in language.

It was meant to be two-way. But it was not the right way as I had been taught. At Yipirinya School all the morning classes were in English. This was wrong. Only in the afternoon did they have language and culture classes run by the Aboriginal teachers.

In the classrooms, the Aboriginal teachers were working in closely with the new white staff to show them our ways. The work was supposed to be shared equally. But it proved hard for the Aboriginal teachers to be heard. The white fellow teaching ways ended up becoming the boss teaching culture. The white teachers had to report back to the government that the morning subjects were done in English, and that was what got done.

So we lost our great curriculum development processes for making our own reading materials and having our outdoor teaching processes. From the time the school got registered, the Aboriginal teachers and the Yipirinya School Council lost their voice and struggled to keep control. We started losing our Aboriginal teachers, our family volunteers, our proper 'vernacular' bi-lingual model and all our community curriculum development frameworks. We also sometimes lost kids and families from the school altogether. And they didn't go back into the public school system. They ended up without an education.

·········

My youngest child, Lloyd, was the only one of my kids that started his schooling at Yipirinya. He was a funny little boy, always up to mischief, making me laugh even now when I think about him. Maggie Wallace was his first teacher; he would run to her when kids tried to hit him for being too much of the joker or when he was acting a bit defiantly. When some other teachers told him to do something he'd say, 'You're not my teacher! My teacher is Maggie.' For a time he also had his uncle Malcolm, who was one of the school bus drivers, to run to if there was trouble. Maggie still rings me sometimes to find out how my Lloydie is going.

Malcolm had left his first partner Yaritji and his kids after they moved into town. Life became difficult between them when Sally Anne was diagnosed with polio. It left her with paralysed legs. They were in and out of hospital a lot. It became very tough for them both. They were still both young, with young kids, including a sick baby. Malcolm started drinking heavily with extended family and not going home much. Sometimes the kids stayed with me and Sandra. In time he said he was finished with Yaritji, and had started a new relationship with Alice Gorey. He had a baby, Antonio, with her in 1984 and they ended up living together in Aileron. Yaritji and the kids moved back to Ernabella. They'd catch up with us and Sally Anne would stay with us when she needed medical treatment in town.

·········

Thirty years on, and Yipirinya School is a much bigger school, with secondary school classes. It has lots of new classrooms, a swimming pool, library and gymnasium. I'm still on the School Council; so are the Stevens and Ferbers and many of the same old families. We did a great job getting that school going. But we lost the battle about keeping the school leadership and the classrooms Aboriginal controlled. We're still working on that, but politics in education and funding are never easy.

There are no bi-lingual programs anywhere now. Just 'bridge over' programs from language to literacy. Bridge over into English, that is. So there is no need for language programs in maths or science in this way. Kids are just expected to be taught and to understand them in English. But the Yipirinya School Council is still fighting for more Aboriginal language curriculum. We want two-way learning all the way through – from primary and secondary into tertiary schooling.

Thomas Stevens at a demonstration to stop the dam at Werletye Therre.
Courtesy of Jenny Green

CHAPTER 25

Land claims and Ngkarte Mikwekenhe

Aboriginal land claims were happening all through the late 1970s and 1980s. The senior men and women from all over Central Australia worked with the lawyers and anthropologists of the Central Land Council (CLC) to get the individual claims finalised. But the Liberal–Country Party government and the pastoral industry were fighting every one of them. The courts couldn't keep up; everything was being delayed. These claims covered the entire Central Land Council area, from the South Australian border all the way up to Wave Hill Station, 1000 kilometres north of Alice Springs. Meetings were held in Alice Springs as well as in the tribal areas to develop these claims and to fight for the rightful owners and custodians to be recognised for their own proper homeland and a place to live.

It wasn't always a happy process. The legal rules were complex and didn't follow traditional Aboriginal understandings of relationships to land or Aboriginal ways of thinking about these things. Having white lawyers trying to decide who was the right person or family in the claim often led to some bitter fights between families that had traditionally shared everything. Many communities were torn apart. It was impossible for many of us to understand, especially families that were excluded. Some felt their land was being stolen away again. But this time it was by their own family and tribal groups. And the Stolen Generations kids got left out again.

For the Anmatyerr and my father's mother's family near Ti Tree there was talk of claiming a homeland called Pmara Jununta at Six Mile Creek. This was close to my grandmother Jenny's birthplace. Her country was around Ti Tree Well where the roadhouse had been built. But Ti Tree Well was excluded from land claims because Ti Tree was gazetted as a town with a school and a clinic and new houses for government workers. So the CLC lawyers said the families should claim their old Six Mile Creek camp south of the town.

Many of these families were also the ones kicked off Aileron Station when the Ten Mile camp was closed by the Aileron Station bosses. They had relocated 80 kilometres north to Six Mile Creek camp and other camps around Ti Tree. This was the story behind my walk with Uncle Charlie and Aunt Ruby as a child. All of the land between Ti Tree and Aileron was part of Anmatyerr homelands. But the stations were excluded from being claimed under the 1976 *Northern Territory Land Rights Act* because they had been given away to cattle station bosses as pastoral leases in the 1880s. But the stock routes remained Crown land and were claimable. Eventually our families were granted their small community homeland at Pmara Yununta on what was part of the old stock route.

....

In the 1980s I got invited to go up to Pmara Jununta to talk with some of the senior people about them building a proper bi-lingual school for their children. This was before they had built any of their houses there. It was all just humpies and tin sheds still, with a little bush health clinic nearby, and a bore with taps providing good clean water at last. All the people were very happy, really proud at last to have a small bit of their own homeland back. They were talking excitedly about getting their school. But in the end the government spent the money instead on expanding their Ti Tree town school.

Uncle Charlie and Aunty Ruby had moved back to live at Six Mile from Santa Teresa by now. A lot of my Heffernan family was coming back. My old teacher and friend Nancy Archdeacon came up from Santa Teresa to participate in building the school discussions. She wanted to meet all my family and see the place. She also wanted learn about our traditional Alwekkere and the circles of women caring for kids. I was really happy to see all my family and they welcomed us both to their new homeland. They gave us spaces to sleep with them in one of the humpies. It had been built of bush timber, sheets of iron and a tent.

My older sister-cousins and their daughters asked if Nancy wanted to go out with them looking for wild berries and hunting for honey ant and witchetty grubs. Nancy was very excited to see this country and learn more about our bush foods. We had some happy days there at Pmara Jununta. Nancy got to see the women living their everyday lives, sitting in their Alwekkere teaching all their young women and looking after the young kids within their circles. She saw what my early life was like and started to build her understanding of the Aboriginal people's ways of being in the world. Later she was able to tell her family and friends about what it was like living in humpies and going hunting. A week later we could stay no more and waving goodbye we drove back to town and Santa Teresa.

Nowadays the families at Pmara Jununta have their own proper homes. Not enough of them though. The place has grown and it's a much larger community. Ti Tree is surrounded by other Aboriginal homelands, including a community at Ti Tree Station. I go back there sometimes to catch up with family. Like everywhere, there have been lots of changes because of the new technology. Kids grow up differently. There is the usual problem of not enough work and too much grog. Ti Tree has a pub, but it is a happy place mostly and the families are proud of what they have made out there on their own home-land. There are lots of big ideas for the future, especially about building new jobs for their kids.

And even today the old women are still gathering in their Alwekkere, taking their young women and little ones hunting to get the bush tucker. They are still sitting around their tiny campfires talking in circles while they feed little twigs into small flames. They are still teaching their young ones. Those women are still gathering their fuel, one stick at a time, lying low in the back blocks of Central Australia, to eventually re-take all of their country and culture back.

· · · · · · · · ·

I was still spending a lot of time with Sister Robyn. She was a very good friend. I remember her calling in one night when little Lloydie was sick at home. She bundled me and Lloydie into her car and raced us to the hospital. But the police saw her and started chasing us. They pulled her up because they said she didn't have any lights on. I was worried for her, but she talked her way out of being charged. Sister Robyn, like lots of nuns, had this way of talking to police that seemed to work. We got to the hospital without any more excitement.

Another time we all went to the drive-in movie; I think it was *E.T.*, a special showing for town camp kids. Sister Robyn picked us up at Hidden Valley. It was our first time at the drive-in. The car was a little overcrowded but Sister Robyn just closed her eyes as more and more kids squeezed in. Then off we went.

At the end of the movie Robyn waited and waited until it seemed everyone else had driven away before she started her car and reversed back. But we found out there was still one car there when she bumped into it. We were all scared. A big man got out of his car and said, 'Look!' He was looking down at his fancy car.

We ducked down as Robyn bravely got out of her car. But there was barely a scratch on his car that she could see. Even so, he made Robyn write down her name and address. He said he'd get back to her and started back to his car. We all relaxed a bit until Robyn pipes up saying, 'Put your name down here too please.'

He turned around and wrote down his name on her bit of scrap paper. She put it in her pocket. He grunted and got in his car, taking off noisily.

The next morning at the office Robyn tells me the name on the paper said 'Constable Fitzgibbons, Australian Federal Police, Pine Gap'. She put orders out to the young girls in the office. 'If anyone rings asking for me, SAY NOTHING!' We all laughed and laughed. Luckily none of us ever heard from Constable Fitzgibbons again.

In 1986 Sister Robyn got Rosie and me invited to an Aboriginal Spirituality conference. It was at a place called Shalom College at the University of NSW, near where I'd first studied linguistics. We had about three or four really good days sharing, talking and saying prayers with about forty people, mostly older, including some priests and some nuns, and a few younger people.

At the conference we told a parable told to us by a wise old Arrernte man we called Harold or 'Wheelchair' Ellis. This was a funny story about how the gum trees were created. At the conference we talked about Alice Springs and our spiritual relationship to our land and country. We talked of the caterpillar dreaming stories, and other ancient stories explaining the creation of our land. We talked about our struggles and hopes for us Aboriginal women. Hopes for our families and children. It was a very special time.

………

Ngkarte Mikwekenhe (NMC) was formed in the mid 1980's to help build the social and spiritual wellbeing of the Arrernte Catholic families in town. Sr Robyn Reynolds helped us to get it all going at Jemma House, in the old boarder's accommodation behind presbytery in Hartley St. I became its first president. We would visit people in the hospital, or who were struggling at home.

Not long after this our Pope John Paul 2 said he would visit Alice Springs in 1986. Fr Phil Hoy was sent to Alice by the MSC order to help organise it. He was very inspiring for us Arrernte people. With Sister Robyn we started talking to our families. Lots of people attended our meetings, and we became part of the local management of the Pope's visit. We asked all local Catholic people to help set up for that day. Elders from our church went out to ask our senior Aboriginal people, both Catholic and from other churches, to come to meet our Pope. We got mobs of people helping with making the Alice Springs Showgrounds beautiful for the Pope and the mass he led.

The Mayor, councillors and politicians were all there to meet him at the airport. We had our own Aboriginal leaders greeting him too. Thomas Stevens did the 'welcome to Arrernte country' ceremony. Lots of our senior people helped out; Amos Golder, Basil Stevens, Rosie Ferber, MK Turner and many, many others. It was a wonderful day. Lots of our kids turned up to hear the Pope talk. Ngkarte Mikwekenhe and our Catholic community became much stronger for us becoming part of organising everything with our white church mob. It was a good year when the Pope came.

After the visit, Sister Robyn, Sister Carmel, John Pettit and Fr Phil all worked with us to sort out how the social support roles would operate. We met after Sunday Mass. Bob Capp started running a adult education program during the week in Jemma House. Mike Bowden helped out too, setting up the Ntyalke Unit at the Catholic High School. There were lots of meeting, and talk, talk, talk. MK Turner and Leonie Palmer might visit sick people at the hospital. Others would go see old people stuck at home or in the nursing homes. Some started translating pamphlets, making videos and using them to go around talking up Ngkarte Mikwekenhe's ideas. We were trying to help our whole Arrernte community to become stronger and spiritually healed. It was our way of using 'two ways' both our old keep our culture strong, and the new ways of living to keep our faith strong. But it was an uphill battle with the grog and the poverty. Our families were struggling with town camp living. These stresses are still problems today.

When Fr Hoy left, we were forced to move. Congress Farm gave us an office. Later we went to the St Francis Centre where the nuns stayed. We had Mass at David Perry's warehouse in Elder Street, outside at the Traeger School

Campus and on Town Camps. Fr Pat Mullins was our chaplain. In the late 1990's, the Bishop said we could move into the Santa Teresa Town House at 40 South Terrace. It had been built by the Santa Teresa Parish Community as places for sick people or visitors to stay. In 1999 NMC finally had an Office and a large room for saying Mass. David Woods got the job as Coordinator.

Around this same time, Nicole Traves was developing an Aboriginal school for secondary age Arrernte kids with Tangentyere Council. Nicole had a strong relationship with Arrernte people from her years teaching at Santa Teresa. She wanted to start a 'whole of family' and community school with Aboriginal teachers in every classroom. After talking with Ngkarte Mikwehenhe families and Tangentyere Council they moved the school to our new No. 40 South Terrace offices. We called the new school the Irrkerlantye Learning Centre, named after the brown falcon, a symbol for the land east of Alice Springs. They used a community development model with health and wellbeing, language and culture, work programs, and enterprise. Felicity Hayes from White Gate, Carol Turner from Hidden Valley and later Bruce Stein from Cairns were trained Aboriginal teachers. Irrkerlantye was a very happy place to go to school; and for people to visit.

For a little while it was like our Arrernte families had all come back together again. Irrkerlantye Community Arts was funded to support our local artists. A CDEP program looked after the grounds and repairs. It was named the best school by the Commonwealth government. The next year the NT Government closed it all down, even though we fought to keep the school.

·········

Sister Robyn, Ngkarte Mikwekenhe and the whole local church community also helped us out organising events in the bicentennial year of 1988. The big event was hosting 700 Catholic schools girls from Melbourne who came to Alice Springs for a reconciliation gathering. This included twenty busloads of students who were camping every night on their drive up the Stuart Highway.

We worked hard to make sure all us Arrernte Catholic mob were well prepared for their visit. One busload was sent to Amoonguna, one busload went out to the mission, another one out to the local Catholic high school and so on. We had every bus going to somewhere with senior Arrernte people as tour guides on each of them. They would welcome the students and look after them when they set up their camping places.

We all had a great night out at the Telegraph Station, everyone all together, with all of the Melbourne schoolgirls sitting around their Arrernte helpers, and the rest of us as a mob. We had local volunteer drivers and buses given to us from local agencies. The visitors had a chance to ask questions and talk with senior Arrernte leaders and our school kids. Leonie Palmer and MK Turner gave a very powerful welcome to these students.

Another strong memory is of Sister Robyn's birthday party one year. She organised Sister Marie Therese, me and some other IAD teachers to come into one of the Alice Springs restaurants in the town centre one night. It was the end of the year for us all but we weren't people who went to fancy restaurants in town much. Sister Robyn got us all dressed up and the party kicked on until the place told us we had to leave. It was pretty late.

After we were kicked out Sister Robyn decided that Sister Marie Therese hadn't yet seen the newly built casino. So she insisted we all took her there. We were walking up to the casino when a bouncer at the door took a look at us and said, 'No, you haven't got the right clothes on.' Owen, one of the men with us, had jeans on. 'No!' the bouncer repeated. 'You can't come in with those jeans.'

All us Aboriginal mob started walking away. But not our Sister Robyn. She fired right back. 'You stupid man. These people own this country.' That got them right off side. 'We can't go all the way back to Santa Teresa and get a pair of trousers,' she went on. 'It's a stupid rule. That's for people in casinos in Sydney and Melbourne, not in the Territory.'

We turned back around for the Sister Robyn show, all of us grinning a bit, but edging away a little too, in case reinforcements arrived to lock us all up.

'Go and get your manager,' she told those two men. 'I know him. He's my friend.'

So off one of them went, and we waited. Finally the bouncer came back. 'No, he's not there.'

Reluctantly, Sister Robyn had to give up, muttering she'd get some pants from someone. Then when we were walking back to the car Sister Robyn spoke to a man walking past. 'Excuse me? Do you live in Alice Springs?' she asked him.

He said something like 'What's that to you?' and Rosie and me started giggling.

But luckily she decided not to ask him for his pants and we all got back into the car. Driving through town, Rosie started teasing Robyn as we drove past other men, saying, 'No, that man's too tall' or 'Nah, that one might be a little fat'. Anyway we drove to the Marist brothers' house. I thought she was crazy, it was really late now, but Sister Robyn said the Marist brothers still had their house light turned on. She marched up and knocked. But no-one came out.

Then she had us driving right out along Larapinta Drive to a friend, Michael Bowden's house. By this time I think she was the only one left that really wanted to go to the casino. But it was her birthday and we were having a great laugh, especially me. I really loved Sister Robyn's crazy determination. Anyway, she got out and knocked on their door. Michael's wife Judy came out like she was sleepwalking. 'Hi!' Sister Robyn said. 'It's my birthday.'

Judy gave her a big hug. Then Robyn asked for a pair of Michael's trousers. Judy just nodded her head, turned around, went inside and came back carrying a pair of trousers.

We all stayed in the car watching and laughing. She took the trousers and we went around to my place where Owen changed. Michael's trousers fitted him nicely. Then back we went to the casino. They didn't stop us this time, and we had a great night.

Over the years we had a lot of really funny times. Sister Robyn could be so energetic and bold. I loved her. She was a little bit bossy too, just like teachers.

Another time we were visiting together at the hospital, late one night. Coming out I gave Robyn back her grinding stone that we had used for making some rubbing medicine. These two American tourists were walking past and said to us, 'You getting any witchetty grubs?'

Robyn talked really slowly saying, 'Yeah, we bin eatim witchetty grub. No worries. You eatim witchetty grub too? We likem witchetty grub, we got plenny ere. With dis stone you can finem plenny witchetty with this stone, no worries.'

They were watching us carefully, looking very surprised. We had a bit of a laugh when they left. Those Americans will believe anything.

Sister Robyn shared all our anger about the racism in the shops and streets. Us Aboriginal mob were all used to it and knew we had to be careful. Some things I didn't hardly notice. But not Sister Robyn. It might be the health centre or the day care place or in shops or government departments or even at the police station; it didn't matter to her. When people started serving Sister Robyn out of turn, she would always pretend to be looking around or at the ceiling. Or she'd turn away so that they'd have to talk to me.

Sometimes she'd start talking in Arrernte in front of them. She might say loudly 'Re arerte nthurre' or something like 'Log cabin anyente'. The shop people wouldn't know 'anyente'. But, I'd say 'Log Cabin' and hold up a finger, saying 'anyente'. Sort of force them to learn a bit of Arrernte. Always the teacher she was. When they gave her change she'd say, 'Keleye. Kele mwarre.' Thank you very much.

Margaret Heffernan and her grandsons.
Courtesy of Frances Coughlan

CHAPTER 26
My diabetes and stroke

I remember when they first told me I had the diabetes disease in my body. In the early days growing up, I never thought of going to see a white doctor to get a check-up. They didn't exist for us. Doctors were only at the hospital, nowhere else. And my experiences of doctors as a young woman in hospital recovering from my burns and with Gilbert's birth were terrifying. They were just bosses that got nurses to do painful things to you. It was not something that made me want to talk to any doctor or even nurses again. Even the mission hospital had been a scary place. So I didn't use the white medical system. We had our own healers. My father and lots of my family had died after white medical treatment.

So I never heard about diabetes. I never went to the mission clinic. And I thought I was healthy and living a good life. But in 1986 I nearly died. It was only after that and being tested at the Alice Springs Hospital that I was told about my diabetes. I got better, then got very sick again when I was giving birth to Lloyd.

Before Lloydie's birth I had been working very hard at the mission school and going into IAD keeping things together. I was getting very tired in the classroom all the time. I thought it was just being pregnant. It was in a way. Gestational diabetes, they call it. During the birth it got worse. Afterwards, for a while, I was too tired to do anything for myself. But when I went home to the mission I was looked after by our old midwives and healers. They got me stronger, making me eat good bush food. So after a bit of a rest, I got up and going again.

Then in 1989, when I was living at Hidden Valley and teaching with the Yipirinya School team, my tiredness got worse and worse. After a while I didn't even have the strength to get out of bed. I was sleepy and grumpy all the time, thinking too much, worrying all the time. My head felt out of control. My sister and family got real worried. Our healers came, found my pain and looked after me. But I didn't get right this time. I got very sick.

Everyone was worried. They called the Congress Clinic who sent a bus to take me to see their doctor. When he examined me, straightaway he said, 'I'm sending you to the big hospital to another doctor there.' The hospital doctor did some blood tests and told me, 'I'd like you to stay here in the hospital for more examinations.' When the tests came back, they told me I was very sick with Type 2 diabetes.

Now I know that some of my family – and that lots of other Aboriginal people – have died from this blood sugar disease. It was probably why my mother became so sick and died suddenly. And now I know the 'white fellow' medicine is good for treating my diabetes. It can help make you better.

Diabetes is the result of our new diet and our less active lifestyle. We didn't have shop food and cars before the white men came. Nowadays we don't chase after food, picking up bush tucker every day like our grandparents did. And because we used to walk around all the time our traditional healers didn't know about diabetes. When everything changed and we started living in towns, eating food from shops, we didn't know anything or have medicine to protect us. Diabetes was everywhere killing our people.

They kept me in hospital for a long time. I couldn't do teaching or go to meetings. I just slept a lot, took lots of tablets and ate what I was told to. No more three teaspoons of sugar in my cuppa, with sweet buns or biscuits for morning tea. No more cakes, scones or soft drinks. Too much sugar would kill me, they said; I needed to eat more vegetables and less fatty meat. The tablets they gave me I had to 'take every day'.

At first when I went home, I was careful. I took the tablets every day. I cut back on eating fatty meat and sweet things from the shop. I even slowed down drinking sweet white wine with my friends. The doctors told me I was getting much better. They also said that I needed to keep on looking after myself, to stop working too hard, and stop getting too stressed. This would be how I could keep healthy.

But slowly my life changed back to like before. It was just too hard to stick to different foods in a house full of family. And I felt well, so it meant I was cured. Wasn't I stronger now than before? Basically, some of the things the doctors wanted me to do were really hard on a town camp. Without a car, going to doctor's appointments and picking up tablets took a lot of time and effort. I couldn't just change what I was doing. People asked me to come back to work, and I did. I started teaching again and being part of the Yipirinya School Council meetings. I thought, 'Lots of people got a little bit sick.' But I was tough. I was a 'good girl'. I had work to do, for my family. There was lots to be done.

Eating the right food was not my culture, and expensive. Nobody else liked more vegetables and less meat. Our families shared all our food anyway. I couldn't say no when someone offered me something they had cooked and I was hungry. I couldn't say no when someone gave me a cup of sweet tea with a sugar biscuit. It would be rude and disrespectful. So I had to eat everything and share my food. That was the way we'd always done things.

After a while I never took much notice of all the diabetes stuff the doctor had told me. The routines around seeing the doctor and taking tablets dropped off. Even though I knew the things I was eating and drinking in my daily life were bad for me, I could only cut a few things down at a time. Soon enough I was back to zooming around doing things my own way all the time, like I'd always done. Except that I was getting a bit older and putting on a bit more weight.

I still didn't go back to the doctor, even when I was feeling sicker again. Even when my head was thinking too much again. I knew the doctors would just get cranky with me. I had stopped getting my medicine from the clinic. I didn't keep an eye on how I was really feeling. I just got up in the morning to do all the things that needed to be done and went to sleep at night when I could. I knew I was tired, and a bit sick. But what could I do?

....

One day I was visiting my son Gilbert who was in Royal Adelaide Hospital with a broken jaw. It was 26 March 1991 and I was nearly forty-eight years old. I remember that day very clearly. I woke up early in the morning. No-one else was awake. But I got up early like I did every day, went to the kitchen to get something to eat, and started to boil the water to make some tea for everyone. I was looking out of the window, waiting for the kettle to boil, when suddenly I knew something was really wrong.

I had a stroke. A terrible pain washed through my head and down through my whole body. Everything went crazy in my head. I started seeing funny zig-zag lines in both my eyes like I was looking at a broken TV. I felt numb and very, very heavy. I tried to move my leg to go over and sit on the chair. My leg felt like a ton of stone and I fell heavily. I tried to get up but I was numb from my head to my legs. I tried to call for help but found I couldn't talk. I tried again to get to the table, but the pain got worse and everything went dark. Then I blacked out.

When I stirred I could see Gilbert's little twin boys watching me closely. I think they got frightened to see me lying down on the kitchen floor. Then I blacked out again. They must have run to tell family. An ambulance was called. I remember them putting me on the stretcher.I can't remember going to the Lyell McEwin Hospital.

I don't know exactly how long I was in the induced coma, only that it was weeks until they woke me up properly. When I got to the hospital they had put tubes into me to help me breathe, and pumped me to get my heart started again. They stuck in a stomach tube to put food into me and another to take things out of me. Then they put me to sleep with their drugs. The nurses said that after a few days I was woken up a little so they could check on me. I can vaguely remember doctors and nurses talking at my bedside, before passing out again. The nurses changed my bed and washed me every day. I was sound asleep. I never realised that I had all those tubes in my body. Every day they gave me medicine that made me sleep so I could heal. They told my son and his family that I needed to get a lot of rest. When they woke me up properly again I was a bit better. I could see all these monitors connected to me making beep noises all the time.

'Do you feel this? Do you feel that?' they'd ask. I would shake or nod my head.

On 19 April 1991, they transferred me to the Hampstead Rehabilitation Centre. I had been at the hospital nearly four weeks.

·········

It took me a long while to recover from the shock of nearly dying. I was still feeling very ill and very, very frightened. I worried all the time I might have another stroke and die. I wondered whether I would see all my family and country again. I wondered if I'd lose everything, all the kids, all my family, all my work and plans. I felt very sad and sorry for myself. I thought, 'Why me?' But then I thought about Lloyd, Joylene and all my kids. They were all too young to lose their mother. Lloydie especially still needed me. Plus I hadn't really spent enough time with my grandkids. I thought a lot about my own mother dying. I especially thought that I needed to get back home again. So I decided to live.

I practised waking up and saying to myself, 'Today, I'm still alright.' Not that I could say it out loud. Just think it really. But slowly I got a bit better. Then when another tomorrow came around, and the next day and the next, and I was still alright, I started to believe I might get better. Every day I thought to myself, 'I'll try very hard to do all my exercises so I can go back home to see my own families. Go back to my country. Go back to see all the people in my life in Alice Springs.'

My stroke left me without any speech. I was still very heavy and couldn't move anything on the right side of my body. I couldn't get my right arm or leg to move. When I wanted to talk, it felt so frustrating. I could only nod and grunt when the nurses and doctors asked me questions. I couldn't get any words out. It took me a long time to learn to stand up again. Later I was able to get my leg to move a little and my right hand to grip things. I had to start learning everything all over again.

At the Hampstead Centre just outside downtown Adelaide they looked after people like me. Slowly they taught me to walk and speak again. They helped me learn to do many of the things I used to do. And I made many new friends there. They were very kind to me.

I started trying to write down little messages to the doctors, nurses and speech therapists. I had to learn to use my left hand. My writing was very messy but I wanted to communicate how I was feeling. And I needed to let people know the things I wanted. Especially I needed to ask them when I was going home.

It took a long time to get a little bit better, and I didn't go home for many months. I was really wanting to be sure that I'd be able to live back with my family. I was feeling 'irrare'. That's when you're really lonely and homesick. I needed my own country and my family.

Right from the start I was introduced to my speech therapist. Sally was her name. She came every day to help me. I wondered if I would be able to do things like I used to do. She gave me hope. First she'd get me up from my bed, holding onto me, little by little. She taught me to walk slowly away from my bed. Every day she did that while she talked about what I needed to do if I wanted to speak again. She never shamed me. And after a while I learnt to walk to another room, holding onto the rails on the corridor walls. She'd walk beside me talking things up, and to make sure that I didn't fall.

It was a long time before I was strong enough to walk by myself. She kept walking and talking to me slowly, from my room into another room, to practise my steps. She also started other exercises to get the strength back in my muscles.

Other people in that room were learning to walk too. Everyone was wearing track pants. I felt worried. I had never worn trousers. But they got me some and I got used to them. There were a few times I was embarrassed. In my culture you didn't tell people to get undressed in front of other people. And I was embarrassed with the way they asked if I had wet or messed up my bed. Aboriginal people don't talk about those things. But I got used to it. They didn't know any better.

Sally used to sit me down at her table. She had pictures to help me learn to talk again. It was like my classroom flashcards. I had to practise the sounds and words over and over again. My tongue and lungs needed to be exercised too. It was like up at Batchelor. Sally showed me how to look in the mirror to teach my tongue and mouth to start moving and speaking again.

At first I found it very hard. It was like teaching little kids in school, learning words for the first time. Sometimes I felt like a very old lady and useless. I was frustrated to have to start exercises just to get my mouth to talk properly again. Lots of times I thought I would never make it. I'd say to the doctors and nurses, 'This is too hard for me.' And every day when the therapy was over, I was so exhausted all I could do was sleep. The next morning it would start all over again. I would see Sally coming, every single day. 'Oh no,' I thought to myself, 'not again. Why can't they leave me alone?' I got so tired of it! But it was a really good thing that they were doing. If they didn't keep bossing me around and making me do it, I wouldn't have got any better.

The first doctors at the Lyell McEwin Hospital had told me when I woke up that half of my brain was dead. It got me thinking so hard. How can I get that half of my brain to work again? Like I'd tell my brain to move my tongue around my mouth. I could imagine what had to happen. But I just couldn't get my tongue to do it.

Sally gave me all sorts of information to help me understand what was happening in my brain. And I tried very hard, making my brain work again using different parts of my body that were still working. I had to concentrate real hard to do the things I wanted my body to do. Eventually parts of my body started to get the idea and I could move things around a little bit. Some things I only got a bit of movement back. Lots of things were never the same.

Talking was the hardest. The sounds they were teaching me was 'm' and 'n'. Plus every other sound they could think of. 'Mmmmmmmmm, nnnnnnnn-nnnnnnnn.' It was very hard but I made myself do it over and over for my own good. I didn't want to think about not being able to speak again; that would be terrible. Even worse than not being able to walk or to be able to do things I used to do. Sometimes everything seemed really too much.

Sally was very good to me and even visited me at the rehab centre on the weekends. Sometimes she took me down to the beach and around Adelaide with her husband and her children. She was a real caring person. A lot of the staff at Hampstead were like that. I had a good time with them. It helped a lot, and I'm very grateful to them all.

Sister Robyn used to ring me on the phone from Alice Springs. At first she couldn't understand me at all. But later she could when I made the high sounds, the middle sounds and the low sounds. She began to read my thoughts and get the idea of what I meant. It must have been like that when I finally spoke to my sister and kids. Sister Robyn picked up Sandra, Joylene, Gilbert, and their kids, so they could talk to me on the phone when I was at Hampstead. They didn't really understand much of what I was saying but it helped me keep going. Hearing them all made my spirit stronger.

At first I went to physiotherapy in a wheelchair. Then after all Sally's work they'd hold me up between bars or give me a walking frame to practise with. After a little while, I was using that frame on my own so they took it away and changed me to a stick. Gradually I was alright walking along on a flat floor with that stick. But I wasn't so good on bumpy ground. I had to learn to be stronger at getting my legs to hold me.

Before I left Hampstead they wanted me to walk a bit without a stick. And I learnt that too. But they made me keep the stick. They didn't want me to be afraid of falling. Sticks are good like that. It was a lot of work but we got there bit by bit. After a long while I could walk without a stick to go most places in the hospital. But I had a bit of a struggle getting in and out of cars, especially high Toyota Land Cruisers. And every now and again I would lose my balance in sand, or especially walking over rocky country. But I was so happy to be walking on my own again. I had been really afraid that I wouldn't be able to look after myself at all, let alone caring for my own family. I didn't want to be a 'poor thing' always waiting for people.

Hampstead also gave me a Canon typing machine with thin ribbons of paper. I could tap away with one finger of my left hand and give people the paper so they'd know what I wanted. I started using it all the time. It helped me a lot. I could type things out on my bed and hand it across when I needed to. It saved slowly telling the nurses and doctors and even my white friends what was happening for me.

I knew I could communicate with my family and Aboriginal people with hand signs. I could still point to things and make noises. I knew I'd feel good about that when I got home. I'd always known hand signs from the old people sitting around the camp with them in my younger days. If my grandmothers wanted water, they could use their hands and fingers to tell me, 'Kwatatje' or 'Go there and get me water.' I could see to do that. 'Kere merne', 'Get me food'. I could sign that too. It would be easy for people to understand me. But I couldn't use my hands to communicate with these doctors, nurses and white friends. So I started to love using that Canon typing thing.

....

I never thought much about my own language at rehab. When I finally came back to Alice Springs I had to learn to speak it again. Even though I had all my own language stored in my brain, I found it difficult to make the sounds like 'ngk' and 'kng' and 'kngw' and 'rr'. Words like 'akngerre' were very hard. When I tried to speak, the sounds just didn't know how to come out. My tongue wouldn't always go to where I wanted it to. That stroke made me lose the ability to speak my own language. It was frustrating. Arrernte has so many difficult and complicated tongue movements.

It made me think about my students at IAD. It was not easy for them to get the sounds either. And sometimes I used to laugh at them. I now realised how hard it was for my students to learn the tongue movements to say these unfamiliar Arrernte sounds. I am sorry I laughed so much. But sometimes those students were really funny. Me and Rosie just couldn't help but laughing. At Hampstead I must have been talking a bit like my old students. I'm glad the staff didn't laugh too much at me. Especially, after they gave me the stick to use. I still had a bit of the storm cloud in me, and might have had to whack them into being a bit more respectful.

When Sally worked with me, she taught me how to speak in English, not my own Arrernte language. The exercises we practised were English sounds. I still find it very hard to say some of the words of my own language. The speech pathologists still don't really have exercises for some of our Arrernte sounds. Before my stroke I was a teacher and it was important to communicate well with all my students and other people. Everybody said I'd made a miracle recovery but I could hardly speak in my own language at all. More than twenty years later I am still finding it hard to move my tongue in ways that allow me to speak my own language properly. I have to keep practising, little by little. And sometimes I have to rely on sign language. But now I could use just one left hand.

It was finally time for me to come back to Alice. I was so happy. My social worker told me, 'Soon you are going home.' My heart jumped with joy. I had been wanting to hear that for many weeks. I felt so excited about seeing my families and friends again. I never slept that night before I left Hampstead.

They took me into the airport in a wheelchair. I still remember sitting and watching all the workmen loading luggage on the jet planes. Finally our plane was ready to board, and they started pushing my wheelchair towards the plane. The forklift driver came over and people loaded me in my wheelchair taking me to the airplane, and lifting me up straight into the doorway. I was so happy.

A few hours later I saw the MacDonnell Ranges come into view out of the window. I could see Old Mparntwe, the land around the Todd River and Mount Gillen, welcoming me home. They unloaded me last and when they brought me into the airport terminal, I saw my best friend, Robyn, waiting and waving, welcoming me back home. My eyes filled with tears of joy and happiness. I felt 'I am home'. My families were there waiting for me. My second daughter Karen was there and she stayed with me. None of the kids had money to come to see me in Adelaide. I had finally arrived home in Alice Springs on 29 June 1991. It had been a long three months.

Gerard, the Community Health social worker, was there at the airport too. He took me in a car to the Yipirinya Hostel to stay for a while, until a place that would be easy for me could be found. Karen, Joylene and Lloydie were all there to look after me. Peter Tait was my doctor. He is a lovely fellow who helped me with everything. Alison Baldock was my speech pathologist.

The Community Health Disability Services organised for me to continue physiotherapy at the rehab centre at the Old Timers Nursing Home. This started as being every day. I would do my exercises, then sit with people at the day centre practising my talking. There were bingo cards and a caller. Someone would help me cross off numbers. We also played cards, but we weren't allowed to play for money. Sometimes we went outside to play lawn bowls on the grass to help exercise our arms. It was good fun there at the day centre.

·········

Some months later I finally moved into a house. But no equipment had been put in to make it easier for me. Territory Housing were supposed to install proper disability taps, disability kitchen equipment, and rails in the toilet and bathrooms to make things possible. Gerard complained but it was no good humbugging them. No good even if the doctors and physiotherapists growled them. Housing just got crankier if you complained. I have been in three public houses in town since I had my stroke. None of them had the proper equipment for people with walking or other disability problems. Housing kept us helpless.

The house had nothing done to the taps to make it easier for me to turn them on or off. I had a gas stove in my first house but I didn't use it because I was frightened of the gas exploding. I could only use one hand to light it. It took them over a year for my gas stove to be replaced with an electric one. They just kept on saying I was on their list. But it must have been a long list. They always said they had no money. Broken things didn't ever get fixed. It was always the same story.

That first house was a nightmare for lots of reasons. It was a newish, white-painted plasterboard place with white shagpile carpet. There were no back verandas or outside spaces off the street where family could sit down or throw out a swag. And it was too far west of town, a long way from my Hidden Valley home where my family and old friends lived. I had no money for proper furniture, and the place was impossible to keep clean enough to make the public housing people happy. They were always coming around humbugging me and my carers.

Lloydie and all the young grandkids sometimes came to stay. They drew on the walls and ran around wildly. The dogs were even wilder. It was so good for me to hear that noise and have that energy around me. But the housing mob didn't like it at all. We had to clean all the time. The family might stay a couple of days or a week. Then they had to be back for work or school or to keep their little children and wives and husbands happy. I would wave them off back to Laramba Station or one of the outstation communities.

Alison Baldock, my speech therapist from Community Health, came to my house one day every week. She taught me to practise pronouncing new words and sounds. I would do one sound first, then another, then put them all together. She worked up my hand signing too. She was really interested in Aboriginal sign language and wanted to take photos and make a list of them all for the therapists when they were working with speech-impaired Aboriginal people.

But then Alison got very sick and had to take time off. Community Health couldn't recruit another speech pathologist. It got harder to get an appointment. Then she suddenly died far too young. She had cardiomyopathy, a disease of the heart muscle. It was very sad. After that, no speech pathologist seemed to want the job. There was only a visiting service from interstate. So for more than twenty five years I have had to wait for speech pathology appointments at the hospital.

·········

It got harder to get family to stay with me so far away from their Eastside camps. Karen and Joylene were living in town, but they were often too busy with their own friendships. They were still young and life had become a bit of a party. Their friends were sharing a drinking circle with them. I often asked Gerard or my own friends from church or IAD to help me find Karen and Joylene. I was always worried about them and wanted to talk to them.

But my girls said they got scared of coming around and causing problems with housing. They said I was always growling them for having too many drinks, or not doing something. Karen could never stay that long. She was married up to Frank Brown and took her kids back home with her. The kids even sometimes said that they were leaving me alone out of respect so I could live quietly. Later they told me they had been telling other family to not go near my house, especially after they had been drinking. They said, 'Don't take your problems to Mum' and 'Don't take money or food off Mum' and 'Don't humbug Mum or use anything that belongs to her.' So, what they thought would show respect, ended up meaning that nobody ever came around much. After a while I found myself often alone at night, and sometimes I didn't see friends for days.

My family and friends hadn't ever been so sick. They didn't know what it's like to feel all alone and sorry for yourself all day. I couldn't talk much. I walked really slowly. I got tired easily. And I was cranky sometimes. So I wasn't always a fun person to hang around with. And I didn't want anyone's pity. So I would tell people off if they started saying things that made out they were feeling sorry for me. People were busy and became a bit scared of coming to see me. It was like old people in a nursing home. I know that story too. Everyone says they'll visit, but it doesn't really happen much without a car.

And after a while I really started missing all the family visits, and the busyness of the camps. I missed working and all the people coming and going. I missed being in the centre of things and spending my time in places where there was lots of talking, drinking cups of tea, laughing and telling stories. I even missed the dogs fighting and people arguing all the time. Everything at Bokhara Street was too quiet and empty.

The physiotherapist started worrying. Then they said I was getting lazier. But everything was a long way away and I needed to get someone to push or drive me around. It was easier for them. But the physios were telling me that I was not walking enough by myself. If I didn't keep using my legs they would stop working at all for me. They were worried that if I lost motivation and strength then I might fall more often. I should start doing my exercises in the rooms at Community Health in Flynn Drive, they told me. This at least meant company of a sort. And they could keep an eye on me. Made sure I wasn't getting too sad or bored or angry.

What I really missed though was going to work and catching up with everyone. As well as coming into Flynn Drive, I was still going some days to rehabilitation with the physio out at the old people's day centre. But my walking was only getting better real slowly. And I was always hanging around with sick people or people looking after us. They didn't want to ask questions about linguistics or check out family connections. They didn't want to know my story and answers. I was just someone they had to look after. I was becoming a 'poor thing' instead of a provider and mother; just another person they had to spend time helping. We didn't share many laughs or have much fun, and my spirit was very sad.

The Canon communicator was okay for a while. I would type in questions and answers. But it was hard with one hand, very slow. I'd spend a long time writing up a list of things that needed to happen, then go in and see Gerard or someone else to see what they could organise. The writing might be two metres of ticker tape. Sometime I might get a few things happening. But I was struggling. Gerard would see me coming with my lists and start making excuses before I even sat down for a cup of tea, and everybody else was working or too busy.

Margaret visiting Lorraine Gorey, Veronica Turner and Margaret Kemarre Turner at Children's Ground. Courtesy of Leonie Sheedy, Children's Ground

CHAPTER 27

The long road to recovery

When Sister Robyn heard David Wilkins, my good friend from Yipirinya days, was coming to visit Alice Springs in 1992, she told him to see me. We'd worked closely when we were struggling to establish the Yipirinya School. He was a linguist and had been away overseas working after leaving our Yipirinya project in 1988. Sister Robin had told David about my stroke and struggles. I'm sure they'd already decided between them that I needed to get back to work. But, like always, when he visited he let me bring up my 'not working' story. We had a great catch-up and discussion about what was happening. Only later did I talk about my sadness and how I was missing my friends and work so badly.

I was still using my Canon text machine and some hand signs to make myself understood. David asked a lot of questions about why I couldn't go back to work. This started me thinking harder about what I could do if I did go back. David made it all seem possible. Afterwards he took me to talk with Alison Baldock at Community Health, and we caught up with the Aboriginal linguists and interpreters who were still working on the Mparntwe Arrernte dictionary project.

All my old friends said they had been too scared to ask me to come back. But when Alison and David explained that I would be alright, and that the linguistic work would be good for me, they cheered up. David talked about how I could use the text machine and hand signals. Everyone was pleased. We talked to the dictionary project managers and they were happy to offer me a return-to-work trial to see how I went. It was arranged that I would get picked up every day to see if I could come into work. I was busting to start.

Work was best treatment that happened to me. It combined my speech pathology and physiotherapy. I was practising and thinking about my speaking all the time. And because I was happy I was doing my physio exercises at work. It was much better than winning at bingo. My work friends made me feel I was useful again.

Being busy again kept me getting stronger. I helped the other linguists when they needed to understand better an Arrernte word and how it was used in a sentence. I used the machine to spell and explain words. Best of all I was back with my friends, being told all the gossip and being teased. I was laughing and having fun again. And I had something important to get me out of bed in the morning. It helped me make big improvements in my speech too. Being busy was the best of all therapies. I wasn't feeling so heavy and sad, and people started visiting me again.

....

Not long after that Gilbert and Rosemary got a place to stay in Larapinta Valley town camp. It was not far away and they would often drop in with the kids. Then the grandkids started to stay overnight so I saw a lot more of them. We'd eat together in the evenings and sometimes in the mornings too. I had an electric frypan and other cooking gear that we used.

But Bokhara Street was a hard place for my Hidden Valley family and friends to get out to see me, and sometimes I still felt very lonely and isolated. I wasn't used to living by myself in a big house so much of the time. I had gone from the Alwekkere to the dormitories to sharing places all the time as an adult so had always felt a bit scared to sleep alone at night, especially after the stroke. Now I mostly needed some company, someone who could check things if there was a lot of noise during the night.

And I wanted to move out. The housing mob were too cranky all the time. Bokhara Street had no footpaths or gutters. It was too far to the shops. And I wasn't really exercising as much as I should. I asked my sister's big daughter, Phyllis Stevens, to see if she could move me into Larapinta Valley, near Gilbert. My cousin-sister, Nancy Lynch, and her husband Don were living there. Some of their kids were close by too.

The Larapinta Valley Housing Association said yes and found me a place straightaway. I was so glad to get out of that Bokhara Street house and into the little unit near my old friend Wenten Rubuntja's place. He was still the chairperson of Tangentyere Council and still important in the Yipirinya School Council. In the early evening I could sit and smell the campfire smoke. That was the sweetest thing. I felt like I was home again hearing the Aboriginal talking, laughter and music. I could hear the dogs barking and kids playing, mothers yelling out for them to come home. I would sit out on my veranda with my grandkids. Sometimes family and neighbours would stop by to say hello.

I had people around me and a busy life again. Even when I was home alone I wasn't so nervous. I wasn't so worried anymore about something bad happening or falling over. It felt like I was getting my spirit back again. Next door was just a shout away. And I didn't have any more humbug from the government mob calling in all the time. They did tell me I had to pay $7000 to fix up the Bokhara Street house or they'd take me to court. But Gerard took me to see a lawyer at Central Australian Aboriginal Legal Aid and together we put a letter into the housing office. My lawyer had a tough talk to some of the Territory Housing bosses, and they stopped humbugging me or saying I owed them money after that. I was very relieved.

At my new place I planted a garden. I also got back into making billies of tea and cooking meals on the campfire. Making my bed and cleaning up became more important to me too. I was even using my walking stick more. It was great for whacking any cheeky dog too! Plus my grandkids stopped with me more often. I became the person to get them on the school bus in the mornings. The bus would pick us up so I could go to work after they wandered off to their classes.

Gilbert and Rosemary moved out after a while but some of their older kids stayed on with me. Sometimes there'd also be visitors from out bush, or other family would come into town. Sometimes my old friends from mission days would need somewhere to stay. It didn't matter how many people there was stopping with me, there was never any housing association bosses talking to me like I was stupid and telling me off about too many visitors. I was so glad. Occasionally the police or night patrol would call in about one of my kids. Sometimes they might drop off grandchildren for me to look after and it'd be the first I'd know that one of my kids was back in town.

....

Some years later I got asked to move into half a house back in Hidden Valley. It was closer to my old family circles but many of our old senior people had left in the ten years I'd been away. Lots of my old friends now lived in public housing in town, and the culture of the place had changed for the worse. Without enough leadership on the camps the drinking was often out of control; and the fighting and humbug could be terrible.

I felt scared sometimes. Often it was the children of my friends, now grown up and very drunk. I'd taught them as babies at Santa Teresa school. Now they had no jobs and not much hope. Hidden Valley also had a whole lot of new families from other tribes. Mostly it was Western Arrernte people married into our families. But sometimes it was Warlpiri or even people from the NPY Lands. Our dream of an Arrernte family village had faded away. Our leaders just left, finding it too hard to work and live in all the humbug.

Yipirinya School had led to our kids hanging out with young people from all the different tribes and town camps. They didn't always even stay with their family at night, going instead to where the action was. This broke down further the parental authority that had worked so well, especially when our adults were sober. The initiated men used to uphold our ancient law. Now the men were often drinking in their own circles, and scattered everywhere. It led to disputes even between old friends and brothers-in-the-law.

Petrol sniffing, inhalants like glue and other cheap drugs started to spread into our Yipirinya school classes. Then they spread through the town camp communities. Our children were often very badly damaged even before they grew up into teenagers. Their brains and movement were affected. Some of them became scary because they could lose control and become very dangerous so quickly. Too much alcohol in pregnancy does this too in what the doctors call foetal alcohol syndrome. Some babies were born without good brains for thinking straight. These drinking problems made trouble for our kids too. Yipirinya became the place where kids would go when other schools wouldn't take them. And some dangerous men started taking advantage of how easy it was to manipulate young people who were addicted. Kids started being lured into sex even when they were very young. Others got bashed, raped and even killed. Some kids committed suicide. Many felt they had nothing left to lose. The whole community had seemed to lose its way.

Tangentyere's night patrol helped where they could. But some families had lost control of their drinking and what was happening to their own kids. It all became too dangerous for me. I needed to get out of Hidden Valley. In the end I called Gerard, who was now working for Congress, and we arranged another public housing place. This time the house was closer to town. But the Gap Hotel was close by. The pub was making its money selling cheap sweet wine to drunks. It was the same everywhere. Sometimes it was my own kids out drinking. Out on the footpath and even on the streets in front of my Gap Road house there'd be drunks in an 'out of control' all night party. There was too much humbug at all hours of the day and night.

Another social worker, Franny Coughlan, who I had worked with in the Tangentyere days, helped me get a transfer to a quieter house in the Eastside. Gerard and Franny both now worked at Congress, in the Social and Emotional Wellbeing Program. Franny became my new social worker.

During this time I kept on with my rehabilitation. I was now speaking slowly but much more clearly, in both English and Arrernte. This helped me communicate all my complicated ideas. People just had to be a little bit more patient listening to me, that's all. I kept up my appointments with the specialists from Adelaide, and the therapists from Community Health. I also got to the Congress Clinic more often to check out the diabetes and get my medication. I changed my diet too, and walked around more.

All of this made me stronger. I started feeling like my old self, confident and with lots of ideas about what needed to happen next. I got my 'boss' voice back. I started to go to community meetings and talk up things again. And I went back full time into my Catholic church groups to try to get things happening in our parish again.

It is still hard for me though. Sometimes when I'm talking to people from some other government department or organisation they don't give me time to say what I want to say. Or they talk over the top of me. If I'm in a wheelchair they might speak to the person who's been pushing me, rather than to me directly. They might think I'm too slow, or perhaps a bit stupid. But I'd learnt from Sister Robyn by this time and I let them know better, so they'll learn to be more respectful. Sometimes they make a statement rather than asking a real question. They think that this way I won't have to work so hard to answer their questions. Sometimes they think they are helping me because they know about my situation. But I never liked people who think they can ask the question and answer it themselves. Too much like the old days. I get very frustrated.

I have to be careful with my walking stick. Sometimes I wave it around, growling a bit. The government people tend to leave quickly, as I walk back inside shutting the door.

....

I took up learning about my stroke and became a bit of a local expert. It got so I was being taken around to schools in Alice Springs by the nurses and therapists. I'd talk to the students about diabetes and strokes. Later, I went down to national conferences in Sydney and Melbourne. The speech pathologists and rehabilitation experts found my slow-but-continuing recovery very unusual. They wanted to know more about me losing Arrernte but not my English, so I got asked a lot of questions.

Some Aboriginal people still don't understand what diabetes and a stroke really means. Especially people who don't have English as a first language, and have more traditional ideas. Some of our people have a different way of understanding sickness. A lot of traditional Aboriginal healers are still saying I was sung by somebody, causing me to get sick[6]. This is the old Arrernte way of looking at things, and lots of people still follow this. But I want people to know that was not what happened to me. I understand the Western medical side of what happened to me now. And I want all Aboriginal people to understand this too.

Every day, many times over, someone is having a stroke somewhere in the world. It is one of the biggest killers, and not only here in Central Australia. Everywhere it is a big problem, but especially for Indigenous tribes. People who lose their land and have to change everything in their lives. They often become very sad, poor and displaced in their own country. I want Aboriginal people to know this. I can look after myself better now that I know the causes of strokes. But some people have no ears for hearing this story, or they are too busy to listen. They don't hear and get a chance to change their own lives. Just like I was before my stroke.

The doctors call a stroke a 'cerebrovascular accident'. But the big names don't really explain it. Something happens in your brain (akurrknge). Blood goes into and out of your brain, helping to keep all parts of your body alive and healthy. But sometimes there's a blockage in one of the brain pathways and a part of the brain doesn't get any blood. Then that part of the brain starts to die really quickly. If the blood stays blocked too long, the part of the brain stops working forever.

The clots in the blood that can cause these blockages are because of bad diet with lots of fat and sugar. If a blockage happens, your leg or arm might go black, then green, and then that leg or arm rots away. The doctors will have to cut it off before it poisons everything. People with diabetes often have toes and fingers cut off because of clots. Sometimes it is worse and you need an amputation of the leg from above the knee, and then you need an artificial limb.

In the old days, most people who had a stroke just died. But these days, if you get medical treatment straightaway you can be saved. You might still end up paralysed, but this is better than dying without the second chance like I got.

It was a part of the left side of my brain that died. It's this part that is needed for people to move properly and also for them to speak properly. I was numb (tharre) and paralysed (anathe) on the right side. Always I have a feeling of heaviness on this right side. A lot of times I felt pins and needles (tantheme) on that side. For a long time I couldn't speak much at all. I couldn't control my tongue properly and make the sounds that I wanted.

But I could still think properly, and I could write a little bit, and type. I learnt that your brain can recover a bit if you teach it again. Another part of your brain can be taught to work these same parts of your body. So you can sometimes get control of parts of your body again. But it's often very hard, and sometimes impossible, to train some muscles to work properly again.

I first learned about stroke by asking about a medical report I couldn't understand. I had to ask a few times before I understood properly. Our doctors should be trained to know that Aboriginal people might say they understand, when they don't really know things properly at all. They are just being polite and letting you know they are listening. And where there are lots of very hard words, they can become 'too shamed' to say that they don't know what's being said. This is not right. Aboriginal people need to know what is happening and be able to properly understand and talk to their doctors. Medical people have to learn to explain everything properly.

....

I am a respected matriarch, strong in my own culture. But I can't do things in ceremonies like the dancing and singing anymore. The stroke ended that for me. I am very strong in organising though, to making sure things happen in the right way. I've been working really hard at writing down my stories, and passing them on. I want to make sure my own family know the culture stories and can keep the next generations of our family involved in their own culture and community traditions.

I was very lucky in some ways. Adelaide Hospital was not far away. I got really good emergency services and quick medical treatment. The Hampstead Rehabilitation Centre was a great place. And Alice Springs had some good people too. Congress Health Services looked after me and helped out with my family. Tangentyere Council gave me support for housing, banking, meals on wheels and food vouchers. Territory Housing gave me a house, even if they kept nagging me all the time. And the Aboriginal Housing Service helped me look after and clean up my houses, before the government defunded it.

Most of the therapists at Community Health and the hospital were very caring and determined. Lots of people were generous with their time and energy. I often think of Sally, my speech pathologist, who took me to her home; her whole family treated me so good. But not everyone gets so lucky. You have to be courageous and ask for the right help. It is your body and your life. Make sure people tell you what you need to know so you can make your own decisions about what happens to you.

But most of all, I recovered because I had a strong group of friends that kept me going when I really needed to get back into my own life and work. They helped with my kids and grandkids. They kept my own determination strong, so that I never thought about giving up. Writing my story has been great for working these things out. And I go to The Campfire in the Heart most Wednesday nights for their 'reflection evenings'. This Catholic retreat space is for discussions about the interplay of Catholic and Aboriginal cultural frameworks. I share bits of my story and it gives me confidence for speaking about my ideas in front of lots of people. Who knows what I can do next.

·········

In 2007 I went to Sydney to stay with David Wilkins who had organised that we talk and do a therapy workshop with speech pathologists associated with the Faculty of Health Sciences at the University of Sydney. We made a video to be used in their Indigenous curriculum. In it I spoke of ways to work better with Aboriginal patients.

My recovery from my stroke was seen as different. It changed how some people understood the recovery phase. There was this idea that stroke victims get to return to a level of skill in the first few months but never progress much past that point. This is called 'aphasia'. But I continued to get better a long time after the doctors said I couldn't. I never stopped learning and progressing, whether it was with regaining my hand signing skills and sand drawing, or re-learning Arrernte.

I still struggle speaking Arrernte, but David and I think this is just because of the complex tongue positions used in talking Arrernte. The sounds and complex grammar structures caused my initial problems. David thinks the reason for me recovering English first rather than Arrernte was just because English is so much easier for me to speak and to be understood easily. At the beginning I recovered my understanding of Arrernte and could even write it over time. But still my weak tongue muscles make it hard for me to speak it clearly. So I mostly use English.

David continued to come and see me whenever he was visiting Alice Springs. He is a lovely man, one of the people that helped start me on the writing up of my stories. This was even before I got sick, when we were both working at Yipirinya School. During those five years from 1984 to 1988 we did a lot of site visits, telling the traditional dreaming tracks and making recordings for the class lesson plans. And we did some writing up of my memories from childhood.

After my strokes we added to the earlier autobiographical recordings and writings. David did a lot of documenting of my treatment in Adelaide after my stroke and my rehabilitation at Hampstead. He also started me writing more memories of childhood, taking me back to the places from my past. This was the start of developing my book.

He also took me on travels through my parents' and grandparents' country. I remember visiting Mount Zeil, my grandmother's country, for the first time. It was just like I'd pictured from listening to her stories when I was young. We also went out to Laramba in 1997, looking for Uncle Huckitta. Unfortunately he was away on business somewhere. When we were driving back the old road, we got two flat tyres. I said it was because David was driving and he wasn't careful enough. He says I was hopeless at telling him where to go.

Anyway, as I was correcting David on his driving technique and substandard efforts to follow my directions – watch my fingers and hand signs – and wondering how far he would have to walk if we were going to get back to town, I heard a car coming from an unexpected direction. I silenced David and a minute or so later who should fly through the bush onto the track but my uncle himself. He pulled up resplendent in his flash cowboy suit, complete with black hat, dark sunshades, sparkling gold belt and cowboy boots, greeting us with hugs and smiles.

He had been out hunting. There were kangaroo bodies bleeding off his roof rack. Despite being over seventy, Huckitta had our car jacked up, the wheels packed with grass and us back on the road in half an hour. Huckitta and me both agreed that it might be best if David didn't help too much. The tyres allowed Huckitta to limp the car back into Laramba. David drove Huckitta's car behind us. Huckitta parked the car at the garage and we had a lovely evening hosted by my uncle.

David was a special friend, funny and thoughtful, always very kind. He could make me laugh so much with his shy but stubbornly held comments. He was great at respectfully giving me all the leadership roles, and I treasure all those trips we made interstate and out bush.

CHAPTER 28

Grandmothers' rules: surviving in hard times

As a young girl I sat down with my grandmothers and other senior women. I learned about grandmother 'rules' sitting in these circles. I heard how our families had survived. We looked after each other in the hard times. It hadn't been an easy life for my grandmothers. They had been forced off their own country, away from their water and their sacred sites. Their leaders had lost control of land and the ability to keep going with the traditional cycles of life. Children were dying; others getting taken away.

My grandmothers had grown up in the days of severe droughts that killed hundreds of their family. They had survived the killing times when some white bosses were still massacring our people. There had been plenty of trauma and pain. All that history of losses. The pushing them off their own land, shutting them out of their sacred places. The Stolen Generations. These old women had been through a lot. And they taught us young girls the skills and knowledge to keep getting up and working hard for our family.

In 1984 it became my turn to be a grandmother. And all the old stories and talks from these women's circles came back to guide me. We were taught to hold our grandkids with strong love. Take care of them all. Protect them from danger or sickness. We never let down our grandkids, whether they are older or small.

I had learned these rules about how to be a grandmother from my own grandmothers. I had their stories of how to support my family within the traditions of our ancient culture. I knew how to help my grandkids to learn and understand this balance between power and wisdom. How to stand strong and still bend when times are tough.

But somehow us group of older women who had been young girls from Yambah, Middle Camp and Santa Teresa all largely failed to follow through on our training as proper grandmothers. When we came to town we often talked about creating our own circle of women and we tried to keep things strong for our grandkids. But we weren't powerful enough. Even with all our cultural knowledge from childhood, we found we couldn't recreate the circles of senior women. So we started to search for new ways to respond as older women and carers.

In the past there was never so much grog and marijuana. Our old people didn't know about these things. Today us grandmothers have too many of our family drinking too much and smoking guntja. Today my grandkids act like they are entitled to behave badly. On top of this, many of my own kids don't even listen to me properly anymore. So our grandkids are not being held strongly, so that they can learn. They are just doing their own thing without any real love or guidance. They have no ears to hear our songs and stories.

There is much jealous fighting too. Many young girls and boys are having babies, and too many of them think it is okay to leave their children for their grandmothers to look after while they go off to town to party. I've found it so much harder to look after my own grandchildren, especially when they became teenagers.

My stroke in 1991 meant I couldn't chase after these kids and grandkids anymore. I couldn't run around to save them or to growl them. And they were learning stupid things from watching our own family behaving badly. I had so much trouble with my own children's drinking and guntja smoking. All us grandmothers were sad. We all had so many other things to worry about. We all woke up every day scared for our kids and grandkids.

When I was married I thought to myself, 'What a good thing it is to become a mother.' I thought I did a really good job being there and looking after my own six kids. But when they all got married, they all went away to different communities while I was back in town working too hard as a teacher. So I wasn't always there for them as a grandmother, unless they came to town.

And in those early days they only came back to town when someone was sick, or when my daughters or my sons' wives were having their own babies at the big hospital. As soon as they had their babies they mostly went back out bush to live with their wife's or husband's family. As parents they wanted to show their babies to their other grandparents out there in the communities.

This was okay. But I was sometimes lonely. So when they came back to town I liked having my grandkids stopping with me. I liked the busyness, the sense of continuity and renewal that it brought back to me. Especially after I had my stroke. Especially after I stopped working.

To have children and grandchildren is a blessing from God. It made me very happy.

My three daughters, Pamela, Karen and Joylene all had kids when they were only young women themselves. I became a grandmother for the first time in 1984. My daughter Pamela had a son, Shawn Gibson, when she was fifteen years old. He was a beautiful baby. Pamela had married Alec Gibson from Laramba. He was an older man and a stockman. A good strong man. They had four kids together. My grandkids were all beautiful. When they were young they all lived out at Laramba; Alec and Pamela were living and working on Napperby Station. They were sitting down at Laramba or the Gibson out-station, quietly trying to work within culture.

Karen married Frank Brown from Yuelamu or Mount Allen. They too had four kids while they were living and working in Anmatyerr country. This was good. My youngest daughter Joylene's relationships were more difficult. She had lots of beautiful kids, and so many problems. But it worried me that all my girls were so young to be running around and having babies. I watched them struggle to grow up and look after their kids. Later on I had to step in to care for these kids sometimes. That made me very sad.

I was sorry that my daughters all missed out on running around as young single women in our circles of older women. They were already mothers by then. Because Joylene was the youngest she grew up and stayed in town longer, but she didn't stop with me. She was only seventeen when I had the stroke. She wouldn't let me hold her close. And my circles of women in town was much more fragile than my own grandmothers' circles. We weren't all sharing a campfire at night like I did. We were scattered around too much.

My three sons married three women from different communities. Gilbert married Christine Brown from Mimili in the south. Trevor married Kathleen McCormack from out Mt Allen way. Lloyd married Priscilla Burton from Ernabella. My sons brought their families to town to catch up and the grandkids often stayed with me. It made me very happy to have them home with me. But my sons later struggled to get any work. They got lost to the town without any jobs to go back for.

At the start my sons and their wives would look after their children very well here in town. And after my stroke they stayed to help me out. But everything changed when my sons and their wives started staying in town for good. The stroke made it more difficult for me to care for their kids. At first my grandchildren would be sent back to their other grandmothers on their communities. This might have helped keep the kids in their bush school. But later the grandkids would live with me. It was often only me that got them ready for school and grew them up. Their mothers and fathers often got lost in the grog when they were in town.

Because there was never enough work in Alice Springs and even the bits of work out bush seemed to disappear, after a while it seemed too hard for them to stay off the grog in town. Or they couldn't stay sober long enough to turn up for what little work there might be. They would join each other in the circle of drinkers. Sometimes they were the drinkers dragging visitors into their parties.

They often came home really drunk, sometimes arguing and fighting with each other. Often this was from jealousy. They might have been fighting with other families as well. Sometimes when they were drunk, if someone said one bad word then really bad fighting might start out of nothing. Later some of my own family might be smashed up, even killed. People became scared of some of my children. But this wasn't happening just to my family; it happened to lots of the grandmothers all over town.

Us poor grandmothers often got woken up in the night to try to stop these fights or settle things down. Our own grandkids were frightened. My grandkids saw and heard too many bad things. They saw their own family getting hurt by their own brothers and sisters. They saw cars and property getting busted up for no reason. They saw people crying. They saw the bully boys within our own families bossing everyone around.

It was often very scary and the police would come to drag one of our own away to jail. Ambulances would take smashed up mothers and aunties away to hospital. It was mostly the women that got hurt. The men got locked away. They had to go to court, and ended up in jail. Everyone started becoming sad. Especially the kids. There were far too many funerals for people killed in fights, or people who had committed suicide. My beautiful daughters became smashed up in all this fighting. Their sadness and anger was frightening. Sometimes they were cutting themselves and saying they wanted to die.

Back in the 1970s and 1980s some of us older women thought the drinking would be okay. We said it was like in the old days when the stockmen used to go into town after the muster camps; when they had got rid of the cattle to the trucking yards and got paid up, they would party a bit. Sometimes they would fight among themselves. But when the money ran out, everything would be mostly sorted out. They would come home and settle down again.

Even in the old days there had always been a few who stopped in town for too long. These people sometimes became lost to their country and couldn't seem to find a way back home. They were mostly a small sad mob, hanging around together. We thought of them as poor buggers, and a bit silly in the head. Some would start drinking metho and other bad stuff. They'd get busted up and grow sadder. Then you might end up visiting them in jail, or going to their funerals.

·········

When I came back to live in Hidden Valley the party had already started a long time ago. But I was a proud young mother and a teacher then, and lots of us young mothers thought we were going to change the world. We worked really hard, thought we were all going to be different. We had come back into town to take back our own country.

Sometimes after a long day we would go out drinking with our family and friends, sometimes even with our new white friends from work. It felt like we were all in this struggle together in those days. We thought we were winning some big battles and having a few drinks was okay. But after a while, even for us working ones, it was like if you didn't have the party and a few drinks, then you were missing out. Some people just got greedier and greedier for the grog. It was very addictive. Sometimes you didn't see these people unless you joined their drinking circle.

Us younger Aboriginal workers and parents had often left many of our senior people still back on the missions or reserves to look after country and ceremony. There was not much effective family leadership for us, without a circle of senior people reminding us of the old stories. Even as a grown-up woman I needed senior people as a group holding us all together.

My children grew up when the drinking circles were getting out of hand. A few people, mostly men, would get increasingly angry when the grog ran out.

They threatened people, making them give over their money for more grog. There was too much fighting, and too much mixing up of the different family groups and tribes.

Some families seemed to abandon their young ones. And somehow some of our mob had given away our spirituality and our culture of respecting everyone and caring for each other. We lost a lot more than we knew. Soon the white bosses were back in control. Soon enough we became the ones putting our hands out for rations again. We had to get permission to be making the decisions in our own Aboriginal organisations. This happened over and over and over. But we didn't seem to learn.

The white bosses with their government money were telling us what we needed to think and do. Families stopped working things out together anymore because there had been too much fighting between groups. Things had been said and done that even the old leadership couldn't sort out. Our own people were hating each other, telling secrets about each other, dobbing each other in to the old white bosses. Aboriginal organisations were split apart and fighting with each other.

Even when services were defunded no combined Aboriginal voice was raised to complain. There was not much respect left. The white bosses could pick us off one by one. They started funding the churches instead of our own organisations, and nobody complained.

Young people out in the communities started to think it was more important to come to town to party, rather than to get an education. Education and hard work didn't seem to be getting Aboriginal people ahead, so they thought selling grog and guntja to each other was a better way. Just like the American black gangs that they listened to on their music videos. Staying at home out bush was stupid. It was missing out. Going to school was for losers.

Coming into town to have a drink became a personal 'right' for everyone. It became like 'land rights'. Us Aboriginal people knew we should get our land back. Now some people thought our civil rights had expanded. They thought they should be able to get drunk whenever they wanted to. They thought no-one could stop them drinking. Not even their own family. It was their right.

·········

In the meantime, the grog was getting cheaper and cheaper. More and more young people stayed in town longer and longer. Then some families started to take lots of cheap grog back to their communities. Some even started making money selling it, sometimes even to young family members. Soon every community had its own boundary fence and grog camps where people got drunk every night of the week.

It got to the point where if you didn't want to drink and get drunk with your family you were seen as being somehow culturally disrespectful. Drunken bully boys started saying that proper family culture was about buying the grog and looking after the drunks. The drunks were acting like it was okay to be taking their 'kids' money' for grog. They told the grandparents, 'Don't worry about feeding our kids. Just make sure the grog doesn't run out.'

And they'd bash people if they didn't get their own way. Bash up old people and steal their money. Steal their blankets and food too. I heard about these things. It was shameful.

·········

Our grandkids saw all this. And soon they started acting that way too. Even when they were living with their own mothers and grandmothers, these young people were not showing respect. They were looking for the next party, even before the last one had finished. And it wasn't just the grog. Somewhere along the way guntja started selling really big. And petrol sniffing started too. Any old cheap drug to make you feel 'better' for a while. Younger and younger kids started looking for drugs everywhere. It became another civil liberty.

Lots of these kids went silly in the head. Newborn babies started to be born funny. Their brains didn't work properly. Their bodies didn't work. More and more babies were being born with foetal alcohol syndrome. None of us really knew what it was at first. Welfare started taking these kids away and sticking them into disability houses away from their own families. These kids couldn't learn properly at school. And they often died too young, without having any chance of a future.

Lots of kids didn't have much family to help them out. Sometimes they didn't even have a proper place to stay or get fed properly. Nobody was there for them. They started hanging around as 'gangers', looking after themselves. And they got into lots of trouble. They sometimes got fed grog and drugs that saw them sexually abused. They even started having sex with each other and making babies, even though they were only little kids themselves. Nobody had been there teaching them how to be part of a family. There was nobody who could pull them into line.

·········

I knew my children were drinking far too much and fighting with other families, and their partners were sometimes even worse. Their marriages fell over. My kids all ended up in trouble, and my sons all ended up in jail one time or another. They all got into fights, hurting people and getting hurt themselves, ending up in hospitals sick and damaged. The grandchildren often ended up staying with me for months, often barely seeing their parents sober.

Meanwhile me and the other grandmothers were trying to keep our own grandchildren safe and at school. It was all a bit exhausting. Soon the grandkids started getting angry and sad themselves. Some of my own grandkids would want to be drunk or 'stoned' all the time. As teenagers, it got so I couldn't get them up to go to school. If they left the house it was only to hang around with their mates. Later they couldn't even be bothered trying to find work. They couldn't do anything to help their family out. And they couldn't be bothered keeping up with friends who didn't drink or smoke. Soon they too started getting into trouble. They too sometimes got badly hurt and damaged.

For some families most of their money started to go on grog and guntja. Sometimes the sad ones took it all to gamble. And there was a lot of humbugging for money and food. These lost ones never chucked in for anything themselves. They were often humbugging their grandmothers for money to keep on drinking.

This happened not just to me, but also many of the other grandmothers. There came lots of times in the 1990s and 2000s when we got no rest in our lives. We weren't just helping out with our grandchildren, we were acting like their full-time parents. It got so it was easier when your kids left you alone and you only had to look after your grandkids. At least then you could take them to school, feed them and all that. At least then you might get some sleep.

Everyone knew our culture was going the wrong way. The kids didn't have grandmothers, they had grandmothers acting like mothers and telling them what to do. Instead of us teaching our grandkids with love and kindness, we were telling them off and saying 'no' all the time. It got so they didn't have someone who would just love them up and give them presents. Us grandmothers became the 'tough love' ones. It was the kids' drunken parents who might sometimes call in to chuck them a bit of money or buy them a present. Sometimes my grandkids missed school so that they might catch up with their drinking parents when they were coming out of the bank on cheque day. Sometimes that was the only way they could get some 'love' off them.

None of this was proper Aboriginal grandmothers' law. It wasn't what I learnt growing up around the Alwekkere. We had been taught by our elders that as grandmothers we take care of our grandchildren. Not for money, but because they are part of us. It was what we should do: hold our grandkids strongly, with love. Help keep them close to their family, so that they don't forget who they are. Be there so they know that we will love them forever. We were told that, and we had felt it as kids ourselves. Now we feel it so strongly for our grandkids.

We knew that grandmothers didn't turn down their grandchildren, that grandmothers were the safety net for the whole family. It was like that in the old days. Grandmothers were like the hidden-away waterholes for the really dry times. The places that even the worst droughts didn't empty. Families were okay as long as the grandmothers still looked after the kids. That is what we thought.

But us grandmothers started getting to where we couldn't do anything without feeling bad. We'd started looking after our grandkids full time. Welfare was coming around telling us to keep them close because our children weren't up for doing anything except drinking and partying. We have got very strong feelings for growing grandkids up and making their lives strong, but we never thought our own kids would be abandoning their kids for the grog.

If you got drunk all the time, behaved badly, didn't turn up for work, didn't look after your kids, then people were going to think you were useless. Not just the government mob, but the Aboriginal family leaders too. Some family would even start to hide away from you. They might even be secretly glad when the government mob would hunt you down and lock you up. They might even be happy when the welfare mob and the courts took away your kids. Because you weren't looking after them properly. You were just looking after yourself.

Us grandmothers can't look after all our children's kids on our own. Our kids have to be standing up more, taking proper responsibility. Me and my fellow grandmothers weren't strong enough before. And now we are much older and sadder. A lot of our own grandkids grew up and became lazy like their parents. They too couldn't get up and turn up. They couldn't seem to show proper respect. And when they got older we couldn't chase after them anymore. They were too fast, and there were too many places for them to hide.

....

In 2007 in the Northern Territory there was the Commonwealth government 'Intervention', the 'National Emergency Response' to the Little Children Are Sacred report. The story was that our children were being abused and weren't getting looked after. I was shocked when I first heard about the Intervention. The government had got the army to come in to run the communities. Everyone was really surprised. Some families got scared and took off out bush. They thought the army might lock everyone up and take their kids away. I heard of some people going across into Queensland and down into South Australia.

Even before the Intervention, no-one much trusted John Howard. And many of his government people weren't much better. The whole lot of them hadn't even said 'sorry'. Mostly that government just talked rough about our people. But nobody really thought they were going to bring the army in. They said it was because of the little children being 'sacred'. We'd been saying that for a long time. But we weren't telling them to steal them all away. That was a terrible idea. Anyway they were going to build houses, they said. That sounded okay. Lots of us had been asking for that for a long time. And they were going to stop the 'rivers of grog'. That had to be a good idea.

But what were some of our people most angry about? The drinkers protested about not being able to get drunk whenever and wherever they felt like. They said it was an attack on their human rights. The lazy drunks were outraged that the government quarantined their 'kids' money' to make sure it went on feeding their kids. I thought quarantining was a good idea. It might stop some of them wasting the kids' money on gambling and getting stoned.

But how did it get to all this?

I can't describe all these worries and hurts. It is sometimes all too hard. But I'm saying this from my heart. I think it is in every mother's and grandmother's heart. Fathers and grandfathers too. We are all feeling the sadness and pain from too much partying. We have Aboriginal kids not being looked after. We have some fathers and mothers who are really hurting their kids and their own family members too. Some fathers and even the mothers are so sad they are committing suicide. It is time for our families to wake up. Time to get the grog under control and fix things for our grandkids.

I once saw a big card written up in a white man's office talking up 'caring and sharing'. So now it was the white mob telling that to us. It's a shame job. In our culture we know how to be sharing and caring. But still our own kids don't seem to know how to look after their kids. They didn't seem to care how strongly us grandmothers are feeling this shame. When my grandchildren are in trouble with the law, or in any sort of trouble, I feel it within me like my heart is being torn apart.

It was never like this before. When my people had their own country and their own work, they looked after their families first and stayed away from too many bad spirits. Our families had their ancient rules, their sacred stories, their language and culture, their strong family leadership and their sense of being responsible. Today the balance between power and wisdom is in big trouble. We need to straighten it out. And we need to do it ourselves. We need to do it proper way, and with proper respect. It is our own children, our own families that we need to straighten out. It is our own hopes and dreams for our future that we need to save.

Sometimes us grandmothers get together to talk about our sons and daughters. We are really sad about what they are doing with their lives and our grandchildren's lives. We try to support and comfort each other. Share our ideas. But us grandmothers can't control our kids' lives. Even when they are grown up, and they are grandmothers or grandfathers themselves, our children are still drinking and partying. But they don't seem to have any ears to hear what we are saying. They don't hear our prayers, or take any notice of our tears.

Some parts of culture are starting to get stronger again now. But there is a long way to go. The government mob need to work with our senior family leaders. We need to all pull together more. But it isn't always happening. I still see the drinking circles every day. Every night in town, on our communities and all along the roads going back to our communities there are drunks making a mess in their own country. We've seen it for years. It has got to stop. It's everyone's trouble. In this country and in this town, there is too much drinking, whether it's legal or not. Kids are drinking too.

Even on the communities there is sometimes too much grog in our ceremonies. We are still losing our elders to the grog. They are dying out. We are losing our stories with them. There aren't enough senior people passing on their sacred knowledge and wisdom to their own family and children. And it is very sad for everyone.

Margaret with Joylene, Aaron, Tommy, Pamela, Andrina, Karen, Sherina
holding Jeremiah, Laquisha and brother Malcolm, 2017.
Courtesy of David Woods

CHAPTER 29

Aboriginal spirituality and the Catholic church

Living in the girls' dormitory at Santa Teresa mission with my sister-cousins and the Sacred Heart nuns was a good time for me. It was another circle of women looking after me. Those nuns were like our grandmothers and mothers. There was the teaching with love, the sharing and caring with strong rules. Like in our circle of senior women, the nuns were leading us 'best girls' into a world of stories that came from their sacred book. I am grateful for these nuns. They stood up strongly for things they thought were important. And they gave me so much courage to stand up for what I thought was right.

I am very proud that I learnt these rules about how to stand up strong for my beliefs. The nuns taught me how to understand a bigger world and to become a part of it. These days I continue my church going. I go to our gatherings for discussions around faith. These gatherings have helped with getting these words on the page. They have taught me how to understand and forgive people. Not that I'm perfect at this. But I'm still working on it.

When I was growing up at Middle Camp with my parents and the rest of my family and relations around there, all us kids went to school at the Old Telegraph Station. We ran around in our Aboriginal camps. But on Sunday we went to the Catholic church to hear the good news about God and the creation stories. I also grew up listening to my grandmother's stories of culture and law in the circle of our senior women. Both cultures had 'Altyerre' or creation stories. On weekends nearly all the Arrernte mob came into town from the camps to go to these Catholic masses. At the ceremonies and rituals we learnt about the God in the Old Testament, and the new stories of hope and renewal about Ngkarte, Jesus, in the New Testament gospels.

I was taught by the missionaries that God was the creator of everything. He was the Father, the Son and the Holy Ghost. He made things from nothing. They taught us that God was the creator of the earth and sky, the moon, the sun, the stars, the trees and the animals. Everything was made by God in six days. From Monday to Saturday. Then on Sunday he rested up. We were told we had to be respectful and give time to learning on this seventh day. We were taught the Catholic rituals of how to listen and learn. And we were told lots about all the things God had done for us. He sent his Son down to die on a cross in a place called Jerusalem to save all the people from sin.

When the priests and nuns came into Alice Springs and Central Australia in the mid-1930s, it had been hard times for my grandmothers and grandfathers. The white people had taken control over lots of our lands and waterholes, places that were important in culture and for keeping our families alive. Many people had died. The stories were being damaged. The elders in our tribe were searching for ways to keep our culture strong. To keep faith with our own Aboriginal sacred knowledges and truths. The religion these Christian churches offered was a way forward for many Aboriginal people. The churches were able to save people; not just their souls, but keep them safe from the bully boys and cheeky ones.

At the mission it was Sister Marie Therese and Sister Robyn who saved me plenty of times. They taught me how to keep on going, strong in my faith. They made me laugh and they talked things up. And they hold special places in my heart. They have always been very good friends to me, keeping me strong and looking after me during some very hard times as an older woman. Their ability to keep our friendship going has been very important to me.

But their lessons in standing up as strong women have also been really important. They stood up even when things were scary. They taught me that a bunch of women can argue back against angry men. Like my aunt Mompy and other strong Aboriginal women, they could stare down the bully boys even when they were frightened. The nuns were very brave. They even talked back against their priests. I have followed their leadership and done that many times now, standing up strong at meetings. I've stood up against policemen and courts. I've fought for things to change. I'm teaching my own granddaughters this. You have got to stand up strong and be proud of your beliefs.

When it came to culture and ways of being in the world, there were plenty of shared ideas between the faith of the church mob and the ancient culture and laws of my own people. A sharing of creation stories where both talk of relationships between God, people and our land. A shared system of thinking where unchanging laws are handed down from ancient times through rituals and stories. A similar priesthood group of old men taking leadership in interpreting law and culture. The same circles of women fulfilling the central caring and nurturing roles within a constantly changing world. Both Aboriginal and church leadership have shared enemies. These include people inside and outside that choose to break the unspoken, unheard sacred rules for their own advancement.

·········

In the 1930s it came to pass that some in the Aboriginal leadership took their families into the Catholic church. Many Christian missions had been places of safety for my people from being murdered or starved to death. The missions had even saved some of our people from the station bosses, the police, the government men, the miners and the carpetbaggers who all wanted to steal things away from us Aboriginal mob. Now some of the Arrernte families wanted to become Catholic church insiders and part of this new spiritual community.

In Arrernte language, the spiritual ideas for creation and culture are called Altyerre, Ngkarte and Utnenge. God is time, place and spirit. God is everything. Altyerrenge – 'in the time of God'; this was when the earth was created. Like in the Bible, our Dreamtime ancestors created the earth. Even before the church came, before the mission, Aboriginal people believed in Altyerre. They knew the Altyerre. When the church came, we heard about their God. And it seemed much like the same God that created our own world in the Dreamtime.

Over the years we have talked about Altyerre and the creator God we were taught about by the missionaries. We think they are the same. When we talk about the trinity – Father, Son and Holy Spirit – we say Akngeye, Alere and Utnenge. When we talk about Jesus we say Ngkarte Jesus. Ngkarte is our word for God. We also call priests Ngkarte because they are representatives of God. The apostles are called Kwertengerle Jesus.

That's how it all came into being. Altyerre and God are the same, but appear in different forms. Aboriginal people can know the creation stories and the culture of the church both ways, from our Christian teachings and from the stories passed down in our Aboriginal sacred knowledge. This is because they come from the one beginning.

Before we learnt the Bible we all believed that everything came through the Dreamtime spirits. Altyerre is something we try to understand in our own dreamings. But God and culture is without ending. You can never fully understand it. That is why it's known and unknowable. Because we are looking for its meaning from within our own dreamings. And we never know everything.

Altyerre means the unknown in the same way as God is really unknown. Altyerre is the creation. This God makes himself known through Ngkarte Jesus and Mary. This unknown spirit creates everything in different ways, in different forms and in different places. In Aboriginal way, our people are connected through the Altyerre to our land and to all the places, plants, animals and other people that are there. This is talked up differently in the different languages. But it's the same spirit. Altyerre arratye. It is by tapping into the Altyerre that our Aboriginal healers, the Ngangkeres, both men and women, know about healing the spirit in the body. That's what Aboriginal people believe.

When we die our soul, or 'utnenge', leaves the body and goes back to the places of its own dreaming. This might be the father's country, or mother's country. It might be the place where the person's mother and father had originally found it. The place where conception and life begins to exist: 'Ampe akweke alkngirreke ikwere-artweye-atherre-ke'. The person's soul, all of it, goes back into those places. My old people say this. Sometimes they can see the spirits of those who've passed away at their dreaming place or heaven. Sometimes they can talk to people in their dreams.

The old people say that some men can change into another form, like the 'kurdatye' or 'inentye' man. These spirits have been given special powers through ceremony to carry out the ancient laws. It is like the grace of the Catholic sacraments. Some might be avenging angels called forth by our spiritual leaders to maintain the essential balance. But most are kindly guardians from the spirit world. These might be the same as the angels and saints.

An Aboriginal person may see the spirits of people who have passed away in their dreaming place. The Bible says we'll see Jesus, Mary, angels, saints and also other people who have passed away. We will see them again in Heaven, after we ourselves have been lain to rest. I believe that too.

Our sleeping dreams are not like this. These dreams are not reflections of the Dreamtime or of Heaven. At night I can dream of anything. It is nothing about God. I'll only really see the Dreamtime, the Altyerre, when I die. I'll see Mary and Jesus when I die. I'll know the unknowable from Altyerre when I die.

We might try to understand our Dreamtime. But this story is without ending. We learn and look for meaning in our Dreamtime because this is important. Learning and looking can shine a light on our own pathway through life. It is unknowable, this Altyerre, this God. But trying to learn and find meaning is very important. It creates the sacred, and talks up the storylines that we need to understand and follow.

Sometimes I see family members who have passed away in my dreams. I can talk to them. It can seem real. You can learn things that you don't know about. When I wake up, I remember, and I can know these same stories. You can try to tell people your dreams. But you can't really get to the middle. You can't know it all. It remains unknown. Without clear understanding.

The Dreamtime and Altyerre are like that. It never changes. Altyerre and God never change. But people change. What our people grow to understand, can be changed. They can come to know new things. Things that always were. Things that are Altyerriperre; things that belong to the Dreaming. Our dreams, the ones we wake up from, are sometimes one way we come to know something new about Altyerre. But as I've said, the whole story can never be fully known. The culture is always changing and always remaining the same.

Within my Catholic church my feeling is to be close to Mary. She is the Mother of Jesus. She helps us to get close to God. We learn about the Holy Trinity through Mary. We learn how we can feel the spirit in ourselves: this Father, Son and Holy Ghost. But it was harder to find a way of helping our men. And that battle goes on. We are not losing this battle; but our men are often too stubborn, and angry to listen to their hearts.

Margaret and family at Campfire in the Heart, Christmas 2017.
Courtesy of David Woods

CHAPTER 30

Reflections

As an old woman looking back on my life, I know I've seen too many changes. I have great joy and pain. I have the excitement of work that is important. I love work, and I meet and work with many clever people. I have so many wonderful friendships. Every morning I get up just busting to get back to work. Christmas holidays were always too long for me.

Sometimes people ask me what has kept me going through all the challenges in my life. My answer is my family, my friends and my faith. These things have guided my decision-making and kept me strong through many hard times. Every morning as a child, I was loved and cared for within my circle of women.

I get to hang around with people who are energetic and funny. I'm not always good at telling jokes. But my friends are generous storytellers. They can keep me laughing. They are bold. And they teach me how to stay strong. My friends love me because I am always wanting to find out more. I love learning new things. And they rely on me knowing things. I was adventurous even when I was scared.

Sister Robyn and David Wilkins are like that too. So was many of my family, my Aunt Mompy and my grandmother Jenny were both brave and energetic. I heard my grandfather Big Foot was adventurous, and it probably killed him in the end. My grandfather Brandy and his mates were brave, always wanting to learn more. I had good family like that.

....

My memories of growing up in the Todd River bed at Middle Camp, at Yambah and later in the mission dormitory, are happy ones. All us kids – my brothers and sister, cousins and friends – ran free, watched over by our parents, aunts, uncles, grandparents, many caring adults. There was always someone looking out for us, keeping us safe and sometimes growling us to be careful. I was always surrounded by friends and family, even at school at the Bungalows and in the dormitory.

By the time my family moved to the mission in the 1950s, there had been many forced removals of Aboriginal people off their country. Many kids were taken away from their families. It's only now, writing my story and understanding more of the history of that time in Central Australia, that I realise that my family, along with all the Aboriginal people, were being swept up in the policy of assimilation. They were forced to move to missions and settlements away from Alice Springs to be educated and trained to fit into places given to us by white fellow society.

When I finished school and survived the crisis of my promised marriage, my education opened doors for me. I loved those years working with the teachers and linguists, learning about the sounds and structure of languages. I feel happy when I think back on those busy years.

Even though I do not have a paid job anymore, I still find myself having to speak up for my families and other people. One day I had to write to the police boss here in Alice Springs, telling him about the rough treatment of my grandsons by some of the young police coming to my house. They were being bully boys and getting away with it. But I'm not the kind of woman they think I am. I'm not mad and wild, but as an elder in my family I'm not going to let them get away with it.

The police kept coming to my house, banging on the windows, waking us up, shining torches in my face through my window and asking questions rudely. I told the policeman boss that when the police behave like this they make people scared and they don't want to answer their questions. I told him that the police need to learn good manners and show respect; then people will feel they can work together with the police.

I admit that one time I told off the police with a bit too much force and found myself in the back of the paddy wagon on a cold winter's night. The magistrate was surprised to see me in court the next day. He was used to seeing me in the court to support one of my children or grandkids. Luckily my good friend and old colleague Russell Goldflam, now a lawyer, helped me. I got a fine and they let me go again. The magistrate told me he hoped next time I came to court again it would be to support the young people in my family.

I grew up learning Arrernte/Anmatjerre way and later learnt white people's way. I learnt some very powerful Aboriginal knowledge and values. And I learnt some really good skills and ways of being in the world from my white teachers and friends. Sometimes the 'two ways' don't fit together very well in my head. Sometimes it becomes a struggle and I can feel trapped living between these two worlds.

White government people say to me, 'Don't let your family stay in your house.' They say my children are just using me. And it is true they don't always help with the rent, or behave very respectfully. They sometimes make too much noise, get drunk and cause trouble. The government people say I need to tell them they have to go. But they have nowhere else to go. And my culture and Christian values tell me you've got to care for your families, sharing with them anything you got, small or big. You've got to keep sharing with love. Caring and sharing is good for everyone. I can't shut my door on them. I have to show them I care by welcoming them into my home. I have to share my food and blankets. This is what Jesus did. It is hard. But it is still the 'proper' way.

·········

One of my biggest worries for my kids is their struggle with grog. Right now my three sons are all in and out of prison. When they are sober they are good men, kind and strong, and I love to be with them. But once they start drinking they change. They become angry. They threaten and hurt people, especially the people close to them. They turn on the people they love. When they're sober again, they regret what they have done. They feel really sorry. But it's too late.

My three daughters have also had the same struggle with the grog. They have all been in relationships with men who hurt them and sometimes they too get wild with the grog and hurt other people. This has been very hard for my grandchildren. Some of them have been taken into care by child protection services. All of them have had hard lives. Much harder than my own life. I watch my grandchildren struggle as the grog and other drugs get in the way, stopping them from being better people and parents. This is very hard for me to say.

Drinking too much grog is destroying their lives. I watch the government blaming my people for the grog and all the trouble it brings. They make new laws and put everyone in the prison. But they also make the laws allowing people to sell grog. They hand out the licences and pocket money on every bit of grog that is sold. I know lots of white people getting rich from selling grog. It is the same with gambling; it's the government and the casinos making the money. Our people are wasting their lives in the pubs and clubs having their money taken away. There must be a better way forward.

It makes me sad that the promise of education never reached out to help my children or grandchildren into employment as it did for me. This is the same for many of my colleagues from back in those days at IAD and Yipirinya School. We were all hardworking teachers, health workers and managers. It made us feel proud. But our children didn't grow up with these same chances. Our dream was that we were paving a way for our children and grandchildren to become the teachers and lawyers and workers for our people. But for all of us, our children have really struggled. I have thought a lot about how this happened. I have spent a lot of time talking with people about what went wrong. This is why I'm writing this book, so that I can share these thoughts.

My kids have got no home. After all that struggle to get our land in town, and our camp Ewyenper Atwatye, now my kids have nothing again. Governments are always changing their rules. We've had the Intervention now for nearly ten years. The government decided to become the boss of our camps and our houses, the boss of who can live where. They now decide where each house is built. They have cleared our valley with graders and turned our creek into a drain.

I left Ewyenper Atwatye after my stroke more than twenty years ago but all the time I thought I could go back there anytime. I also thought my children could go back there when they were ready. But I was wrong. My families are not living there anymore. They have been pushed out. All different families are living there now, people who do not recognise our traditional ownership for that place anymore. The government says they don't have to listen to our families who worked for that place and got it started. We all worry about this. I had to beg them to let me go back. It took years before I could get a house there again.

I want our people and the government to really think about these things. We need our families to have a place to call home. We need them to have work.

We need our children to get a really good two-way education to lead them safely into the world. They need skills and opportunities to get work. And it is important that real jobs start to be created again. It's exhausting to argue and fight all the time for our rights in our own country. It is hard to keep asking for support to build the opportunities for meaningful changes. We've been doing it for a long time. And I'm getting tired now.

·········

In the 1950s and 1960s, there was a lot of the old men and women to carry on our culture. They still knew the old stories and the law. They did the growing up and teaching of our young people. But there are fewer senior men and women now to carry on their teaching and the telling of the sacred stories.

Today you hear our Arrernte language spoken only by the old people as part of ceremony time for the making of our young men. Ceremony happens mostly every year now. But even when the ceremony is on, and the dancing takes place, we don't seem to be able to remind everyone that the Kelenthwelkere people need to learn the knowledge of their old people before they pass away. They need to learn their own language, and the sacred objects that the old people held onto so strongly.

But do the young people want to be the owners and custodians of this sacred knowledge? Do they want to learn the old languages enough to save them? Do they have any love for the old ways of Aboriginal culture? During ceremony, with its dancing and the telling of songs of my grandfather's country, I am reminded of the losses of Anmatyerr power, the loss of language, and the dangers to our culture and its ancient traditions.

Our young people nowadays seem more interested in new cultures. They listen to the new music and the young voices coming out of America and elsewhere. But this new group of younger leaders needs to embrace their own cultural identity and make it useful in their own lives. We need people of energy that are respected by their own children and families because they hold their community with love and strength. They are the ones that can reach out and teach our young ones about traditional knowledge and values. They are the ones who can adapt it to our new world. Without these younger leaders respecting our elders and our ancient culture, it won't be saved.

Recently, the Arrernte people of Santa Teresa had a meeting to talk about all the deaths. Most of the senior people had died in the past couple of years. There are now no older men in their sixties or older. All that knowledge and history has died out. They decided to ask my uncle Huckitta Lynch and other senior men to come to Santa Theresa to share some of their stories of growing up in the 1950s and 1960s. They wanted Huckitta to help teach our young ones our ancient law and culture.

As an elder, Huckitta, is a senior man in our law and culture. He still travels around in the circle of our senior men. But Laramba is now his home, and he is in his eighties. Like a lot of those old stockmen who had worked on country he is still fit though.

The old people at Santa Teresa are worried about what might happen for future generations if our stories are lost. This is why they have asked Huckitta and his old mates to come. They want the senior people to sit down with the younger leadership. Perhaps my own sons can join their uncle in the stories of the Kelenthwelkere people and help these stories continue to live when us old people have passed away. A message has been sent out and hopefully this gathering of the senior men will happen.

....

When I was a young girl our families taught us our kinship lines and circle connectedness. They taught us to respect our ancient culture and its ways of operating. These rules kept families at the centre of everything. We still need to keep strong these ancient teachings about the proper ways of growing up and of belonging in the world. And us senior women need to keep growing up the circles so we can pull our young girls back into their families again, back close to us. But how to do this, is the big problem. If it was easy, we'd have done it already.

We tried to do it when we created our Aboriginal classrooms at the Santa Teresa school when my kids were little. It was the same thing that we tried in our classes in town at Yipirinya School. We were always hoping to re-create these ancient Aboriginal, inter-generational circles of women sharing their knowledge with the young ones.

When I was young sitting around our family camps, often one of the senior women would be the right one to take up teaching the young ones through her own stories. As a group, the senior women would be working out ways of holding onto their own kids and growing them up better. There was no 'one way' for doing this. Everyone was different. These senior teachers were trained in being able to interpret the readiness that ran through each individual and the group. Sometimes the grandmothers would talk about their own childhood. Or they might talk about their own grandchildren. This was to hold the group and tease out its moods. If it wasn't time then you changed the storyline.

Us grandmothers do that all the time. As the senior teachers we dance and play with the curriculum. It is our young ones that we have special responsibility for. They are our children's children, no-one else's. So the responsibility to grow them up in culture and law is powerfully held.

Sometimes for the senior women the talk might be about what members of our own family were doing with their lives and in their children's lives too. The talk could be of the good things that were happening but they also sat down to talk about family troubles too. They'd try to sort out these troubles. For grandmothers it is the holding of family together that is the most important thing.

Sometimes it might be a story from the distant past. But it was not really the story that was the lesson. It was always the details of the discussions. Within these circle classes, the younger ones were offered the proper ways to think and behave. And it was important for everyone to know the rules. You didn't have to agree. But you needed to know when you misbehaved. To muck up would be to disrespect your own family. And the circles that held you and that you were living in, would want to talk with you strong way about this.

Today these grandmothers' rules that we learnt about as young people, and got more understanding of as we grew older, mean that we have responsibility to continue the culture. We need to look for ways of sharing our circles with our daughters. Giving them better ways to sort out their own lives. Teaching them how to hold strongly the people they love. We try to do this for our daughters, and especially our granddaughters. We look for ways of doing it for all the women in our family. But it is hard. And we are not always winning.

Our sons too need to sit in the traditional circles of senior men. But the senior men are struggling even worse. The circles of men sometimes became the drinking circles. The hunters of kangaroos adapted to become the hunters of the next drink. And the drink made them silly. They didn't know what they were losing. They didn't seem to find a way back home.

Today some men are thinking more about this. More senior men are coming back more often, and standing stronger for longer. Nothing else can work with our own boys and young men. They need to be led into their world by their own grandfathers, fathers and uncles. They need to be taught the skills and knowledge to be self-disciplined. Watch and learn the ways of how to be good men within their own families. Nothing else can hold these men and teach them proper love, the proper ways of being good fathers and brothers, and how to be strong men again in their own family and community.

. . . .

The late twentieth century saw many things changing too quickly for a lot of our families. We were fighting to be more powerful. We were trying to be part of the new world. And when we started winning a bit of power, we started thinking lots of other things were possible. That is what we hoped. That we could be in control and be the bosses for ourselves. Even us young women began to think we had the right to be the boss. We began to think we could make things better. That we would get big things happening for our own families, and especially for our own children.

We sometimes had good jobs in this new world. We became more confident. We had new circles of friends. We thought we could do this all by ourselves. But we lost a lot of the things that had always kept our families strong. We moved into modern houses that they said didn't have room for our big families and our visitors. We gave away our circles of women and our meeting spaces.

We became dependent. We thought we were 'entitled' but we had to follow the white fellow rules. Instead of independence we got more white people bossing us around, telling us that our old ways had to change. Part of this saw us taking the 'sit down' down money they said we were entitled to. But if you take their money, you have to follow their rules. So you had to turn up for their rubbish training, and do their useless Community Development Employment Program (CDEP) jobs. There was no pride in these things. The old men were dismissive of the new skills. The jobs were seen as garbage collecting, or worse. The young men chose laziness. They forgot how to get out of bed. They lost their ideas about how they could do things for themselves and their family, do things their elders would respect.

We knew that the new white government men were often the same as the old government men. The new generation of white cattle station bosses still thought much the same as their parents and grandparents. Everyone had their own traditions and stories to explain the past. And no-one would be giving anything away to us. Someone would have to pay. No-one really wanted to say 'sorry' or admit that their own ideas were stupid. No one was wanting to lose face or give away their own power and positions if they didn't have to. No-one was really going to let us do what we wanted. That would be too scary.

Somewhere along the way we forgot to persuade our young ones to look after their own traditions of family and relationship circles. We forgot the culture and forgot the knowledge. We lost the ways we had of keeping ourselves safe.

Even when I was young, some senior men and women were worrying that younger Aboriginal men and women were getting too silly. That the white fellows were only giving us jobs if we gave away our culture. The old people kept reminding us that the ancient rules of language and culture were being lost.

We didn't listen. We didn't support or respect them enough. Even back then we were being told that us young mob were losing the ability to sit quietly to listen to our own language and family values. We were all too busy trying to get ahead in this new white fellow world that had opened up for us.

Today, our leadership needs to find ways to build men's pride and culture back into their lives. The government should get on board. It is good that our land councils support ranger programs and employing our men to look after their own country. It is good that governments support these things. Everyone agrees that it will be a great day when a lot more of our men are working for country and at home looking after family, than are locked up in our jails or detention centres.

........·

We share a lot of our history and stories now with other Australians. As a mother and grandmother I have often sat with them and heard them talk of their own worries and losses. We need to share our beliefs and ways of being in this country. We need everyone to share their stories, their faith and their dreams for their children. This is the way forward for my people. And it is the same everywhere. We need to be working together strongly, and we need to hold our little ones with love.

Our circles of women have been holding up our families for a long time now. Our men need to get back into their meeting circles. They need to re-learn the joy of cultural togetherness. Re-establish the sitting quietly and listening to each other. We all have something to share. It is no good that these circles are in our prisons and detention centres. Men have to get up in the morning within their families and communities, and make things happen. I'm not talking about getting enough grog for themselves. The white sugar poison has been part of destroying our hope. We all know that. It puffs us up, then makes people angry and weak. We don't need self-pity. Our men need to stand up strong in our culture and our family stories again. They should be there with us leading the dancing and ceremony again. We need them to be looking after themselves; and showing each other respect.

No need to wait for government money to get strong. Us senior people can do that in our own circles. We don't want you men to join our Alwekkeres. That would be terrible. You need to rebuild your own circles where you talk things up and help each other. Start living your lives with your hearts full of energy, respect and hope. And then we meet again as families and communities to grow up strong children, held with love. We need you men to rekindle your own spirits.

I'm talking too much now, and I've got to finish this book. My next job is starting to write people's stories of their strokes. And I'm still working with translations of gospel texts. I need these projects to get me up in the morning. Being busy helps me live in hope. It stops me worrying too much about my own broken body. My dancing days might be behind me but we all have to celebrate the life we have. And together we should keep using our stories and our sacred knowledge to teach each other. We need to share our cultural understandings.

As senior women and men we need to have all our families with us. We can't do it alone. We've got to grow our futures together. All our different communities in Central Australia need to remember this.

1　Baldwin Spencer and FJ Gillen The Native Tribes of Central Australia, MacMillan, London, 1899

2　From data from Peter Donovan; Alice Springs: Its history and the people who made it. Alice Springs Town Council -1988. Annual Report of the Government Resident of Central Australia Commonwealth Parliament papers CPP 151-1929/30 p9

3　Annual Report of the Government Resident of Central Australia Commonwealth Parliament papers CPP 151-1929/30 p9

4　Glenville Pike, Frontier Territory: A history of the Northern Territory: Pinevale: 1980, p.221.

5　Margaret Heffernan & Thomas Stevens (illustrations), Ampe Urreye Artnerrentye Akweke Akerte, The Crawling Baby, Yipirinya School Council, Alice Springs, 1989.

6　[ayeng-arle arrpenhe-le alyeke arrwengkelthe-le (I-THAT other-ERG sing-past bad. magic/disease-with)].

*　Still images courtesy of AIATSIS, Thomas Sidney Dixon collection, item DIXON_T001- FC00496_1-13b

Moving Back Home To Hidden Valley

In early March 2015, I fell in the bathroom and broke my hip. My granddaughter Makisha found me and called the ambulance. I was in hospital for nearly 3 months. It was a long time because other things happened to me too. My hip got infected, and they told me I had pneumonia and a series of silent heart attacks. I got very thin. Everyone thought I was going … never getting better. But I had faith and trust in God. All the time I was happy, not sad. I met my families and my friends coming to see me every day. That made me happy.

I didn't know what was happening to me. The doctors thought I was dying, but I am alright. Everything in my body was alright. I had the strength in me to trust God. If he wants to take me in my life, that's OK, but I still have work to do, like helping with the Bible reading, translating the words for everyone, thinking about the work that's not finished, my work with the Bible.

They put me in a separate room thinking I was dying. I was thinking, 'What are they doing with me, putting me in a room by myself?' My family came to see me. They knew that room was for the very sick people and dying. I was peaceful. They never thought I was dying.

I don't know what got me to stay alive but they moved me to the ward. But after my time in the hospital, lying in a bed all the time, I couldn't walk any more. They gave me a wheel chair. I made myself move around from side to side, getting up, trying to stand up, to transfer myself to the chair from the bed. I was doing that.

Doctors told me, 'Now you can move to Flynn Lodge at Old Timers nursing home.' First thing I noticed when I there was that the doors were all locked. That was no good. I didn't want to stay locked in. I had thought that there would be a lot of happy people at Old Timers to talk to me like old friends; and I would be happy there. But most of these people couldn't talk. They had no memories left. I was very sad, very lonely, and very bored. The staff were real bossy too. They had no time to talk; and no ears to listen. I told myself, 'I've got to go out from here.'

But that wasn't easy. If I was to go anywhere else I would have to have someone from my family to look after me and it didn't seem like anyone was able to do that. I stayed at Flynn Lodge for 6 months. I missed all my family when I was there. I was outside the Gap and it was too far for them to walk to come and see me.

I thought that one of my three daughters could look after me, if I went to Topsy Smith Hostel. Two have got their own flat. I thought, Pammy is the one who is good to look after me. She agreed and we moved into the Hostel together in the middle of November 2015. They gave me a key and I could come and go with my friends. I was happy to meet with other Aboriginal people and mix with them. I was pleased to sit around and talk to families who came to Eastside Shops. They would come over and talk to me.

But something was still missing … my home … I wanted to move back to Hidden Valley, where I lived before I had my stroke. But there were no empty houses. Everything was full up. One day I decided to move. My nephew, Benedict, had a house there. I asked him if I could shift into his house. 'Any room?', 'Oh yeah, you can come back,' he said. My daughter was with me and helped me to move to my nephew's house. Pammy and me had a room to ourselves. It made me very happy, sitting around with my grandsons and nephews, just like old times. I was back with family again.

Benedict was very good to me. His wife lived there with him and the house was very full of her families with lots of other people coming and going. I got to thinking that now I had been there for a while maybe I could get my own house in Hidden Valley and gather my family around me in our own place. So when we heard that a house was vacant, I went along with Benedict to a meeting of the Executive Committee where he asked if I could have the house. Pammy came along to support me. They said that was alright.

Shawn, Pammy's son and his partner were the first ones to shift in with us. Now Lloydy and his partner come and stay when they are visiting from Ernabella. Lots of my grandsons come in and out. I feel at home with my families around me, whether they stay or go.

I had left my own house in Plumbago Crescent when I broke my hip 18 months before and now I was going to have my own place in Hidden Valley where I always wanted to be. In all that time I had hoped that I would get my own place again. I had been very sick and it didn't seem possible and with the support of my friends and family my dream came true.

I belong here. I am thankful for everything in my life.

Margaret Heffernan and David Woods, December 2017